P9-EMG-831

parenting
today's
adolescent

parenting *today's* adolescent

HELPING YOUR CHILD AVOID THE TRAPS
OF THE PRETEEN AND TEEN YEARS

Dennis &
Barbara
Rainey

with Bruce Nygren

THOMAS NELSON PUBLISHERS
Nashville

Published in Nashville, Tennessee, by Thomas Nelson, Inc., Publishers.

Unless otherwise noted Scripture is taken from the NEW AMERICAN STANDARD BIBLE®, Copyright© The Lockman Foundation 1960, 1971, 1972, 1973, 1975, 1977. Used by permission.

Scripture also taken from *The Message : Psalms*, Copyright © 1995 by Eugene H. Peterson.

Rainey, Dennis, 1948–
    Parenting Today's adolescent : helping your child avoid the traps of the pre-teen and early teen years / Dennis and Barbara Rainey with Bruce Nygren.
        p.   cm.
    Includes bibliographical references (p. 336) and index.
    ISBN 0-7852-7084-1
    1. Parenting. 2. Teenagers. 3. Preteens. I. Rainey, Barbara. II. Nygren, Bruce. III. Title.
HQ799.15.R35   1998
649'.124—dc21   98-29878
                                                                    CIP

Printed in the United States of America.
1 2 3 4 5 6 - 03 02 01 00 99 98

Contents

Part I
FROM THE GOLDEN YEARS
THROUGH THE PERILS OF PUBERTY

Part II
STEPPING AROUND SNARES

Part III
PRAYERFULLY PERSEVERE

Dedication

This book is dedicated to our Sixth-grade Sunday School Classes,
1986-1997

1986-87
Cary Carter
Penn Dodson
April Fain
Matt Finley
Josh Gettys
Jessie Gray
Rob Henry
Ann Hiller
Amy Hoag
Lee Ann Hoggard
Elizabeth Langston
Laura Maack
Jill Richie
Ashley Rainey
Sarah Smith
Brian Sternberg
Betsy Tucker
Hollie Tucker
Julie Warner
Amber Wellons

1987-1988
Kristin Atterberry
Bryan Alexander
Laura Bass
Becca Bochetti
Ivy Bowden
Brad Cruse
Mark Current
Bryan Fuller
Robert Fuller
Max Heathcott
Ty Henry
Brad Hill
LaRhesa Hughes
Tommy Keet
Jana Lackie
Elizabeth Lovelace
Chris Mano
Michael Milton
Jenni Orahood
Paige Perritt
Dylan Potts
Benjamin Rainey

Lauri Rees
Robert Rice
Rachel Robinson
Nathan Rollins
Scott Scruggs
Krissy Seaman
Richie Sessions
Betsy Sevier
Brandi Skrivanos
Jennie Stowers
Abe Taylor
Dawn Walker
Jay Watkins
Sarah Wellons
Jennifer Willis
Karen Wunder

1988-1989
Meredith Anderson
Eric Asbury
Allison Bramhall
Rachel Bruns
Brooke Burrell
Nathan Darby
Joanna Festa
Stuart Finley
Angela Foster
Steven Guy
Joi Gwin
Christa Harrod
Greg Henry
John Hiller
Katherine James
Jamie Johnson
Brad Jones
Missy Larson
Elizabeth Lewis
Matthew McCraw
Nicole Norris
Jill McDuffee
Carrie Orahood
Suzannah Plunkett
Chuck Reynolds
Brady Ring
John Snider

Joshua Squires
Mark Warner
Todd Weber
Adam Williams

1989-1990
Allison Arrington
Erica Atterberry
Keri Barker
Teri Barker
Niki Barnhart
Cullen Bowden
Liz Carter
Katy Cobb
David Dalporto
Hunter Davis
Meredith Davis
Cam Demmerle
Clay Freeman
Sarah Greenwood
Seth Harrell
Brian Hughes
Anne Holland
Chase Keet
Michael Lubansky
Eric Lynn
Jeff Markus
Laura Martin
Elizabeth Milton
Emily McCaskill
Matt McClard
Chris Mueller
Ben Newton
Dan Parkinson
Michael Parsons
Samuel Rainey
Pam Rees
Mary Linda Roberson
Jeff Rochelle
John Mark Rutter
Brian Scott
Spencer Session
Ryan Skinner
Philip Walter
Laura Williams

Anne Wilson
Brent Woodall

1990-1991
Emily Appleton
Meredith Asbury
Brianna Boyd
Natalie Cameron
Andrew Crow
Jamie Evans
Sam Finley
Morgan Foster
Mary Helen Gettys
Sarah Haynie
Adam Heathcott
Star Hy
Scott Knight
Jim Knox
David Lasater
Ryan Lee
Rebekah Lewis
Mary Marsh
Tricia McCauley
Kyle McCraw
Sarah Morse
Piper Mueller
Kenyan Norman
Allison Oberste
Megan Orahood
Betsy Oxley
Sara Peeples
Ryan Rice
Rhea Rushing
Evan Sewall
Rebecca Short
Melissa Singleton
Hunter Slaton
Amber Smith
Chad Smith
Matt Thorpe
Caristiana Ulmer
Chris Watkins
Laurie Wunder

1991-1992
Nathan Allison
Troy Braswell
Lissa Boschetti
Ashley Bridwell
Guy Byars
Natalie Carbonaro
Sarah Carter

Stephen Crain
Peter Crow
Brooke Cyphers
Lindsey Daniels
Kyle Driggers
Saul Farris
Kelly Ferguson
Carrie Furr
Kurt Garland
Kirby Goff
Zachary Govia
Carla Harrod
Ben Holman
Corrie James
Brooke Johnson
Geoffrey Lessel
Courtney Lessenberry
Edward Lovelace
Philip Lynn
Mary Marsh
Kirby Mano
Rachel McClard
Dale McDaniel
Scott McWilliams
Jay Mitchell
Kara Newton
Matt Paulus
Court Perrin
Anthony Pilcher
Jessica Platt
Allison Powers
Michael Reding
Cliff Richardson
Ryan Ritchie
Chad Roberson
David Robinson
Garrison Roddey
Anna Rutter
Hannah Smith
Leanne Snider
Andrew Steger
Coy Stewart
Brooke Stowers
Ragan Sutterfield
Courtney Tucker
John Turrentine
Celeste Wilson
Ben Wright

1992-1993
Mitzi Alley
Brad Alexander

Lindsay Baggett
Julie Baskin
John Bass
Morgan Bowden
Matt Boyer
Crystal Brooks
Carlee Brown
Joshua Burrell
Sean Carney
Christian Cash
Jimmy Couch
Lindsey Cope
Bethany Current
Wade Davis
Ashley Earl Marshall
Leah Elrod
Allison George
Chris Hartig
Anne Holland
Jennifer Honea
David Hudson
Abby Jack
Bethany Johnson
Paige Kinslow
Katherine Anne Knight
Joey Larson
Susan Leggett
Jeff LeMaster
Brad LeNarz
Amy Lepine
Sarah Loescher
Anna Martin
Mary Catherine McClendon
Sarah Beth Northup
Jay Orahood
Nate Perry
Jim Phillips
Rebecca Rainey
Aldo Reyes
Mollie Richardson
Peter Richmond
Nick Ring
David Rollins
Charles Rogers
Matt Scroggin
Anna Sewell
Lyle Sewell
Caleb Shamlin
Angela Sherrill
Damon Singleton
Anthony Smith
Marci Sudduth

Wes Thorpe
Elizabeth Turrentine
Megan Wallraven
Mary Kathryn Wells
Lindsay Williams
Nate Wilson
Chris Zelnick

1993-1994
Christina Alessi
Rebecca Asbury
Emily Baker
Jeff Baskin
Janie Bass
Kambru Bickings
Brittany Boyd
Lindlee Bullock
Courtney Callan
Britt Carter
Ruthie Cobb
Brandon Coleman
Molly Collier
Jason Connolly
Douglas Dalporto
Justin Ferguson
Danielle Gates
Hunter Goff
Matthew Greenwood
Stephanie Haggard
Stephen Harper
Katie Holland
Kara Howe
Heather Hutchinson
Susan Hyatt
Brooke Ivy
Susan Jack
Lee Jines
Matthew Kielczewski
Danny Knox
Bret Lasater
Jacob LeMaster
Justin Lessel
Garrett Lewis
Heather Lubansky
Lindsay May
Molly McCaskill
Maudie McInnis
Courtney McLellan
Rebecca McWilliams
Emily Mesko
Taylor Moore
Bob Myers

Jake Newell
Daniel Oberste
Mallorie Oliver
Amber Outlaw
Ray Peeples
Jeremy Perrone
Matt Perry
Jamie Platt
Amber Raley
Ashley Reynolds
David Rice
Amanda Rich
Steve Roberson
Cory Roth
Amber Runnels
Elisabeth Rutter
Jay Sawatski
Sarah Selby
Chris Short
Jacob Slaton
Isaac Smith
Dawson Smith
Luke Stanton
Scott Steger
Sarah Stewart
Lauren Sudduth
Spencer Sutterfield
Ashley Taylor
Julia Thompson
James Watkins
Ben Wellons
Travis Williams
Christy Williams
Katie Wright
Jessica York
Ben Zook

1994-1995
Travis Abbott
Amy Alexander
Ashley Anderton
Lee Aronson
Claire Benson
Bethany Boehi
Wyn Bowden
Sarah Bowman
Matthew Bridwell
Kelly Buchanan
Bryan Bucari
Amy Butenschoen
Mark Caruthers
Adam Charlesworth

Johanna Clayton
Kristin Conklin
Christopher Conn
Cara Cox
Lauren Daniels
Aaron Davis
Jonnathan Davis
Aura Diaz
Chris Dinwiddie
Aaron Elrod
Chad Farneth
Joshua Fisher
Kelly Furr
Alex Gilbert
Whitney Guenard
Whitney Hall
Aubrey Hansen
Joshua Hartman
Andrew Henry
Hailey Hoggatt
Julie Honea
Stephen Hudson
Carrie Johnson
Andrew Kella
Chase Kinslow
William Knight
Ann Marie Kooistra
Lissa Malcom
Andrew Marsh
Lindsay May
Brad McCray
Katy Mendelsohn
Jonathan Mobbs
Hannah Moore
Matthew Morgan
Mary Katherine Northup
Debra Owens
Stephen Paulus
Mary Helen Peeples
Brad Phillips
Lesley Phillips
Lindsay Porter
Colin Potts
Chris Prichard
Michele Rambo
Ashley Reddick
Philip Richmond
Adam Robelot
Melissa Scates
Scott Schuchard
Stacey Scroggin
Elizabeth Searcy

Megan Serbus
Sarah Sevier
Jay Snider
Sarah Sturdivant
Brandy Thompson
Lauren Vinsant
Austin Walters
Jenny Wilkes

1995-1996
Catherine Alessi
Ashley Allred
Jill Anderson
Mary Virginia Bain
Hunter Benson
Ashlyn Bickings
Jacob Brown
Corbi Bullock
Brad Burnette
Carly Calhoun
Tim Camp
Andrew Carter
Barak Cheney
Molly Clark
Adam Crabtree
Brian Cyphers
Ryan Darks
Lauren Davis
Lindsey Davis
T-Kay Dillaha
Daniel Duvalian
Steve Eades
Rachel Eddy
Matthew Ellis
Amber Fleck
Mickey Heard
Magan Herr
Daniel Hooper
Mary Beth Kiningham
Seth Latture
Mary Susan Martin
Ashley McCafferty
John Connor McInnis
Joshua Miller
Bethany Pilcher
Karen Pritchard
Deborah Rainey
Whitney Rich
Thomas Rogers
Grant Rollins
Elizabeth Rorie
Stacy Roth

Hunter Scott
Michael Seaman
Jennifer Sherman
Jordon Smith
Lindsay Steward
Cameron Tull
Cara Willams

1996-1997
Justin Adams
Candace Archer
Elizabeth Baker
Blake Barber
Danni Birdsong
Bo Boschetti
Nicole Boutiette
Daniel Burrell
Adam Butenschoen
Patrick Callan
Matthew Camp
Rick Campbell
Kimberly Church
Melissa Conn
Josh Connolly
Stephen Daley
Justin Davis
Andrea Duensing
David Engle
Lindey Fox
Ashley Gates
Stan Gover
Danny Harrison
Kate Hinman
Adelphine Hy
William Hyden
Jamie Jackson
Ashley Kella
Dustin Kopf
John Lawson
Peter Marsh
Bess Matthews
Roddy McCaskill
Bradley McColey
Ryan McCracken
Matt McKenzie
Jacquelyn Mendelsohn
Ashley Millheim
Elizabeth Millsap
Landon Monnahan
Lindsey Monnahan
Nathan Moore
Natalie Morrison

Kathleen Mosley
Trey Oliver
Caleb Olson
Matthew Osteen
Allyson Outlaw
Bobby Paine
Sarah Phillips
Philip Pounders
Laura Rainey
Erin Rambo
Dallas Rentch
Will Richardson
Anthony Riggan
Myles Roberson
B.J. Rogers
Carson Roncketto
Trevor Rossi
Katherine Rutter
Lauren Saint
Carla Sawatski
Mary Margaret Schuchard
Jeremiah Schultz
Nicole Slayton
Emily Spadaro
Jimmy Spice
Jeremy Spyridon
Katie Stowers
Shawn Tait
Jonathan Tucker
Karen Tuttle
Jarin Walters
Drew Westbrook
Rachel Wilkes
Missie Wooten

Acknowledgments

In the past we have written some small epistles in thanking our team here in Little Rock. This time it is going to be short and sweet.

Bruce, thanks for your incredible labor on this project—the equivalent of two books! You are a good man. Thanks for mining the tapes and manuscripts and finding the ore. We appreciate you for hanging in there with us.

Dave Boehi once again proved to be an objective sounding board and tireless worker in reshaping many chapters. You are a lifesaver.

To our team at FamilyLife, a special thanks goes to Merle Engle for standing in the gap so we could write in private. To Dorothy English, Matt Burns, Sharon Hill, and Arlene Kirk, thank you—you are a great team and one that I deeply appreciate.

To the radio and materials team that contributed much to this process—Betty Dillon, Pat Claxton, Marty Paine, Julie Denker, Bob Lepine, Keith Lynch, Mark Whitlock, and Blair Wright—thank you. And a special thanks to Tom Clagett for the research.

ACKNOWLEDGMENTS

A hearty word of thanks and appreciation to Michael Escue for his thoughtful research and for being such a great addition to our family.

And to our children, who provided so many great illustrations and stories, you are the best. And no, you can't get paid royalties on the stories in here. We love you.

Foreword

Growing up these days is tough.

I base this conclusion on nearly four decades of experience in ministering to young people throughout the world. As probably never before, adolescents now need parents who understand the challenges teens face in a hostile, frequently dangerous, and trap-filled culture.

The insight and hands-on advice included in Dennis and Barbara Rainey's *Parenting Today's Adolescent* provide a very practical guide for parents who eagerly desire to prepare their teens to triumph over temptations related to peer pressure, sex, drugs, and a host of other issues.

I've observed Barbara and Dennis as both colleagues in ministry and as fellow parents who are still raising their six children. You could not find better "fellow strugglers" to help mold your child from a practical, yet thoroughly biblical perspective.

A unique focus of *Parenting Today's Adolescent* (a perspective I enthusiastically share) is the emphasis on helping parents develop their own convictions on issues before attempting to shape the convictions of their children. It is impossible to make the old "do as I say, not as I do" routine work with today's young people. They just won't buy it—and shouldn't.

If you want help on how to prepare your child to live for Christ through a holy and productive life, this book's for you. I expect you will return again and again to seek Dennis and Barbara's warm and often witty wisdom as you walk beside your child in the incredible journey from adolescence to maturity.

Josh McDowell

Introduction

What words would come to mind if we asked you to share your feelings at the thought of parenting a preteen or teenager?

In preparing to write this book, we asked nearly two thousand parents attending FamilyLife Marriage Conferences across the United States to identify the feelings they most often had about raising an adolescent. Here are their responses:

Challenged	61 percent
Optimistic	53 percent
Excited	44 percent
Fearful	33 percent
Worried	33 percent
Confident	26 percent
Inadequate	21 percent[1]

Can you identify with this mix of hopeful, yet uneasy attitudes? We certainly do!

The same survey asked what "great concerns of parents were related to their preadolescents or teenagers":

Spiritual growth	54 percent
Self esteem and identity	43 percent
Peer pressure (negative)	42 percent
Turning away from the Lord	39 percent
Dating—relating to opposite sex	39 percent
Character	34 percent
Safety—protection from violence	34 percent
Back-talking	31 percent
Rebellion	29 percent[2]

These issues resonate in our hearts too.

In *Parenting Today's Adolescent* we have attempted to address all of these feelings and concerns—as well as many others. We trust that God will use our experiences, mistakes, insights, and successes to help prepare and guide you and your child through the challenging but exciting years of adolescence.

Before we begin, two matters of style and approach in this book require comment. First, to enhance readablility by avoiding the constant use of *he or she* when referring to a child, we have chosen to use male pronouns. Our language just does not provide a simple, gender-neutral pronoun or uncluttered wordage to refer to either a girl or a boy.

Second, most of the anecdotes about our family in this book are told by Dennis in the first person—that is, *I*. The stories related by Barbara are identified as such. Again, we have done this to make the material more readable. In reality every word in this book represents our combined thought and effort, like most endeavors in our marriage, parenting, and ministry.

When the Lord picked Joshua to lead the Israelites into the Promised Land, He urged the new appointee to be "strong and of good courage."

No more appropriate words were ever spoken for those of us wanting to honor God as we parent today's adolescents.

Part I

From the Golden Years
Through the Perils of Puberty

1

Stepping Through Traps

What Children and Their Parents Face Today

The scene caused a chill to trickle down my back.

On an outdoor stage in Denver, Colorado, with fifty thousand Promise Keepers watching intensely, a fifteen-year-old boy—blindfolded and barefoot—began stepping cautiously toward a dangerous obstacle course filled with a dozen steel animal traps.

Directly in front of the boy lay the grim, gray jaws of a huge bear trap that was so powerful that it could crush his leg and so large that setting it had required three men. Several feet to the left of the bear trap lay a smaller device, a beaver trap—quick and potent.

Next to me, twenty-five feet away from the blindfolded young man, stood the boy's father. This unusual demonstration was my closing illustration in a message entitled "Turning Your Heart Toward Your Children."[1] I wanted to make a visual point that children need their dads to guide them through the challenging terrain of adolescence and life. On each of the traps I had fastened labels representing the "traps" of adolescence, words like *peer pressure*, *alcohol*, *drugs*, *sexual immorality*, *rebellion*, and *pornography*.

The boy took two tentative steps and was about to take a

third—directly toward the bear trap—when his father, Tom, screamed into a microphone, "Trent, stop! Don't take another step. I'll be right there!" His order echoed through cavernous Mile High Stadium. The air seemed to suck out of the arena as an eerie silence replaced the normal fidgeting and low-grade hum of the throng.

No one moved. Except Tom.

Trent sure didn't move. He waited obediently as his father circled the trap field and stepped in between his son and the bear trap. Tom whispered instructions to Trent, then he turned his back to the boy. The young man eagerly placed his hands on his father's shoulders.

Slowly, taking small and deliberate steps, Tom maneuvered through the trap field, his son nearly glued to his back. Trent's hands gripped Tom's shoulders, his shuffling feet often clipping his dad's heels. Tom stayed as far from the traps as possible, not taking the slightest risk that Trent might bump a trap with his bare toes.

One man's tentative clapping broke the silence in the stadium. Soon others joined in. A chorus of voices yelled encouragement to the father and son. Only a few yards, a few traps remained.

When the two reached me and the blindfold was pulled off, Tom and Trent hugged each other. Applause and cheering started at one end of the field and swelled to a thunderous, standing ovation, rolling like a tidal wave across the stadium.

Above the roar I shouted over the sound system, "Men, that's what God has called us to as fathers—to guide our children through adolescence, the most dangerous period of our children's lives!"

THE TRAPS OF ADOLESCENCE

Although they seldom admit it, deep down, most teens desperately want their moms and dads to come alongside them and say, "You know there are some things I wish I had told you earlier, but

I want to tell you now. I want to be a part of your life as you go through these teenage years. I want to be there for you. I want to help you avoid the traps of adolescence."

Thankfully, God's desire matches our own. He wants the best for our (His) children too.

But those traps, what about them? How much of a threat are they?

We are convinced that far too many parents are lulled to sleep during the tranquil elementary years. Unaware of the approaching perils of adolescence and of how quickly they arrive, parents are caught without a defensive and offensive game plan for the teenage years.

Imagine your child at a school assembly for junior high and senior high students. Studies show that if the teacher asked the following questions and got honest answers, here's what would happen:

- "How many of you who are 15 or younger have had sex?" *33 percent of the boys and 27 percent of the girls stand up.*[2]
- "How many of you who have finished eighth grade have used alcohol?" *77 percent of the students shuffle to their feet.*[3]
- "Those of you who are older, 16 to 18, how many of you have considered suicide?" *29 percent of those students rise from their chairs.*[4]
- "You older teenagers who drive—how many of you have driven a car while drunk?" *21 percent stand.*[5]
- "Now we're really going to get personal. How many of you who are 12 to 19 have genital herpes?" *Ignoring the snickers of their classmates, 20 percent of the assembly rises.*[6]

Would your child be among those standing? What are your plans to make sure he would stay seated? Do you know what the traps are and where they are located?

These snares, and others like them, such as drug use, teenage pregnancy, and gangs, are the newsmaker traps. But there's another whole group of traps that don't get as much press but are just as perilous to our youth. In this book we'll talk about subjects like peer pressure, "attitude," deceit, false gods, busyness, media, appearance, mediocrity, anger, and more.

Your child needs you to lead the way through the trap field. Grab his hand. Grab God's hand. Watch your step. Move out together.

TRIPPED UP BY TRAPS

A child once got caught in these traps.

The boy had everything going for him. He was not the oldest child, but the first son born into a close, godly family. They lived in a cozy home near a national forest that had hundreds of acres of hills and hollows where the boy could fish, hunt, and play cowboys-and-Indians with his friends.

The father was successful in a worldwide ministry requiring frequent travel. But he spent as much time as he could with his son, and the two adored each other. The boy's mom was devoted to her children, reading Bible stories at night and frequently interrupting her day to pray for her family.

The son knew all about God. Growing up he had learned Bible verses and went to Sunday school and church every week. But in his heart he had begun to stray. As a child there wasn't anything blatant, but there were some fights at school, and he just would not keep up with his schoolwork. And in spite of threats and escalating punishment, he continued to torment his sisters.

He carried this disobedient, rebellious trend into high school. Increasingly worried and frustrated, the parents opted for a new environment, sending their son to a prestigious Christian boarding school. The boy missed the woods and home and hated the new school. Covertly, some bad habits solidified—like smoking and sneaking a beer now and then. He struggled in the tougher academic environment and was nearly expelled for rule violations.

Giving in to his persistent begging, his parents brought him home to finish high school. There were more fights at school, and a speeding encounter with a local policeman almost landed him in jail.

Although glad to be home, he refused to give up bad habits and was always pushing the limits. With his window wide open, he smoked in his room and blasted his much-loved rock music throughout the house.

A foul-up in course planning caused him not to graduate from high school as planned. He took a summer job in Alaska and ran with the construction crowd working hard all day, drinking hard all night.

His parents set up another opportunity. He enrolled at a Christian college. This went well for a while, but again he began pushing the envelope on rules and he was expelled.

Now on his own, the young man's prodigal spirit reached full bloom. If there was a way to show rebellion against the beliefs and lifestyle of his family, that's what he did.

On his twenty-second birthday, after a meal with his parents, his concerned father took him for a walk and confronted his sin: "You're going to have to make a choice either to accept Christ or reject Him. You can't continue to play the middle ground. Either you're going to choose to follow and obey Him or reject Him."[7]

Billy Graham was one frustrated dad, fed up with the foolishness and dangerous rebellion of his son, Franklin.

You may know "the rest of the story," as Paul Harvey would say. Franklin came home to Jesus Christ and his parents. Today he leads a ministry called Samaritan's Purse that aids some of the most needy people throughout the world. And he is taking over the reins of his father's worldwide evangelism ministry.[8]

But if Billy and Ruth Graham's boy could step in a trap, so can your son or daughter—or one of ours. There are no guarantees; our children are not robots.

An adolescent in today's world must develop an ability to recognize and maneuver through traps. Some of these snares are small, like a mouse trap that will sting your finger but only cause momentary pain. Yet others, like the two-foot-wide bear trap, can tear skin, crush bones, even hasten death to its victim.

ARE WE READY FOR THIS?

What can we parents do to prepare our children for the challenges they face?

We know they're not perfect, and like everyone dressed in human skin, they must go through good times and bad, the inevitable mountain tops and sinkholes of life. But we ache for them to avoid as many traps as possible and to have lives of happiness, meaning, purpose, and achievement.

Ultimately, more than all else, we want our children to know, glorify, love, and obey God.

But how do parents get from here—our dreams and longings—to there—children who become adults who are mature spiritually, emotionally, morally, intellectually?

We have spent the better part of our twenty-six years of marriage seeking answers to that question. Although this book is not intended to be a dissertation on parenting, we do have a thesis statement. It's found in the Psalms: "Unless the LORD builds the house, they labor in vain who build it" (127:1).

This is the ultimate answer: God is the Crafter of each child's life. He alone knows the blueprint and the kind of house being built—the outcome of all our parental blood, sweat, prayers, fears, hopes, and tears.

God wants to help you raise your family. He wants to equip you. He wants to guide you. But He demands that you be utterly dependent upon Him. How is this to be accomplished?

We believe the critical tasks of being a God-honoring parent fall into three categories:

1. *Know and walk in the truth ourselves.* We need to know what we believe, our convictions, and stay out of the traps as adults.

2. *Shape the truth in our children.* We build convictions in their lives so that they can identify the traps and stay away from them.

3. *Monitor the testing of the truth in our children.* We encourage and guide them as they "test" their convictions in real life situations while still living under our roof.

And when our children are ready, we release them to their own journey of living and following the Truth.

Doesn't sound simple, does it? When we signed up for parenting, most of us didn't read the fine print.

Can you name a more demanding career than being a godly mom or dad? Air traffic controller? That's a nap in the park compared to a mom landing and dispatching four teenagers from an after-school holding pattern. Brain surgeon? Would you rather poke around in a sedated skull in a fully staffed operating room or try by yourself to soothe and heal the tangled feelings and thoughts of a teenage girl who wasn't invited to the prom or who failed to make the drill team?

On top of all the challenges of parenting, there's something far more sinister taking place: We're in a spiritual war and are operating like guerrillas behind enemy lines. The paths we walk, and the trails our children must walk, are dangerous—littered with traps set by a spiritual enemy that you can't see, an enemy who wants to destroy the souls of children before they become adults.

In the years while your child is at home, you can help him successfully navigate the trap field. Often you'll need to go first, showing step by step the way around those deadly snares. There's hope. It really is possible to raise a godly family in this family-unfriendly culture.

PARENTING TODAY'S ADOLESCENT

We do not have a tidy theory on parenting. No equation. No recipe.

We've written this book as honestly, as openhandedly, as efficiently as we can. Without sounding simplistic, we want to share what we know—so far—about getting youngsters ready and helping them through adolescence.

We have some scars on our hearts put there by our children and our own mistakes. We have knees bruised while praying the Prayer of the Helpless Parent. We have some bedrock convictions and insights that have been hammered out on the anvil of everyday experience.

And we have humility. With six children, we have *plenty* of humility.

God blessed us with ample opportunities to test parenting theories and continue the process of growing up ourselves. The names and ages (in early 1998) of our children are Ashley, 23; Benjamin, 22; Samuel, 19; Rebecca, 17; Deborah, 15; and Laura, 13. Our younger three are still at home, and only Ashley is married (July 1997).

Although still learning, we are well on our way to our own home school doctoral degrees after more than twenty-four years of research in bandaging, correcting, cleaning up, staying up, training, pleading with, listening to, crying over, praying for, hugging, crying with, laughing with, coaching, fussing over, wrestling with, loving, and asking forgiveness of our children.

Our desire in writing *Parenting Today's Adolescent* is to help three types of parents (pardon the baseball analogy—Dennis just can't hang up his spikes for good):

- **Rookies.** You have a child, probably ten to twelve years old, and you see the teen years on deck.
- **Minor leaguers.** Your child is thirteen to fifteen. Already you have had to try to hit some curve balls pitched by your adolescent, and maybe you whiffed on one or more.
- **Major leaguers.** You're in the big leagues; your child is a full blown adolescent, sixteen or seventeen, going on twenty-five. You need some tips to improve your parenting batting aver-

age. And you want as few errors as possible in the remaining games of the season. Maybe you feel like you are in a "losing season" and just need hope.

In addition to fitting in one of these categories, you may be a single parent or a part of a blended family. Most of the ideas in this book apply to all parent-child or blended-family situations, but occasionally we will offer particular thoughts or words of encouragement directly to the single parent. This book is for all parents who want to do their best to fulfill the assignment in parenting that God has given to them.

The way our ideas are presented in *Parenting Today's Adolescent* resembles an airplane trip. In Part I, From the Golden Years Through the Perils of Puberty, we lift off the ground to get a clear view of the big picture. Here are the scripturally based principles and other insights we've learned that moms and dads need to know about their children and themselves to achieve parenting success.

In Part II, Stepping Around Snares, we bring the plane back down to earth as we discuss what we believe are the top fourteen traps of adolescence. The section overflows with practical advice on how to establish your convictions on critical issues, as well as how to shape and help your preadolescent and teenager test his convictions. An alphabet of topics related to adolescence is presented here: anorexia, chores, clothing, curfews, dating, diets, friends, grades, Internet, jobs, money, movies, music, pornography, conflict resolution, rooms, sex, smoking, sports, stress, youth group, and more.

Last, in Part III, Prayerfully Persevere, we offer encouragement and hope for the remaining years of adolescence.

This may sound intimidating. Trust us, it's not. We've tried to write a book that even the Raineys, often running at top speed to keep up with six children, would have time to read!

Two hard-won, heartfelt conclusions underlie all we say in this book:

11

First, parents must be connected relationally, emotionally, affectionately to their children. This ongoing attachment and involvement are absolutely essential as parents encounter the challenges of raising their children to maturity.

Second, the reason so many Christian parents are struggling today is that they do not know what they believe and have not determined the standards, boundaries, and convictions for their children.

Thankfully, God doesn't expect perfect parenting from imperfect people. He doesn't want us to have our eyes fixed on who we're not and how we've failed. He doesn't leave us to flop around and flounder out of what may be dysfunctional backgrounds. He asks us only to look at Christ, the Author and Perfecter of our faith, the One who will see us through a child's adolescence.

We want to give you courage that you can help your child avoid the traps of adolescence. No matter what you may have done wrong or will do wrong, do not quit. No matter what kind of family you have come from, no matter what hand you've been dealt, hang tough.

NOT MANY CHEERS, BUT PLENTY OF REWARDS

I didn't quite finish telling the story of what happened that day at the Promise Keepers gathering in Denver.

After the demonstration with the traps, a large stream of boys began pouring into the stadium. Most of these young men, who had been listening to another speaker, had come to Promise Keepers with their dads. I had asked the men in the stadium to be quiet and reverent while the boys filed in.

As the young men entered a totally silent stadium, their fathers stood, baseball caps in hand. Here was the next generation—their own sons. These were boys who would depend on their guidance through the traps of the teenage years so they could grow to become men of God.

Then on cue, I said to the men, "These are the leaders of the families of the future. These young men are our sons. Let them hear what you think about them!"

A full-throated roar erupted. You can imagine it, much like a last-second winning touchdown scored by the home team. Fifty thousand men applauded and cheered wildly.

My throat tightened, and tears filled my eyes as the unbridled clapping, stomping, yelling, and whistling continued for several minutes—a high tide of enthusiastic affection surging through the stadium. If I live to be a hundred, I'll never forget that scene.

On occasion I've reflected that it's too bad that rearing children can't always be as exhilarating as those stadium moments. Life and raising families take place on a playing field that's lonely at times. There are no cheers by the masses. Only challenges. No headline records a parent's victory. No TV anchor interviews a child who makes a winning choice in a deadly situation.

Parenting is much broader and deeper than a magical moment in a stadium. Attempting to be God's parents is hard work. Long hours. No guarantees.

But there are plenty of rewards. Nothing can compare to the joy of seeing a child grow up to walk in the truth—"I have no greater joy than this, to hear of my children walking in the truth" (3 John 4). Nothing is as exhilarating as watching our children bravely walk through traps and snares, advancing the banner of Jesus Christ in their generation.

Being a parent is one of *the* supreme privileges of life.

2

Mining Ore During the Golden Years

Never Underestimate Your Child's Potential

If there ever can be such a thing as pure pleasure in parenting, preadolescence is it.

The terrible twos are a fading memory. Your child now dresses and feeds himself—even takes a shower without nagging. You and your child have conversations in which he expresses his thoughts and wishes. And best of all, he *admires* you!

We call this oasis of tranquillity in the parenting pilgrimage, when the child is nine to twelve or so, the golden years, a time as blissful as a lazy boat ride down the river on a pleasant summer afternoon.

Sure, you know adolescence is just around the bend, and there may be some rapids ahead, but for now parenting is *good*.

Life was good, too, for three people who pushed their boat away from a river's edge on a hot July Saturday in 1960.

One of the passengers was a seven-year-old boy named Rodger. This was an exciting outing for him. Rodger's dad was a carpenter who moved his family frequently while following construction work. Without permanent roots, Rodger was learning to appreciate special opportunities like the boat ride when they came.

Having lived only months in this, another new town, Rodger

didn't know much about the place or the river. He was just glad to be away from his family's trailer house on a blistering summer day. The twelve-foot aluminum boat belonged to Jim, who was his dad's foreman at the construction job. Jim had stopped by and asked the whole family to go for a boat ride, but Rodger's mom and dad had things to do so only Rodger and his seventeen-year-old sister, Deanne, had gone with Jim.

"Remember to wear your life jacket," Rodger's dad had told him as they left. Rodger was just learning how to swim.

The air was cooler on the river, but the life jacket made Rodger sweat. He asked Jim if he could take it off—there seemed to be little danger. Jim shook his head, no.

The boat, powered by a small Evinrude outboard motor, made its way slowly downstream. Rodger became bored, and as the craft went under a bridge, he turned and asked Jim if he could steer. Jim shook his head again. Not now, the river was becoming more turbulent.

Rodger looked ahead over the boat's prow. In the distance he noticed an odd mist rising from the river. *What is that?* he wondered. Before he could ask, he saw a small island in the river swarming with birds. This held his attention until the boat began to rock as it met larger waves.

The boat's motor, which had been droning on faithfully, suddenly began to whine. As Rodger turned to see why, Jim killed the motor and tipped the propeller housing out of the water. The propeller blade had hit rocks and broken the shear pin. The motor was useless. As Jim grabbed for the oars, he yelled for Deanne to put on her life jacket.

Jim rowed furiously, and Rodger saw fear in his eyes. Deanne screamed, "What's the matter?" Jim didn't answer.

Rodger looked ahead. The river's current now pulled the boat swiftly toward the mist. Water churned and crashed around them. A huge wave struck the side of the boat. The boat turned nearly on its side but then slid upright in the trough. Rodger gripped the sides of the boat. "I don't want to go swimming!" he cried out.

15

"Don't be scared," Jim yelled. "I'll hold you!"

Another wave smashed the boat, and this time it overturned, dumping everyone overboard. Jim grabbed Rodger while Deanne tried to hang on to the capsized boat.

Rodger clung to Jim, but in seconds the vicious torrent of water ripped them apart. Rodger slammed into a rock, then swirled away into the wet chaos. Now he was alone, speeding through the rapids of the Niagara River, just hundreds of yards away from the deadly Horseshoe Falls.

Deanne lost her grip on the boat. As she bobbed in the wild surf she saw a man standing ahead on an island. He was waving and yelling at her, begging her to swim with all her might. She kicked and paddled weakly toward him.

"Kick harder!" the man screamed. Deanne did, and just as she was about to be swept away, she reached up and caught his thumb and two fingers. With one leg wrapped around an aluminum guardrail and the other teetering on a small lip of rock, the man held her. But the force of the water—rolling over into the abyss just fifteen feet away—was too strong for him to yank her to safety. The two held on amid the drenching mist and thunder of mighty Niagara Falls.

"Help! Help!" the man screamed, and another tourist came running. He leaped over the rail and, swaying on the slippery bank, pulled both Deanne and her rescuer to safety.

"My brother! What's happened to my brother?" she yelled.

The second man, who had seen Rodger and a mangled aluminum boat pass over the falls, could only say, "Pray for him." Deanne dropped to her knees, tears streaming down her face.[1]

HIGHER EDUCATION FROM THE
SIXTH-GRADE CLASS

Preadolescence is much like Rodger's boat trip. The river can be deceptively calm. But you need to be prepared for what lies ahead. Put on your life jacket.

16

When our oldest child, Ashley, was about twelve, we were drifting blissfully down the river called preadolescence. God often seems to give parents a bit of a free ride with the first born. We were enjoying our relationship with her immensely. Maybe this teenage thing was something that happened to other, perhaps less-skilled, parents? We weren't arrogant; we just hadn't been in the river long enough. Yet.

Not that Ashley, or any of her brothers and sisters who followed her into adolescence, has been a terrible child. We just were clueless as to the magnitude of the changes that churn through the bodies, minds, and emotions of the typical child headed into the teen years.

It took a unique experience before we fully realized the incredible opportunity parents have to prepare their children for adolescence in those golden years. There's almost no current, the river is as placid as a sheet, there's no waterfall creating a roar that makes hearing one another difficult. It's a great time to talk calmly about what lies ahead.

And the child will listen! That delightful son or daughter, the one who still occasionally sits on your lap and thinks you are the source of all wisdom, will listen to what you have to say about the new, exciting, sometimes trap-infested adolescent life waiting just around the bend.

Our naive river cruise was interrupted in an unexpected way when we volunteered to teach sixth-grade Sunday school class. I will never forget that first Sunday. Our church is larger now, but back then all the sixth graders could fit around the big table in the board room. Twelve preteens were waiting for us.

From the very first, Barbara and I sensed they were ready for some meat, not the macaroni and cheese we might have stirred up for them. They seemed primed to have their convictions challenged, shaped, and tested—to really grapple with truth at a profound level. So we plunged in, at the same time paying close attention to learn what our students' issues were.

Over time the curriculum evolved into discussions of issues like peer pressure, drinking, drugs, smoking, and sex. It was astounding how sharp these sixth graders were in understanding truth and making applications, even though they were not emotionally and relationally mature. They were fully capable of making life-changing decisions.

A Surprising Survey

A huge boost to our understanding of these preteens came the first time we did a survey. We asked a provocative question: "If you could ask your parents any question, but I would ask it for you and then give you the answer later, what would it be?"

One year we received these responses (remember, these are from *eleven and twelve year olds*):

"If I become pregnant before marriage, what would your reaction be?"

"Did you have sex before you were married?"

"How old will I be before I can kiss?"

Four students requested that we ask their parents: "How old were you when you first had sex and who was it with?"

Two more requested: "Mom, why do you have sex?"

"What qualities should the person I marry have?"

Another time we asked in what areas they felt peer pressure. These were children living in middle-class suburban families, and many of them attended Christian schools. Here are some of their answers: Making fun of other people, cut-downs, music, cigarettes, cussing, clothing, leaving one movie theater to slide into another movie, stealing, cheating, and being mean and saying bad things to other people. Going places I shouldn't go, dares [that was a big one], drugs, alcohol, insults, money, and hair. Just being tempted to do wrong things.

After seeing children respond in the same ways year after year, we could not help but conclude that a whole lot was happening beneath the surface in these "cute" little boys and girls. Seismic shifts were jolting their brains and bodies. Yet, they were now old enough intellectually, emotionally, and spiritually to begin grasping the significance of the life experiences awaiting them in their teenage years.

After we taught the class for several years, another benefit surfaced. We were able to track what was happening to some of our alumni. Was this training doing any good? Our students went on to junior high and high school and some came back to report. Occasionally we would hear, "Thank you, Mr. Rainey, for teaching that material. It really helped prepare me for junior high." Sadly, others we knew about ignored what they'd been taught and fell into a number of traps.

Yet the good fruit of our efforts made us more confident. After starting with the bar of expectations at a modest height, we raised it higher, getting more and more specific around issues and challenging these youth to higher standards.

We never felt we were rushing these young people. The parents were another matter. A few would come to the class at times when Dennis was teaching and sit with folded arms and furrowed brow. You could almost read their thoughts: *Why is he teaching my little Jimmy or my little Susie all of this material now? My child is not facing that.* And they were right. But what they usually didn't know—what we were learning ourselves—was that these issues were just around the corner.

Our guess is that 99.9 percent of all parents look at their child at eleven or twelve and don't have the foggiest idea that he or she is beginning to grapple with adult issues. Preadolescents don't know how to connect all the dots—they may only understand the basic facts on sex, for example. But their own sex drive is emerging, and they are sensing a new, often frightening, need to be accepted and appreciated by the opposite sex. Life is in full gear. Determinative life choices are about to be made.

This is no time for parents to curl up on the couch for a nap. Instead there is a twelve- to twenty-four-month window of opportunity in the fifth- and sixth-grade years to prepare the child for the rapids of junior high.

Many parents believe that the truly significant, foundational choices are made when a child is well into the teen years. Our "research" in the laboratory of our sixth-grade Sunday school class, in ministry with youth and families since 1971, and in years of field testing in the Rainey home leads us to believe *the most pivotal choices are made during the age span of about eleven to fifteen. Wrong choices can tragically alter the course of a child's life.*

A NAVIGATION AID FOR PARENTS

Is there a proven way for parents to steer children safely through the turbulent waters of adolescence?

We've learned there isn't a single strategy that will guarantee no rapids in your child-rearing stream. However, we—and other parents—have been helped by the insight that every child seems to move predictably through what we call the "zones of adolescence." An understanding of these zones can serve as a navigation aid for proactive parents.

Just like the cycle of the seasons in nature, certain attitudes and behaviors seem to appear on cue during the preteen and teenage years. If you know what zone your child is in, and what will happen in the next zone, you can be prepared to meet the needs of your child, as well as be better able to maintain your equilibrium as a mom or dad.

The Innocence Zone (Age Ten Through Twelve)

A preteen in this zone is still largely unstained by temptations and evil. "Hormonally speaking," the child is not yet experiencing the confusing signals the body will soon send his way. For the most part, he will still listen to what his parents have to say.

During this zone parents need to seize the opportunity to do two things: First, mom and dad must secure the relationship with the child. Second, they need to aggressively begin to shape the child's convictions *before* adolescence hits in full force.

Don't make the mistake of many parents who severely underestimate the amount of convictions that can be transferred to a child in this zone. (Part II of this book, Stepping Around Snares, contains extensive instruction on how to shape and test your child's convictions.)

The Danger Zone (Age Thirteen Through Sixteen)

We believe this zone is *the* most dangerous phase of your child's life. The junior high and early high school years are when most families lose a son or daughter, although the actual loss of the child may not become evident until later.

To this point your child and his friends have been essentially under the control of their families. Many parents assume, incorrectly, that the children their sons and daughters have relationships with at church, at school, and in the neighborhood have similar values to their own.

This is a very, very dangerous assumption.

In the danger zone, however, the family values learned and lived-out behind closed doors that may have seemed so similar are now exposed for what they really are—often a murky, bland adaptation of the world's values or a startling absence of values altogether.

With the onset of the teenage years, when children are experiencing greater freedom, the peers who once were a good influence may now be banding together to test the limits of their parents. As a result, by the time they reach fifteen, many "good" children are out of the control of their parents and will soon be out of control in their lives.

For many young people, the junior high years become a fork in the road where they either continue down the right path or take the wrong one, testing things that are harmful. Sadly, many stay on the disastrous path, and the results won't be evident until later in high school, college, or even adulthood.

The problem is that choosing the wrong path is usually not a one-time decision or a huge event. It's a slow, slippery descent into compromising situations. If it occurred overnight, parents could spot it and react.

The wise parent recognizes this danger zone and is careful to not give a child too much freedom too soon. Just because a child is beginning to look and act like an adult by making some "right choices" does not mean he is really ready for adult responsibilities and corresponding freedoms.

Parents with a child in the danger zone often have intense feelings of hopelessness. Their feelings may be articulated as, "Will the teenage years ever end?" or "We've lost our relationship with our child!" or "We are raising a juvenile delinquent!"

Don't quit! This is a time for perseverance in love and your efforts to shape your child's convictions.

The Release Zone (Age Seventeen Through Nineteen)

Assuming a successful passage through the danger zone, this final phase of adolescence results in the child having increased responsibility and freedom. In our family this zone has arrived during the second semester of the child's junior year in high school.

The increase in privileges is a reward for mature, trustworthy, and faithful behavior by the teen. Failures will occur from time to time, but the child is proving himself worthy of adultlike responsibilities, such as later curfews, more freedom in the use of time, and fewer restrictions.

Our goal is to release the child slowly, so that by the last semester of his senior year in high school, he is free of many of the restrictions of his earlier teen years. We have felt it was better to release these older teens bit by bit while they are still at home. Then as they make mistakes, we are still there to coach, encourage, and even correct. Releasing a child does not mean you stop being the protector, provider, and parent.

The exception to this would be a child who has not proven himself worthy of this trust. At this point it might be necessary to establish a written contract with the child to clarify restrictions and responsibilities.

Stay Involved

As we watched one wave after another of our sixth graders in the Sunday school class move on, we observed a pattern: If the parents were not engaged and involved on the important issues in their child's life, those youngsters were more at risk.

Some time in the early teens, a spiritual erosion can occur, and often there is an emotional drift towards isolation. The teenager naturally pushes away from his parents, and if the parent allows his child to push him out of his life, the child will end up in a vulnerable place: overly influenced by peers.

That's why it is so important to start talking about the big issues in the ten- to twelve-year-old age frame and to establish good relational connections. Then as you actually face the issues later, the communication lines will be in place and you will be able to review information discussed before.

On the other side, involved parents, the ones who taught the standards and values we reinforced on Sunday, tended to see good choices and pleasing results in their children. For example, one family had five boys. Every one of those boys turned out stouter than horseradish (in a good sense), because they had a mom and a dad who engaged their sons around the issues, set clear standards, and didn't back off. All of these young men tested their parents' limits repeatedly. These boys were not perfect. Yet all of them today are strong Christians.

The Alumni Return

One of the favorite sessions for the class occurred when we asked some of our alumni, now in high school or college, to come back and share their ideas and experiences as part of a panel. The sixth graders would sit on the edge of their seats when an older teen spoke. These older youths' comments have affirmed the wisdom of presenting our real-life curriculum.

Here's a sampling of quotes made by graduates of our sixth-grade "life training institute":

23

- "My dad wanted to make sure I treated my mom and little sister with respect before I was able to date. So, if I learned to treat [with respect] the ones that I live with, I should be able to be a good leader to go out on a date." (Young man.)
- "The main thing that kept them [parents] trusting me was that I had a very open relationship with them. I would share with them about the things I would be doing on a date . . . I kept them in touch with what was going on." (Young woman.)
- "I think that the guy should have enough leadership to ask the girl out." (Young man.)
- "As far as your standards, you had better make your decision before you go out on the date. Everyone does have a sex drive, and if you don't set standards for yourself on a date, you can fall into something that you never wanted to do and never thought you would." (Young man.)
- "I think it's really neat to have a dad who wants to interview your date." (Young woman.)
- "Ladies, you shouldn't think, 'If I want this guy to like me, I need to kiss him.' You are not obligated to do that. You need to set your standards." (Young woman.)
- "Don't do anything to a girl or girlfriend that you wouldn't want done to your sister. Don't paw over her! I don't want anyone touching my little sister." (Young man.)
- "When I was about your age and on through junior high, I was ashamed to be with my parents. I just didn't want to be around them. I thought they weren't cool . . . If I knew then what I know now, I would do it differently. I would spend time with my parents. I realize now that I will be gone in about three months, and I messed up the better part of my life with them because I wanted to be cool." (Young man.)
- "You have to give your parents something to trust." (Young woman.)

With comments like that, you can see why we're so sold on injecting an immense amount of truth about life into preteens.

Most adults reading this book won't go out and start a sixth-grade Sunday school class, although we couldn't offer a better suggestion for obtaining a real education on preadolescents. (Does your church need help?[2]) But all parents can implement a strategy to help their children prepare for adolescence.

This book is intended do just that. Your approach may be as basic as a weekly breakfast with your child where you connect and communicate about the critical traps of adolescence. Whatever you do, it will be one of the best investments ever made in the future success of your child.

RODGER FINDS HIS ANSWER

Whatever happened to Rodger, the boy who was swept over Niagara Falls?

On that horrifying afternoon, below Horseshoe Falls, about two hundred feet back from where the falls empty into the gorge, a boat sat—filled with tourists who were snapping pictures and enjoying the cooling spray. The captain was about to back *The Maid of the Mist* away when a passenger yelled, "Man overboard!" About fifty feet away in the whirling current was a child wearing a red life jacket.

The captain circled the boat. A line attached to a life preserver was hurled toward the small body. The first time it fell short, the second time Rodger grabbed ahold. Moments later he was safely aboard.

"My sister! Where's my sister?" he asked.

Standing on the observation point, more than 150 feet above, one of his sister Deanne's rescuers had watched Rodger's retrieval onto the deck of *The Maid of the Mist*. "Your prayers have been answered," he told her.

The body of the boat owner, Jim, was found down river four days later.

Rodger grew up, went to college, married, and became a father. Later he returned to Niagara Falls twice with his family to show them where he had almost died.

But a question nagged at him. Why had he been spared? Others would say to him, "Somebody must be watching over you; somebody has something special planned for you."[3]

Years passed, but he still had no answers. Then in 1980, twenty years after the incident, Rodger, after being invited to church by a friend, prayed a prayer acknowledging Christ as Savior.

In 1990, on the thirtieth anniversary of his plunge over Horseshoe Falls, Rodger returned to Niagara Falls and spoke at a local church. In part he said, "Something happened thirty years ago that was very, very special. I lived. Why? So that I could live again . . . so that others would come to saving knowledge of Christ and have the gift of eternal life."[4]

In many ways, parenting is like Rodger's story—all of it, not just the miraculous escape.

None of us wants the ride through adolescence with our child to be as turbulent as Rodger's river adventure. But whether it is or not, there's Someone who knows all about it and has things under control. We just need to wait a while before we understand how God will shape the outcome of our child's adolescence.

3

If We Had Just Thirty Minutes of Your Time

Seven Priorities for the Effective Parent

Do you ever feel like your brain might explode if you have to remember *one more thing?*

It's no wonder—we've got a lot to remember. The password to get into the computer. A code for voice mail. A secret number for the ATM at your bank. Phone numbers at work, at home, in the car. And our child's number at college—it changed again this year.

Do you long for the good old days (maybe the mid 1980s or early 1990s) when you didn't have to answer the phone while driving, and you only found mail in the box at the end of your driveway—not in your computer, spewing from the fax machine, or in an overnight packet on your porch?

Our brains need braces for the information overload. People who study such topics say that a single weekday edition of *The New York Times* has more information than a typical person living in the seventeenth century would have encountered in a lifetime![1]

Parents certainly feel the pain brought by information glut. Everywhere we turn someone is offering more advice on how to do it right with our children.

We know this book is full of ideas but in this chapter we will simplify the priorities to focus on as you craft the life of a preadolescent or teenager.

Let's pretend we are old friends who, after years apart, have just bumped into each other while making connections at O'Hare Airport in Chicago. After exchanging greetings, you tell us your oldest child will soon be a teenager. We nod and smile—"Been there. Done that. Several times."

"Say, what can you tell us about successfully raising a teenager?" you ask with a nervous laugh. "Some of our friends tell us it's horrible."

We all look at our watches—thirty minutes until you board your flight for Hawaii and we head back to Little Rock. You offer to buy the Starbucks Coffee.

Here's our best shot—seven guiding priorities to embrace every day of your child's preadolescent and adolescent years.

The coffee is hot, your pen and notepad are ready, here goes.

PRIORITY 1: PRAYER

This one probably does not surprise you. But before you glance at your watch and start tapping your foot, *please consider carefully what we have gleaned from parenting six teens.*

The sobering news about raising children is that we really have no ultimate control over whether our child will choose the narrow gate "that leads to life" (Matt. 7:14) or the wide gate that leads to destruction. If other experiences in life have not humbled us and shown us how dependent we are on God, then parenting a preadolescent or teenager will.

But understanding our desperate need to depend on God is the good news. Once we give up the naive idea that we parents can dictate the choices our children will make and the spiritual gate—narrow or broad—they will walk through, then we are ready to slip on the knee pads and get serious about prayer.

What have we learned about prayer for our children as they prepare for and enter adolescence?

Pray regularly. Bring every concern, dream, desire about your child to God in fervent, persistent prayer. (Luke 18:1–8 contains a great parable on persistent prayer that must have been told just for parents of teenagers.)

Two of the best times to pray with your child are on the way to school (assuming you drive him) and at bedtime—regardless of age. We live about five miles from our school. Every morning we would pray about things most important to our children—tests, friends, teachers, activities. As the car topped the hill right before the school building, we always concluded with the same request: "And Lord, we ask that you would keep Rebecca, Deborah, and Laura from harm, evil, and temptation this day. That they would experience You at work in their lives and be used by You to influence others for Your Kingdom. Amen."

Now that our teenagers drive themselves to school, we use breakfast for this prayer time.

Bedtime prayers can be more personal for each child. Pray for his future mate, relationships, activities, challenges, temptations, and heart for God. Don't assume that even a teenager is too big for you to kneel beside his bed and stroke his face and pray.

Pray offensively. Before your child hits adolescence, pray for his peer group—that he will have at least one strong Christian buddy for the teenage years. Ask God to protect your child daily from others who would be an evil influence. Also consider asking God to help you spot your child doing things right so that you can encourage him in making right choices.

Pray defensively. On more than one occasion we have sought the Lord's help in removing a friend of questionable character from a child's life.

From time to time we have felt that one of our teens might be deceiving us, but we could never be absolutely certain. In those situations we have asked God to help us catch him if he's doing something wrong. God seems to feel sorry for parents who pray this prayer!

Pray intensely. One of the most misunderstood spiritual disciplines of the Christian life is prayer accompanied with fasting (the giving up of food for a prescribed period of time). Although fasting does not earn points with God, He nonetheless assumes in Scripture that we will fast and pray (see Matt. 6:16–18) and promises to reward us if we do it correctly. We know a couple who have set aside each Monday to fast, sunup until sundown, and pray for their struggling fourteen-year-old child.

Pray when God brings your child to mind and burdens you. It may be at that very moment your child is facing a circumstance of critical importance. Some friends of ours were burdened one night to pray for their daughter. At the very time they slipped out of bed and to their knees, a police car was driving by their daughter's car on a remote mountain road where she and a girlfriend had gone to look at the city lights, eat a sandwich, and talk. Unknown to them, an escaped prisoner was hiding underneath the car. The prisoner was apprehended, and the girls drove off unharmed.

Pray with your child. It's easy for prayer to become an exclusive dialogue—you and God. Why not do what one mom, Nina, did with her teenage daughter, Natalie, and become prayer partners. Natalie's teenage years were filled with special moments where she and her mom knelt together and prayed over Natalie's struggles and challenges.

Pray together as a couple. For more than twenty-six years of marriage we have ended every day we're together in prayer. No spiritual discipline has protected our marriage and our family more than this daily time of communion together with God.

Three of our six children have made it through adolescence. With that behind us, you might think we are tempted to coast to the finish line? Hardly. We've been humbled so many times that we know how impossible it is for us to shape the hearts of our children. We pray more than ever for our children—all of them.

God wants the same thing for you and your child. *Talk to Him*.

"The effective prayer of a righteous man can accomplish much" (James 5:16).[2]

PRIORITY 2: STANDARDS

We are amazed at how many moms and dads have never had a focused conversation on what the specific boundaries and standards will be for their child during the preadolescent and teen years. Regularly in our sixth-grade Sunday school class we were shocked by the choices children were making. One Sunday over half the class of sixty eleven- and twelve-year-olds admitted that they had viewed an R-rated movie in the last three months. Many watched the movie with their parents.

Have you and your spouse talked about dating, driving, jobs, grades, curfews, friends, and after school activities? The list seems endless at times. We promise this: *If you don't nail down your own convictions ahead of time, your teenager and his peer group will establish their own!*

If you have not agreed as a couple upon guidelines, your child will soon hit you with the divide-and-conquer strategy. Children are experts on whether dad or mom is the easy touch on certain issues.

Even when you know you should be united as a couple and clear on the rules, you may still stumble. I took one of our daughters shopping for some shorts. As I waited outside the dressing room at the department store, another child, who looked to be about thirteen, came out to model shorts for her mom. Those shorts were aptly named—they looked incredibly short to me. Then our daughter came out. Compared to what I had just witnessed, her pair seemed acceptable.

When we got home, our daughter modeled her new outfit for the rest of the family. One of our sons said, "Dad! I can't believe you let her buy those. They're too short!"

Barbara agreed. In the area of clothing, we have a policy—a particular piece of clothing must pass the approval of both parents (an opinion of a brother or sister is appreciated—usually—but is not a binding vote) before it goes into the permanent wardrobe. I had blown it but was saved by our shared conviction. Amid frowns and protests, the shorts went back to the store.

PRIORITY 3: INVOLVEMENT

We are not suggesting that you become the ultimate soccer mom. That's not bad—being there at all of your child's activities—but involvement means much more than driving the carpool and never missing a dance recital.

Involvement means crawling inside your child's head and heart. Involvement is moving from the outside to the interior of an adolescent's life. Involvement means diving into the turbulent currents caused by emotions—the child's and the parent's. Soul to soul. Heart to heart. This can be scary and uncomfortable.

The sobering truth is that you can be in the same house, the same gym, but be clueless about what's really going on in your child's life. Although it's a humbling thought, consider beginning with this assumption: *"I'm not involved in my child's life. I don't really know what's going on in his life."*

Author John Trent tells a powerful story of how important our involvement is in a child's life:

> Recently, a woman grabbed my arm after I'd finished speaking at a conference on the enormous need we all had for affirmation.
>
> "Dr. Trent, can I tell you my story?" she asked. "Actually, it's a story of something my son did with my granddaughter that illustrates what you've been talking about."
>
> "My son has two daughters: one who's five, and one who is in the 'terrible twos.' For several years, he's taken the oldest girl out for a 'date' time, but it wasn't until recently that he'd asked the two year old out.
>
> "On their first 'date,' he took her to breakfast at a fast-

32

food restaurant. They'd just gotten their pancakes, when he decided it would be a good time to tell her how much he loved and appreciated her.

"'Jenny,' he said, 'I want you to know how much I love you and how special you are to Mom and me. We prayed for you for years, and now that you're here and growing up to be such a wonderful girl, we couldn't be more proud of you.'

"Once he said all this, he stopped talking and reached over for his fork to begin eating . . . but he never got the fork into his mouth.

"Jenny reached out and laid her little hand on her father's. His eyes went to hers, and in a soft, pleading voice she said, 'Longer, Daddy . . . longer.'"

"He put his fork down and told her even more reasons why he and my daughter-in-law loved her. 'You're very kind, nice to your sister, full of energy . . .'

"Then, he again reached for his fork only to hear the same words again. A second time . . . and a third . . . and a fourth time . . . and each time he heard the words, 'Longer, Daddy, longer.'"

That father never did get much to eat that morning, but his daughter feasted on words every child longs to hear. His words made such an impression on little Jenny that a few days later she spontaneously ran up to her mother, jumped in her arms and said, "I'm a really awesome daughter, Mommy. Daddy told me so!"[3]

The Jennys in our families will never grow too old for this kind of affirmation.

Throughout this book, we will offer advice on how to connect heart-to-heart with a preadolescent or adolescent. It takes time, courage, perseverance. And it takes energy. Lots of energy.

It may mean trying to get into your child's life and being thwarted by the child. Pushed out. Locked out. The child, emotionally confused, doesn't know what he wants or needs. We've been there.

You may have to endure a time or two when your child is screaming at you, when you just want to say "You're grounded for a month" and run from the messy details of a relationship. This is hard, and it's why so many parents give up.

Involvement also means not losing heart when you don't see immediate results. When a child is not living according to what's acceptable, many parents surrender. They settle for less. Lower their standards. And stop pressing the child. They end up compromising, shrugging their shoulders, and saying with a sigh, "Maybe my goals and standards for my teenager were unrealistic. I guess what he's doing is not that bad."

Connecting with your teenager may be one of the most demanding challenges of your life. Even after raising three adolescents, I still struggle with involvement. Just recently, after Barbara told me I was too busy, I sensed my relationship with a daughter was slipping away. I was losing touch. I've had to commit myself to reconnection. I overhauled my schedule. I'm back doing things she wants to do, like taking her fishing, having date nights, and just hanging out talking.

Reconnecting can be something as simple as walking into your child's bedroom and just sitting there and asking a few questions. Then listening. Really listening. Like recently when Barbara went on a date with Rebecca: They sat at a Sonic drive-in, munching on fries, and Rebecca soaked up the one-on-one time. She needed the attention.

Pursuing a heart-to-heart relationship is usually rewarding. Although some of the information may be unsettling, you will *know your child*. And in knowing, you will be able to pray with power and minister to your preteen or teen's needs.

PRIORITY 4: TRAINING

The best parenting is proactive, not reactive.

The reactive parent stays in a defensive posture, continually reacting to a child's mistakes. A proactive parent goes on the offensive and does what is necessary to become the child's trainer.

Effective training involves at least three parts.

First, *parents need to see clearly the goal.* They need to know what they are trying to achieve. Most parents have never written a mission statement for what they are trying to build into their children. It's no wonder so many parents feel like failures and don't really know if they've succeeded or not.

Shortly after we started our family, I recall how I began to develop a list of everything I wanted to teach our children. I started with a list of twenty-five things that soon ballooned to more than fifty. It was a good exercise, but it was overwhelming. In addition, Barbara was frustrated with me because I had developed the list and she hadn't really been involved in shaping it.

Months later we went away for a weekend and wrote down separately what each of us wanted to build into our children. Both of us ended up with a prioritized top-ten values list. We then got together and worked our way through a unified list of our top-five values. That list has proved to be the North Star for our parenting.

Second, *effective training involves repetition.* A Green Beret once told me, "As Green Berets we train to learn what to do in every conceivable circumstance—over and over and over again. Then in times of battle we know what to do. It's just second nature to us."

That is a picture of what we parents should do. We train our children and instruct them in making the right choices in the circumstances they will face. And we do it over and over.

Repeated training situations should begin early in your preteen's life. Seize the window of opportunity—the eighteen months or so when your child is ten to twelve—to run your own boot camp to prepare him for the traps. Do not underestimate the capability of a child this age to understand truth and develop personal convictions.

Continue training him all the way through his adolescent years. There's a danger in assuming that the standards don't need to be revisited often as your child advances through high school. You may need to find fresh ways of repackaging what you teach, but don't stop teaching.

Finally, *training involves accountability*. One of the major mistakes made is giving our children too much freedom without appropriate oversight. This is especially true if a family has more than two children. We tend to overcontrol our firstborn child and release the younger children prematurely.

My mom was the master at accountability during my teenage years. She demanded to know where I was and what I was doing. I can still hear her saying, "Where are you going? Who will be there? What time will you be home?" And my dad was right in there with her. The first night that I was allowed to go out alone in the car he wrote down the mileage on the speedometer and gave me a five-mile maximum limit.

There is an old saying, "You can not expect that which you do not inspect." One of our biggest regrets as parents is not doing a better job of inspecting what we expected with each of our pre-teens and teenagers.

PRIORITY 5: COMMUNITY

We have become increasingly convinced and alarmed that one of the most damaging changes that has occurred in recent years is the loss of community in raising our children. We used to look out for the children of others far more than we do now.

I remember when I was growing up in Ozark, Missouri, population 1,300, in the 1960s that if I peeled out from a stop sign at 8:00 P.M. any night of the week, month, or year, by 9:30 P.M. when I parked in the driveway, I could expect my parents to know about it. One night I got into a fight at the Dairy Queen. Fifteen minutes later when I walked through the door, they already knew what had happened.

This type of involvement is rare today. Humorist Garrison Keillor has said, "Adults no longer dare to influence other people's children. You should be able to discipline another person's child, up to a point. Children are supposed to be raised by all sorts of people."[4]

Keillor uses a key phase—*adults no longer dare*. In our age of tolerance, we have developed the philosophy that we have no right to tell another parent about a concern we have about his child. And children suffer from our failure to be involved in the lives of others.

We've called parents about behavior we have observed in their children and had them tell us they "didn't want to hear it." They didn't want to know. One parent angrily chewed me out for calling about something his son had done that was clearly wrong.

We need to drop our defensiveness and fear and encourage others to offer observations to us about how our children are doing when we're not there to see for ourselves. Take the initiative by telling the parents of friends of your child: "If you see my teenager doing anything questionable, you have the freedom to tell me. I want to know."

It took us several adolescent projects in our own family to learn how much we needed the help of others to monitor and correct our children. Friends, true friends, have cared enough to courageously call and express a concern about something they've seen one of our children doing that they know we wouldn't approve of. Those are tough phone calls to make. And tough to receive. But in each and every case we've seen God use these circumstances to help us keep a child out of a threatening trap.

There is a natural community that we need to do a better job of tapping into for our children's accountability—our church. Certainly this group of folks ought to have the right perspective on the value and worth our children possess. We are in this thing together, and that should pertain especially to raising the generation that is the future of the church. Why not call a meeting of all the parents, say fifth through twelfth grade. Give one another the challenge and freedom to look out for one another's children.

PRIORITY 6: DIRECTION

We have found that most Christian parents desire more than anything else to raise children who will grow up to love Jesus Christ and walk with Him. With that overall objective in mind, we have searched the Scriptures to discern what biblical goals we should aim for with our children. The four qualities we developed give us four clear goals to pursue as we craft our children. Nearly every issue or trap our children will encounter can be linked to a young person's need in one of four areas.

Identity: The Scripture records the story of God giving man and woman an identity. The nation of Israel was selected, adopted, and set apart by God to be "His people." Every person is born with a unique, divinely imprinted identity. If we want to properly guide our children to a healthy self-identity, we must acknowledge and support the Creator's design in three key areas: spiritual identity, emotional identity, and sexual identity. We must also communicate with them one of the most important messages they will ever receive—"You are made in the image of God. You are an incredibly valuable child."

Character: From Genesis to Revelation, character development is a major theme of God's work in people. And it's one of the major assignments God gives us as parents. Character is how your child responds to authority and life's circumstances. It is "response-ability," and comes as a result of training our children to submit to God and His Word.

Relationships: None of us was intended to make a journey through life alone. We need the strength, comfort, encouragement, resources, and power provided by God and others.

Try teaching truth without a relationship with your child. It produces rebellion. Similarly, relationships without truth can result in a self-indulgent teen, one who is spoiled.

Children also need parents who will build into them the ability to love others. And this training can occur quite naturally in the context of our relationship. The best school to learn about relationships and resolving conflict is in the University of Family, where the professors teach and train their students for more than eighteen years.

Mission: Every person needs a reason to live, a driving passion or calling that provides meaning and impact. This is a person's mission.

We need to ask ourselves, "Have I more passion for the values of this world's system than for the things of God? What are my goals in life—are they ones I want my child to copy?"

Every child should be helped to understand that life is a dynamic relationship with God that overflows in love to other people—a love that the Holy Spirit uses to reconcile the lost to God. Everything else, as good or innocuous as it may be, is only a prop to facilitating this mission.

PRIORITY 7: PERSEVERANCE

Winston Churchill could have been talking to parents when he said, "Never give in, never give in, never, never, never, never—in nothing, great or small, large or petty—never give in except to convictions of honor and good sense."[5]

Parenting is not a weekend project. We're talking years—the rest of your life, actually. Fortunately, adolescence does have a time limit, but we'll never make it if we have to see immediate results for our efforts.

In fact, so often during the teen years it may seem like you're losing ground. You may be working hard, pouring truth and your heart into a child, and yet one foolish choice follows another. The temptation is to feel that you have failed. It's over. Hang it up. Toss in the towel.

Don't. Don't. Don't. If your parenting boat seems to be leaking like a sieve, keep bailing with one arm and row with the other. Perseverance is the parenting quality that helps you keep doing all the other important things—the praying, training, staying involved, and setting standards.

You will get tired. You will experience pain. The ones we are sacrificing for—our children—will sometimes say and do things that hurt us deeply. They do that because they are still children, and "Foolishness is bound up in the heart of a child" (Prov. 22:15).

At times we may have to endure even a broken heart, but we must not lose heart: "And let us not lose heart in doing good, for in due time we shall reap if we do not grow weary" (Gal. 6:9).

In thinking about the perseverance needed by parents, we smile and take heart at the pithy quote by the great English preacher Charles Haddon Spurgeon: "It was by perseverance that the snail reached the ark."

There you have it, our thirty-minute summary, with probably a minute or two to spare.

Before you run to catch that plane, here's the list of priorities one more time:

Prayer
Standards
Involvement
Training
Community
Direction
Perseverance

These seven big ideas can make the difference between frustration and fruit in parenting preadolescents and teenagers.

Have a great time in Hawaii!

Part II

Stepping Around Snares

4

The Traps of Adolescence

Preparing a Child for the Journey of a Lifetime

Near a coast of one of the earth's vast oceans, a small angler fish was hungry. Not equipped to move at sizzling speed and overtake a slower swimmer, to "do lunch" the angler fish had to resort to trickery and fool its prey.

Angler fish have a flexible, string-like dorsal fin that extends some inches from the body and can be moved much like a fisherman would flick a fly rod. At the end of this extremity is a small chunk of tissue that conveniently looks like a minnow.

Settling quietly in the weeds, the angler fish deftly began to move its "rod," the bait darting in the water just like a miniature fish. The trap was set.

A stranger passed nearby, just some fish swimming about—maybe headed for school or on the way to the fish mall. He saw a small, wiggling, tasty-looking snack. *Oh, why not*, he thought. *Some fast food to eat on the go.*

In seconds it was over. The stranger swam over and lunged hungrily for the bait, but just as his jaws were about to close, larger jaws opened below him. *Gulp*! The angler fish burped, packed up his tackle, and moved on.[1]

All of God's creation on earth, from the tiniest animal to man himself, is susceptible to myriad dangers lurking behind various baits and lures, snares and traps. With the animal kingdom, the threat is physical death, but with God's highest creation, man, the threat is far more subtle. The threat is spiritual death. It has been Satan's mission since the Garden to deceive and destroy mankind, and any opportunity he might have for a relationship with the God of the universe.

We parents have the opportunity and responsibility to train our young in the art of recognizing and detecting the enemy's traps. In addition we teach our children that the best way to avoid being snared is never to go near a snare.

As adults we've learned some basic lessons about staying away or running from the things that ensnare. Our children, however, are young and innocent, naturally curious, eager for independence, filled with alarming arrogance. They are especially vulnerable to traps.

In the following chapters we present what we believe are the fourteen most common and dangerous traps of adolescence. We know the list is not exhaustive, but if every parent helped his child recognize and stay away from these, the journey through the teen years would be much less painful and damaging. Our teens would then stand on the threshold of the adult world with far fewer battle scars, not a walking wounded Christian skeptic, but a hopeful, confident young adult, ready for the challenging plan God has before him.

Following is a list of the traps we will expose in detail:

Peer pressure	**Deceit**
Sex	**Substance abuse**
Dating	**Busyness**
"Attitude"	**The tongue**
Media	**Mediocrity**
Unresolved anger	**Pornography**
Appearance	**False gods**

We expect this section on traps will be used in several ways. Ideally, you should read all of the material, because at some point during your child's preadolescent and teen years, you will encounter nearly every issue we discuss. But if you are interested in particular topics or need information *now*, the chapters on traps stand separately and may be read in any order.

Obviously, many of the issues covered interrelate, and the parenting principles we present often apply to more than one situation. To further assist you in finding relevant information on specific subjects, we have included an index near the end of the book.

All of the chapters on traps contain similar blocks of information. Each one has these three core sections:

1. Determining Your Convictions

As parents, we need to heed the advice given by Seneca, a Roman philosopher, who said, "You must know for which harbor you are headed in order to catch the right wind to take you there."

Our convictions as parents, the captains of the family ship, will steady us when the waves of teenage emotions and persuasions threaten to push us off course. But if you don't have convictions, if you haven't taken the time to grapple over what you believe and why, the undercurrent of the culture will suck your family's ship into a whirlpool of conflicting and confusing values.

At this point, we wish we could step out of these pages and hug you as a parent of a preteen or a teen, fiercely look you in the eyes, and sternly say: *You are about to enter one of the most challenging and rewarding assignments in all of life—raising a teenager. You are beginning the slow, perilous process of releasing your child to handle adult issues and to make life-changing and life-altering decisions on his own.*

Hear us on this one: "Mom, Dad, in just a few short years you aren't going to be there to help him make those decisions. If he's twelve, at best you've got six years of influence left. If he's fourteen, you have forty-eight months!"

Taking you by the shoulders we would plead with you, "Now is the time to begin to hammer out and clarify your spiritual convictions around the real life issues that your child will face. If you do not know what you believe and are not aggressively helping your teenager develop his own set of convictions, *then the world will thoroughly teach and indoctrinate your child. Guaranteed!*

That's why we think this book is so important for you and your teenagers. We genuinely want to help you determine some core convictions that you want to pass on to your children. Each of these fourteen "trap" chapters will give you an opportunity to examine, review, and clarify your own values, standards, and convictions. We'll offer some of our standards and convictions as we go through the book, but it's our hope that you and your spouse will take some time to interact and come up with your own.

It has taken us four teenagers and more than a dozen years to hammer out our convictions, so don't be discouraged if your standards don't come quickly. Pray. Read the Scripture. Decide what you truly believe.

2. Shaping Your Child's Convictions

Our goal is to help you equip your child with the biblical perspective on his life and the choices he will face. We want to enable you to come alongside your preadolescent or teenager and give you the courage and confidence to shape his conscience. Not only will we share what convictions we want our children to embrace, but also how we have gone about embedding these convictions in their lives.

This part of each chapter is based upon one of the keys to the prophet Daniel's strong and unwavering character: "But Daniel made up his mind that he would not defile himself with the king's choice food or with the wine which he drank" (1:8). Daniel made up his mind in advance. He decided what he would do *before* he faced the temptation or the trap.

We want you to have the privilege of teaching your own child how to decide in advance so he won't get caught in traps.

3. Testing Your Child's Convictions

Here we will offer specific ideas and suggestions to monitor your child's progress in handling the traps of adolescence. This is the time to help him learn from his mistakes and to encourage him to pursue maturity and responsibility. This is a time to stick close to your teen—coaching, instructing, training, and cheering him on.

When our children fail the test, by deceiving us, cheating, or breaking rules, we put our arms of love and grace around them. As we correct and retrain them, we explain that we would much rather have them make their major mistakes while they are at home under our training than later after they are gone.

Mistakes can be a tutor for your child to learn invaluable lessons in life. You may actually decide to create a situation that tests your child's character to see if he is getting the picture. Conviction testing is a critical part of your teen's character development.

In addition to the three core sections of each traps chapter, we include three other features in many of them.

FOR THE SINGLE PARENT

We know that many parents find themselves in the unenviable position of having to raise a preteen or teenager alone. We know many single parents who welcome all the support, encouragement, and guidance they can get. That's what we'll offer in this section. We'll share some customized suggestions and direction that we trust will provide some "wind beneath your wings."

UNFORGETTABLE LESSON

Do you remember moments or events in your childhood or teen years that burned a lesson about life into your brain? Often those watershed events were painful because the conclusions we reached as young people came as a result of wrong choices that initially promised life and happiness and fulfillment but later left only emptiness and despair.

As moms and dads, we know our children will have to learn a lot of life's lessons for themselves, but must they all be learned there? No. That's why God left us many illustrations in His Word that say, "Don't go that way, go this way."

For our impressionable preadolescents or young teens, an activity or demonstration that makes a significant, memorable point on avoiding each of the major traps can be a vivid reminder years down the road when a huge trap is directly in their path. Because most children are visual and experiential in their learning, these unforgettable lessons should be fun as well as instructive.

CONVICTION BUILDING PLAN

This section of questions and exercises related to each trap will help you move from just *thinking* about how you should help your preadolescent or teenager face challenges and form convictions to actually *implementing* ideas and solutions.

Most of the Conviction Building Plans involve two steps: Part One is a list of questions each spouse should answer individually; Part Two offers the opportunity for husband and wife to compare answers from Part One and move on to solidify shared convictions, construct a plan, and take action.

With the help of a friend, a single parent also will reap great benefits from the Conviction Building Plans.

What follows is not just a listing of facts, hints, and instructions. Each chapter presents relevant insight and instruction from Scripture. Knowing the need that we all have to see how someone else did something, we have included many stories from our personal experience to add living color to our ideas. In fact, some of the stories do not represent how we did it right; we've made our share of blunders. Like us, you'll learn that some of the most valued lessons that we have passed on to our children have come through our failures.

Preparing our children to face the traps of this world is a demanding challenge, but we are not to be fearful or intimidated. Jesus said, "In the world you have tribulation, but take courage; I have overcome the world" (John 16:33).

And the psalmist wrote about avoiding traps: "I will say to the LORD, 'My refuge and my fortress, / My God, in Whom I trust!' / For it is He who delivers you from the snare of the trapper" (91: 2–3).

May God's favor be upon you as you guide your child through the traps of adolescence.

5

Trap 1: Peer Pressure

Friends Are Major Players in Shaping Your Child's Values

Have you heard a distant rumble?

When your child reaches age ten or so, you will hear the sound—like an approaching thunderstorm. It's the herd!

You remember the scene in many movie westerns: Across the prairie gallops an enormous brown, shaggy, bellowing mass of buffalo, their pounding hooves shaking the ground. The pioneers in their path had better scramble with their oxen and wagons out of harm's way or mayhem, destruction, and death are likely.

For years your child has known peer pressure. Since at least preschool, for example, your child probably has craved the latest popular toy—from Barbie dolls to Beanie Babies to action figures with obscene muscles that make Dad look malnourished. But all of that peer pressure is minuscule compared to what happens in early adolescence. This is when your child encounters the herd.

Individuality is out. Following the masses is in. The typical child learns what everyone else is doing and quietly, willingly complies. This is not the time to stand out or be labeled as different or weird. There's not another point in life where being accepted by a peer group means more.

Some of this peer pressure is innocent. Having a good run with your buddy buffalo is exhilarating. But unfortunately, a fun romp can turn into a stampede that sweeps everyone over a cliff.

Although we've had some fun describing the herd mentality of preteens and young teens, the peer pressure issue is extremely serious.

When you send your child off to the typical middle school or junior high these days, you just can't naively assume that members of his peer group are coming from a family who shares your values. Every school in America is populated with many children who come to class each morning from unhappy or often unwholesome home situations. Some children are so wounded and detached that joining a gang gives them a more stable place of personal refuge than their own family.

Dan Korem, an expert on youth subcultures, has written that members of gangs prey on these troubled youth. Gang members are almost guaranteed to have issues of divorce, separation, and physical or sexual abuse present in their families.[1]

Your child must be prepared to combat the most insidious forms of peer pressure. This literally can be a life-and-death issue. Through choosing the right friends and developing and owning the right convictions, your child needs to learn when it's okay to gallop with the herd and when it's better to graze alone.

Peers—for good and bad—will tug at our teens. Outside the guidance we continue to have at home, nothing will influence our children as much as the choice of their friends. Nothing.

The Bible speaks pointedly on the power of the people we spend time with. Paul wrote: "Do not be deceived: 'Bad company corrupts good morals'" (1 Cor. 15:33).

The opposite is also true: Good company guards against the development of bad habits. Many parents are so afraid of peer pressure they seldom use "good" peer pressure to their advantage.

A Bad Apple

One of my favorite object lessons in the sixth-grade Sunday

school class was the bad apples demonstration. Surprisingly, most youth today have not heard the old saying, "One bad apple can spoil a whole barrel." This phrase doesn't have much meaning when most of us buy apples by the bag, not the barrel.

On a Sunday morning near the beginning of the nine-month class, I would bring some apples. I called them my "buddies." I usually had one beautiful, shiny red apple and a couple others that looked nice but had at least one bruise.

"These two apples with the bruises represent a couple of buddies you really ought not to spend time with in junior high," I would say. "They have a dark side to them, a compromised area of their lives.

"This good apple represents you, a good Christian preteen. The good apple sees no problem with the bruised apples. He says to himself, these are my buddies. They wouldn't do anything to hurt me. They're not *that bad.*"

I continued, "These three apples are going to become close buddies for a few months. We'll check on them at the end of the class and see what happens to the good apple."

Then I would put the apples in a plastic bag, drop the bag into a paper sack, and stick it in the closet. After a few months, several students would become curious about what happened to the buddies, but I wouldn't open the sack until the last class of the year. In that class, I would read 1 Corinthians 15:33 and then invite a member of the class to come up and pull the plastic bag out of the sack.

It never failed—the two bad buddies had really made an impact on the good apple. The identity of all three apples had been lost; the bag now contained a discolored, mushy, apple soup. The youngsters on the front row would shrink back as the plastic bag with the putrid goop was pulled out of the sack.

This lesson demonstrated how bad company can corrupt and even consume the best young Christian. The friends our children spend time with will influence them. And sometimes it's difficult to spot the children with bruises. A child who seems fine may slowly develop a dark side—a missing value, a character flaw, a bad habit—and begin compromising.

You shouldn't expect your child to be discerning enough to perform this apple inspection without your help. Training is needed.

Without consciously realizing it, the herd is undermining the authority of parents. Therein lies some of the great danger that peer pressure places on children:

- Peers will arrogantly and flagrantly ridicule the standards and values that you teach at home. Don't underestimate this one—you can count on it happening among peers, even at your child's youth group.
- Peers will encourage deceit, rebellion, and disobedience to parents. We've seen peers put on a real act to gain our trust. Later we've discovered that they had looked us in the eyes and lied to us.

Parents need to constantly monitor the friends their children hang out with to spot negative peer pressure. We've seen good teenagers ensnared by this trap in a matter of weeks.

DETERMINING YOUR CONVICTIONS

If you desire to help your child resist peer pressure, you will first need to examine your life to make sure the same trap does not ensnare you. Otherwise, you may be giving negative instruction to your child on how to respond to peers.

Nearly twenty years ago I was in a room with a group of Christian leaders, and we were asked to vote on a particular issue. I was seated next to a very close friend who had a strong opinion that was opposite from mine. During the debate that ensued, I kept silent about my convictions.

Finally we were asked to stand to indicate a "yes" vote. I watched my friend stand and thought, *I'm against this, but how can I stay seated when one of my best friends is standing?* I looked around the room as other men stood, and I did what every pread-olescent or teenager is tempted to do: I stood. Only two men voted against the proposal. I still remember them because of their courage and convictions.

Rainey, you're a hypocrite, I thought. *You have just succumbed to peer pressure.*

I learned some very important lessons that day through my compromise: First, I am susceptible to peer pressure. Second, it takes courage to stand for my convictions.

We believe there are several core convictions related to the trap of peer pressure that parents need to hold.

Parents' Conviction 1: The quality of our relationship with our child is the determining factor in how significant peer influence will be.

The world is often a hostile environment for children. Most ado-lescents experience a significant amount of alienation. Some youngsters are extremely popular during adolescence, but the majority really struggle with feelings of being excluded.

The family must become the harbor in the storm. The family must be that safe haven that always welcomes your teens back. No mat-ter what the world says to them, they know they can find love there. We often tell our children, "Nothing you can do will make me love you any more and nothing you can do will make me love you less."

Children *need* to be *needed* at home. They long for approval, for a deep sense of belonging, for importance, for order and secu-rity. If they don't receive these things at home, they will seek them elsewhere.

Parents' Conviction 2: We will never underestimate the incredible impact — negative or positive — of peer relationships on a preadolescent or teenager.

When Ashley was thirteen, she came home from school one day and described the pressure she was feeling from peers. She told us that they were making her feel like she was standing alone on a wall. Some of her friends were on the ground below, trying to get her to do something she didn't want to do, chucking stones, and pulling and tugging on her, trying to knock her down. Others were jeering at her and making fun of her for her standards. And even though she felt horribly alone on that wall, Ashley withstood their attempts.

We told Ashley that when peers try to pull you off the wall they are ultimately trying to get you to drop your standards to fit in with the herd, so that the herd can feel good about the choices it's making. We applauded her for standing strong.

Another way to counteract this negative herd instinct is to use positive peer pressure to your advantage. You may want to consider challenging one or two of your child's friends to be a good influence on your child while at the same time challenging your child to be a positive influence on them.

We approached the parents of one of our teenager's best friends and asked them if we could challenge their two teens to be a positive influence on our child. What followed was a great discussion with all three girls. We talked about how they could encourage one another to do what was right with the opposite sex, how they could be a positive influence in the lives of others at school, how they could pray for each other and hold one another accountable. They accepted the challenge to influence one another positively.

Parents' Conviction 3: We will not relinquish our right to influence and even control our child's relationships.

You are the parent. Realize that maintaining control of those who influence your children is within the boundaries of authority granted by God to you as a parent: "Children, be obedient to your parents in all things, for this is well-pleasing to the Lord" (Col. 3:20).

As friendships begin to take shape, steer your children in the direction of positive peer pressure and away from negative influences. We have made it difficult for our children to spend time with friends who do not provide the kind of influence we desire. In certain cases, we've even declared certain friends off limits.

It isn't wrong to make it more difficult for your children to get together with those who look like bad apples. You need to choose carefully the orchard where your children will do their picking.

We have encouraged our children to invite their friends over, to *make our home the place to be.* We particularly encourage our children to invite those friends that we know are good influences.

If all the apples are hanging out at your house, you can check out the quality of the fruit. You learn a lot when friends spend the night. You can observe how they behave, what kind of language they use, what they talk about. Then you'll have more information to use in steering your child in the direction of the good apples.

If you can, get to know the friend's parents to gain some idea of their values, beliefs, and convictions. One way to begin to get to know another family is by going to their home to pick up their child when he is invited to your house or by offering to take him home.

Also, be especially careful about where you allow your child to spend the night. That's one setting where peer pressure can be intense—to participate in ungodly conversation, for example, or to watch movies or play games that do not meet your standards.

The older your teen is, the more of an explanation your child will need. On one occasion we explained to our son Benjamin (then fifteen) that we didn't feel a certain friend was a good influence on him—the boy's life reflected a home that was very unstable, and it was clear that his influence on Benjamin was far greater than Benjamin's influence on him. He felt we were being unfair, but we carefully explained our concerns. Then we prayed with him for his protection and wisdom in handling this friendship.

You do have to handle this carefully, because if you are overly controlling, you can drive your child away from you and directly *to* the relationships that concern you. We have found that if we are eliminating a relationship our child enjoys, we have to step in and aggressively spend time with our child and meet his needs. Ultimately, of course, as your child grows older he will increasingly choose his friends on his own, and these teaching times will hope-fully influence those choices.

SHAPING YOUR CHILD'S CONVICTIONS

Have you ever stood on the edge of the beach where the waves break? And have you been caught off guard by one of those waves and knocked flat? But if you're ready for the wave when it hits—your feet spread apart, braced, maybe even holding on to a part-ner, you can withstand some pretty good sized ones.

A big wave of testing hits in the first two years of junior high—when your child is most insecure. Psychologist David Anderegg wrote, "The peak of conformity comes at around age 13. At this age, there's nothing more important to a child than being just like everyone else—normal."[2]

It's in seventh and eighth grade when the teens (girls especially) form their cliques. And if you don't fit in, you're alone. It's when the boys, too, start getting together and becoming buddies with two or three favorite others. Then they start competing with other groups to see who can be cool and impress the girls.

We can help our children handle peer pressure by anticipating when the waves will hit and then helping them brace themselves to stand up under the pressure. Talk to your preadolescent about the challenges he will face from peers in the next couple of years. Peers will pressure him to look at pornography, to swear, to drink or take drugs, to rebel against "dumb" parents, and more.

We suggest that the following key convictions related to peer pressure be built into every child's life. (They are stated in first person to illustrate how the child should be able to articulate the conviction.)

Child's Conviction 1: The friends I choose will have a big influence on the kind of person I become.

Your child's most critical conviction related to peer pressure is, "Whom will I choose as my friends?" You will need to set a game plan for how you will help your child find and choose friends. The drive to be liked and included is so strong that you as a parent cannot assume that your thirteen to fifteen year old understands how to pick a good friend.

Teach your child that the essence of friendship is commitment to another person during the good times and the bad, misunderstandings, disappointments, and conflicts. Proverbs 17:17 says, "A friend loves at all times." As parents it is part of our responsibility to teach our children that showing love at all times means being nice even when others may not deserve it.

Take advantage of opportunities to guide your child as daily life unfolds. For example: "I've noticed that you sometimes don't share turns on the computer when your friend comes for a visit." Or, "I noticed the other day that you cut your friend off several times when he was trying to tell you something." Keep training your child in relational basics. This is prime Golden Rule territory; to have enjoyable friends, you need to be an enjoyable friend.

Child's Conviction 2: I won't assume that Christian friends will always be a good influence on me.

Some teenagers have grown up going to church but have never made Christ the true Lord of their lives, and they can easily lead your child astray. If you don't train your child to discern this, your child may go somewhat blindly with Christian friends in the wrong direction. Don't assume Christian friends are always good apples.

Child's Conviction 3: I will try to decide in advance how I will respond to key life choices like drug and alcohol use or sexual temptations.

Often, as a result of what friends are pressuring him to do, your child will face difficult choices on a daily basis. The best insurance against the baited traps of adolescence is knowing ahead of time how to spot the trap and knowing what the steps are for steering clear.

One technique we have used is to play the Decide in Advance game. Only two are needed to play—one child and one parent.

The parent comes up with a list of peer-pressure situations. For example: "You are at a friend's home. No one else is in the house. Your friend produces a pack of cigarettes and asks you to join him for a smoke. What would you do?"

You and your child then talk out the situation—your child playing himself, you being the tempter friend. If your child is struggling with how to handle the situation, switch roles. Do the same for possible situations involving other issues—alcohol, drugs, pornography, cheating, stealing, going to forbidden movies, lying, etc. In fact, peers will use almost every trap we highlight in this book to tempt your child.

Ultimately your objective in shaping your child's convictions related to peers is for him to be able to stand firm in the face of temptation. In doing so, he'll gain the respect and admiration of his peers. Give your child a challenge, a mission to be an influence for good.

TESTING YOUR CHILD'S CONVICTIONS

I will not forget the first time I asked my sixth-grade class, "Whom would you rather talk to about matters concerning the opposite sex—your parents, your brothers and sisters, or your peers?"

The overwhelming response: "Peers." I was stunned. I looked around at the teachers—their mouths had fallen open like mine. These were youngsters who came from some of the best Christian families you can imagine.

"Now wait a minute," I said. "Let me ask you a couple of questions. Let's say you want to find out about sex. Wouldn't you want to talk to someone who understands it? Who has experienced it? Someone who has been there?

"Or let me put it this way. Let's say you were traveling from Little Rock to Dallas, and you had never been there before. Who would you go to for directions? Someone who has never been to Dallas and never even looked at a map, or someone who has been there several times and has the route memorized?"

Teenagers can be very illogical, even foolish. They may refuse to wear a raincoat or use an umbrella in a downpour because they think their friends "would think I'm stupid."

Your child is inexperienced and his immature heart may impair his judgment. His emotions may be out of control. He needs you to give him perspective, even though he won't admit it.

Here are some ideas you can use over time to test how your child is holding to his convictions.

Ask your child to tell you about some of the groups at school. What are they like, how do they act, who is their leader, what's their music, why are people attracted to them? Ask him what group(s) he's in and what it's like.

Be observant. If you see subtle changes in dress or appearance, find out what's behind the new look.

As your child's freedom increases, don't be afraid to inspect what you expect. If you've given your child freedom to go get a pizza with friends, ask who went, what time your child left the pizza place, where did he go? Did he pair up with the opposite sex?

When failure occurs, make sure you talk through the situation and gently help the child articulate in his own words what went wrong. Your child will make some mistakes and succumb to peer pressure. With a force this pervasive and powerful, this is to be expected. As you deal with these failures, remember that some good testing of convictions is exactly what you want to occur when your child is still at home—where you can guide, correct, and instruct.

Role-play the situation to help the child understand how a better choice could have been made. Although discipline may be required, balance it with forgiveness and encouragement. Being a young person is very challenging. He needs to know you're on his side.

Applaud your child's good choices. When your child does make the right choice, put on your cheerleader outfit, grab the megaphone, and go crazy: "Way to go! Give me a high five!" We often get too excited about the wrong things. Sure, the touchdown or basket scored in the ball game is worth cheering. But what should get us up for a standing ovation are those choices our children make that reveal their convictions and character. Trophies tarnish; character doesn't. Character glistens. Character is what lasts into the next generation.

Don't always try to rescue your child from loneliness. Nothing has saddened us more than watching our children make right choices—and then have to stand alone. Every one of our children has experienced different levels of loneliness in junior high and on into high school. It also carries over into young adulthood and college as well. And with the wide range of standards in the Christian community today, sometimes they don't have the support of other Christian teens either.

The very pain of loneliness that we would rush in and rescue our child from may end up being what He uses to grow our children into strong warriors for Christ.

Be sure to provide abundant love at home. Your children should look forward to coming home. The best way to reduce the appeal of the herd is to keep the pasture at your house green, lush, and tasty.

FOR THE SINGLE PARENT

Resist the temptation to engage in drop-off parenting, leaving the child with friends at teen hangouts. However, if your child wants to be in after-school activities, find situations that are effectively supervised by adults.

You may have to work even harder at relationship building. With incredible demands on time, this is a real challenge. But even a few minutes of focused one-on-one interaction a day is much better than none at all.

If the child spends time with the noncustodial parent, seek to establish consistent guidelines on how much time is to be spent with friends and doing what activities. Share information with your child's other parent on which friends are the best influence on the child.

If possible, through your church or perhaps with the parents of one of your child's friends, form an unofficial parenting partnership. Encourage the other family to monitor your child's attitudes, actions, and speech while in their home and to feel comfortable in reporting observations to you.

CONCLUSION

At times you will be tempted to think you're being too harsh by urging your child to form personal convictions and resist romping with the peer herd. Don't back off! The ability to stand against negative peer pressure will be used by God to embed convictions, courage, and a stand-alone faith that will help your child become a difference-maker for good in our culture.

UNFORGETTABLE LESSON: Bad Apples

I believe in the power of strong, visual lessons to drive home truth to a child. The bad apples lesson I described at the beginning of this chapter is a good example; it's amazing how well preteens remember it.

One mother told me about a conversation she had with her daughter (whom I'll call Sara) who had attended our sixth-grade Sunday school class about three years earlier. A thunderstorm had moved through Little Rock, the lights were out, and they were talking about peer pressure.

Sara talked about the compelling influence of bad friends in her life. "Mom, it's so powerful I just want to give in," she said. "I want their approval so bad."

Then there was silence; not much was said for five minutes. Finally, from the darkness, came Sara's voice: "You know, Mom, all I can think about are Mr. Rainey's apples, and the picture of what happened to the good apple when it spent all that time with the bad apples. I know what I need to do."

You can duplicate this lesson very easily. Here's what you need to do:

1. Obtain three apples. Make sure at least one of them has no flaws and that the other two are clearly bruised. (Bounce them off the floor if necessary to create a bad apple.)

2. Show the apples to your child, and explain how the good apple represents the good teen. The other apples are friends who have some flaws—bad attitude, filthy mouth, poor habits, etc. Tell your child that this lesson will show what can happen when the good apple hangs out too much with the bad apples.

3. Put all three apples in a plastic bag and seal it. Put the bag away—ideally in a non-refrigerated place.

4. Leave the apples locked up for six to nine months. Then show the bag to your child and talk about how this illustrates bad peer pressure.

5. Identify the "apples" in your child's life—both good and bad. You might start by asking your child to do the identifying. Listen carefully to what he observes or what he doesn't observe in his friends.

6. Read 1 Corinthians 15:33 and talk about how bad company corrupts good morals.

CONVICTION BUILDING PLAN

As you continue the process of shaping your child's convictions on peer pressure, use the following questions to clarify your own responses to yielding to the wishes of others.

Part One: Answer the following questions individually

1. How often do you compare what you have with what others have? Are you a person who tries to keep up with the Joneses with things like your car, home furnishings, clothing, club memberships, gadgets, and so on?
2. Are your educational choices for your child based upon your convictions or upon what everyone else in your church or circle of friends is doing?
3. When you have discussions with neighbors and friends, are you able to express your opinions graciously but firmly when you do not agree with what the other person believes?
4. Would you describe yourself as a people pleaser? How might that influence your child's reactions to peer pressure?
5. Think back over your life and list some times when you made poor choices based on pressure you felt from peers. (If appropriate share with your child.)
6. List some examples of positive peer pressure in your own life.
7. How do you think your mate responds to peer pressure? Go back over the preceding questions and answer them for your spouse.

Part Two: Conclusions

1. Meet with your mate to share and discuss your answers from Part One. If you are single, discuss your answers with a friend who can give you wise guidance.
2. How has your child responded to peer pressure up until now?
3. How do you think your child will respond in the future?
4. Summarize your conclusions on how you will seek to model courageous behavior in regard to peer pressure:

*"Now flee from youthful lusts, and pursue righteousness,
faith, love and peace, with those
who call on the Lord from a pure heart."*
—2 Timothy 2:22

6

Trap 2: Sex (Part One)

Set Your Standards High

Centuries ago, a popular queen was interviewing applicants to serve on a six-man team to transport her on a portable throne on long journeys. As she interviewed each man the queen asked, "If you were bearing me along a mountain path, how close would you go to the edge of a cliff with me seated on my throne?"

Some men would answer, "Your Royal Highness, I am so strong I could go within a foot of the edge of the cliff."

Others would boast, "Not only do I have superior strength, but I also have almost perfect balance. I could go within six inches of the edge."

But others would answer, "Your Highness, I would go nowhere near the edge of a cliff. Why would I want to endanger your valuable life by leading you close to danger?"

Guess who earned the job? The wise queen chose men who would keep her far away from the edge of disaster.

We parents should heed that story as we guide our children through the adolescent years. Will we allow our children to walk near the edge of the cliff as they pursue relationships with the opposite sex? Or will we guide them so far away from the edge that we help protect them from potential disaster?

Our friend and coworker Josh McDowell makes the point well: "I would rather build a rail at the top of a mountain than have an ambulance service at the bottom of the valley." The choice between sexual purity and sexual experimentation is an important battleground for the souls of Christian youth today. This deadly trap snares millions of teens, scars their lives, and leads them away from a vital relationship with Christ.

Of course, teenagers throughout history have been tempted with sex. What's different today is the incredible pressure to experience it at an earlier and earlier age.

Our society is permeated by sex. A significant study revealed that each year the average American teenager hears almost fifteen thousand sexual jokes, innuendoes, and other sexually suggestive references on TV. Of these, fewer than 170 present a message supporting responsible sexual behavior.[1] Sex outside marriage is generally portrayed as positive and normal for teens in high school and even junior-high school.

Sadly, very few people in our society seem to be cheering our teens on to the high goal of moral purity. The failure to do this starts close to home—very close—with moms and dads.

DETERMINING YOUR CONVICTIONS

Most of us grew up in a permissive culture strongly influenced by the sexual revolution that began in the 1960s. The goal of that movement was to challenge moral standards and boundaries. Guilt and shame were to be thrown off as repressive, and the experience of unfettered pleasure became the god of our culture.

Christians have not been exempt from this barrage of new thinking. Sadly, we still suffer from its disturbing legacy. We have observed among many Christians, for example, a growing tolerance toward sexual experimentation.

Restrain our preteens and teenagers? To many that truly is a frightening prospect. Have we ever so slightly bought into the idea, promoted by our sex-crazed culture, that to wait for sex until marriage is a nice concept but a bit old-fashioned in the enlightened modern age? Have we become so desensitized to the sexual content of our media that we have begun to accept behavior we would have abhorred twenty years ago?

To determine your own convictions in this area of sex is a formidable task. You will not reach all your conclusions by the time you finish the two chapters we have committed to this lethal trap. We would advise a lot of thinking and communicating as a couple, but above all do a lot of praying and reading of the Scripture.

The first step to take in determining your convictions is to make an honest appraisal of your own history (including your mistakes and regrets) and learn how this has affected your views. Is guilt about your own compromises (past or perhaps present) keeping you from developing conclusions about right and wrong in this area? Are you afraid your child will ask about your own sexual experiences prior to marriage? Are you afraid of looking like a hypocrite if you challenge your child to uphold standards that you did not keep?

Past failures must not prevent us from calling our child to the standard of God's Word. We've all lied, yet we still teach our children to tell the truth. We have all stolen something, but that doesn't stop us from teaching that stealing is wrong. We believe the ultimate enemy of our souls is behind this conspiracy of silence in our homes.

What should you do if you were sexually active outside of marriage in the past? If you have not dealt with that sin, go before the Lord in prayer, confess it, and ask for God's forgiveness.

Unfortunately, the fear of being asked an embarrassing question makes many parents way too tentative in discussing sexuality and sexual behavior. Most children will never ask whether or not a parent was a virgin prior to marriage. However, if you did not enter marriage as a virgin and your child does ask a pointed question, we recommend that you *not give a complete answer*—at least for now. Here's a suggested response:

"That's a good question, and someday when you are an adult and more mature, I want to answer you more fully. But for now, that information is off limits."

If your child is not satisfied and persists, you *may* want to admit that "I made some mistakes I really regret"—but not share further details. But even this much information may not be a good idea.

We believe strongly that children during their preteen and teenage years desperately need role models, chief of which should be their parents. It's better if children do not know much about the failures of their parents when they were young. Continue to hold up a high standard and don't be a stumbling block (see Rom. 14:13).

Remember that during adolescence, children are still extremely impressionable. They may look mature on the outside, but they are immature on the inside. Withholding the whole truth is not the same as lying. When your child is an adult, in the context of an adult relationship, then you can decide how much you want to reveal.

Even then, though, be discrete. Details of past, forgiven sins are not that relevant or helpful. Just say, "I made some mistakes and bad choices. I'm sorry, but I ignored my parents' instruction," or "I did not have a parent who was challenging my standards and calling me to live out convictions based on Scripture."

Other terrible wounds that still fester in many parents were caused by sexual abuse, rape, or some other tragedy. If any of these are in your background, God wants to bring healing to your heart. For your sake and for the sake of your child, who longs for a loving, honest relationship with you, seek the healing you need. (An excellent resource for those sexually damaged is *The Wounded Heart* by Dan Allender.)

In spite of your failures and personal pain, you still have a responsibility to train and protect your child from evil. Ask God to help you and give you the courage to step into your child's life.

Ask Him to help your child understand the importance of following God's commands, no matter how well you did or did not follow them in the past.

Once you have evaluated how you have been influenced in this area, it's time to develop a strong set of convictions as a foundation for teaching your children about sex. The remainder of this chapter will look at four convictions we believe all parents should uphold.

Parents' Conviction 1: Our children need to learn a godly perspective about sex primarily from us.

Where is the best place for your child to truly hear a godly perspective of sex? It had better be at home. Why would we want our children to learn about this sacred aspect of marital love from any one else?

Talking about sex may be the single most powerful way parents have of entering into the lives of their children. It also can be the most difficult. Talking about reproduction and the most intimate nature of what it means to be a man and a woman is not like discussing tomorrow's math test or last night's ball game. When you dare to broach the subject with your child, you communicate, "You are important enough to me that I will risk talking about this uncomfortable topic."

Because you've had this conversation, your child may feel it's safe to talk about other intimate issues with you. It has to be a relief to admit this is a part of his life to someone he can trust, namely his parents.

One survey reported that when thirteen- to fifteen-year-old children were asked how they learned about sex, 67 percent had learned most from friends, school, and entertainment. Less than one-third listed parents as their primary source.[2]

Even if your child does not want to talk about sex, press through your fears, inhibitions, memories, and embarrassment. A few minutes of blushing, stammering, and clammy hands will deepen your relationship and could literally save your child's life.

If you have been faithful in appropriately teaching your child from an early age about sex, you will be tempted to relax when your child hits preadolescence. But teenagers need moms and dads who stay involved in their lives all the way through their teen years by breaking the silence and discussing matters of human sexuality and sexual response.

And if your child has already passed puberty, remember that it is never too late to initiate conversations. He may not act like it, and he won't say so, but he is feeling insecure, maybe even frightened.

Do you recall how *you* felt as a teenager? Teens need to have mom and dad come alongside them and say, "There are some things I should have discussed with you earlier but I want to tell you now. I want to stand beside you as you go through what can be some very confusing years. I don't want to leave you with your peers or by yourself to deal with this issue."

King Solomon had these talks with his son. Huge chunks of the book of Proverbs are dedicated to gritty talks about the snare of sex. For example, read Proverbs 5–7, where the king implores his son to be wise about a seductive young lady.

Men in particular may back off from talking about sex with their teenagers because they just don't know what to say. Or maybe dad hasn't done a good job in other areas of parenting and he feels defeated. Regardless, dads need to pursue their children.

(To help you with these talks about sex, consult the checklist entitled "When to Say What About Sex" at the end of this chapter, page 80.)

Another mistake parents often make in this area is feeling like they can only talk about sex at prescheduled appointments with their children. But it's better to view sex education as another one of those ongoing training opportunities for shaping your child's attitudes toward life. If you take advantage of them, you'll find many opportunities for instructing, asking questions, correcting. And then it won't feel quite so awkward.

I remember an incident when I took a risk to show my daughter my concern. It was Rebecca's first year in junior high. She came home from school one day really discouraged because a boy was making comments about her being flat-chested.

I said, "Really, what's his name?" Rebecca gave me the name—we'll call him Tim. "What's Tim's phone number?" I asked.

"I don't have it but I can get it," she said. "What are you going to do?"

"I'm going to call him."

She was amazed. "You're going to call Tim?"

"Yeah. I'm just going to call him and have a little man-to-man chat."

Rebecca pondered that for a few moments and then her face beamed. I think she actually liked the idea that her dad would seek to protect her.

When I called, Tim's grandfather answered the phone and asked, "Why do you want to talk to Tim?"

"Well, I've got a matter of concern for him," I said. "He is making some comments about my daughter."

"Well, let me go get him." But first Tim's dad came to the phone and asked, "Why do you want to talk to my son?"

"I'm not going to be mean to your son," I replied, "but he is making comments about my daughter's figure. I just want him to know this is not the way he should be treating a young lady."

Apparently that met with the father's approval. "Hang on a second. Here, Tim, talk to this guy."

Tim got on the phone, and I said, "Young man, I'm Rebecca's dad, and I want you to know I don't appreciate your comments about her body. I don't think this is how you should be treating a young lady, and I would like for you to respect her dignity as a woman. I would like for you to stop teasing her about her body."

Rebecca came to me later and said, "Daddy, thank you for making that phone call."

Now, that phone call didn't take much time. But it made a statement to Rebecca about her dignity as a young woman. And down the road when she was older and I needed to talk about limits in her own life, I had some relational capital to draw upon. She choked down my admonitions because she knew she was loved because her daddy cared enough to protect her.

Ultimately sex education is character education and training. That's why the best person to educate and train your child is you!

Parents' Conviction 2: Sex education consists of more than an explanation of human reproduction.

Of course, your children need to know the biological basics. If you've never had a good, explicit discussion of human reproduction with your child, do it now.

But even if you've done a great job of instructing your children about the biological facts of sex, you need to finish the process with moral training. Of all the discussions we've had in our family about sex, probably 95 percent of them have concerned character issues. We've had discussions about God's purposes for sex, the importance of sex and marriage, why you should wait for marriage before you have sex, how to avoid situations in which you are tempted, how different types of media shape our thoughts in this area, the types of movies to see and avoid and why, how to respond when someone challenges your convictions, and many other topics.

We've found that the issues surrounding human sexuality, such as self-control and obedience to God, are the foundational character qualities every parent wants to build into his teenager.

Parents' Conviction 3: We must teach and model true biblical standards of purity and innocence.

If you were asked "What are you teaching your child about sex and morality?" my guess is that you might say something like, "We are teaching him that he should wait until he is married to begin having sex."

How do you think your teenager will interpret and apply, "Wait until marriage before having sex"? Would he answer, "Being a virgin on my wedding night"? Or, "Everything but intercourse"? Or, "?"

In this culture, challenging your child with the goal of virginity is excellent. Off and on since 1971 we have worked with teens and preteens. And in the process of raising our own teens, we have developed a strong conviction that virginity is *not* a high enough goal. Nor is it the ultimate biblical goal. Unfortunately, studies have found that even our Christian teenagers are engaging in sexual activities reserved for marriage, yet are maintaining technical virginity.

This point was underscored during a recent television news report on churches that are teaching abstinence to their teens. One teenage girl who was interviewed was adamant about maintaining her virginity until she was married. Yet in the next breath she mentioned that heavy kissing and petting were okay as long as she didn't engage in sexual intercourse!

Scripture does not command us to preserve a technical virginity. The Bible presents a number of pointed principles to ensure that our relationships with the opposite sex are appropriate and rewarding. The key words underlying all of them are *purity* and *holiness*. Here are several basic passages:

"For this is the will of God, your sanctification; that is, that you abstain from sexual immorality; that each of you know how to possess his own vessel in sanctification and honor, not in lustful passion, like the Gentiles who do not know God . . . For God has not called us for the purpose of impurity, but in sanctification" (1 Thess. 4:3–5,7).

"Flee immorality. Every other sin that a man commits is outside the body, but the immoral man sins against his own body. Or do you not know that your body is a temple of the Holy Spirit who is in you, whom you have from God, and that you are not your own? For you have been bought with a price: therefore glorify God in your body" (1 Cor. 6:18–20).

"Now flee from youthful lusts, and pursue righteousness, faith, love and peace, with those who call on the Lord from a pure heart" (2 Tim. 2:22).

The goal of our instruction with our children is not just protecting their virginity, but helping our children protect their *purity and innocence.* And those two God-given gifts are lost long before intercourse when your child begins to experience the sexual response that God designed for marriage.

Ask yourself a couple of questions that helped us clarify our convictions: Just how much of sex do you want your child to experience before his marriage bed? How much of sex do you think God wants your child to participate in outside of marriage?

Our culture is robbing far too many Christian parents of their standards, convictions, and courage. As a result many of our teens are morally bankrupt of the standards and convictions that will protect and lead them through the most tempting and vulnerable period of their entire lives.

We must set our sights high and challenge our children to the highest standard, God's standard. As parents, don't we want them to arrive at marriage innocent of evil, pure in their sexuality, and with a healthy view of marriage—not encumbered by a lot of emotional baggage from sexual mistakes during the teenage years?

Abstinence is a part of the answer. It's just not the total answer.

Picture a beautiful, exquisitely wrapped package. Inside is the most delightful, untainted pleasures you can imagine. Now, wouldn't you want to give that gift to your child? That's what this gift of innocence is, helping your child understand who he is as a sexual creature reflecting the image of God. Once you make that your goal, it will change the way you think about how you guide your teenager.

Okay, we can hear a parent saying at this point, "But, Barbara, Dennis, you are talking about something that is so far above where our children are right now. I'm not sure we can get there!" Our response? It's better to have the highest goal and fail, than to set a low goal and succeed.

But it all begins with you.

Modeling Purity

No matter what you teach your child, your model of purity will go farthest in protecting your child. He needs to see a commitment to purity in your life.

If there is anything that can disqualify a parent from being able to talk to a son or daughter about sex, it is being presently involved in sexual sin, sexual addiction, an affair, or an affair of the heart.

If any of these issues are ongoing in your life and you have not repented, your sin is not just personal; it *will* have an impact on your children, your grandchildren, and beyond. The Bible warns that *sin will be passed down to not one but four generations* (see Deut. 5:9). Repent and have your conscience cleansed by the forgiveness of Jesus Christ.

Trash the videos. Burn the literature. Put some screening software like Cybersitter on your computer. Stop going to suggestive movies. Break off a relationship with the opposite sex. You will not be able to instruct your child to keep out of the traps if you are not staying out of them yourself.

At this point you may be asking, "Are the Raineys suggesting a return to the Victorian era?" No. But we feel it's past time for parents to reject passivity in this area and to get actively involved in helping their preteens and teenagers stay as far from danger as possible. The stakes are too high to sit quietly on the sidelines.

We as parents have been duped into thinking there is nothing we can do: Teens can't control themselves. We can't help them. They don't want our help. Peer pressure is too strong. It's their decision to make, and we shouldn't interfere.

Is that propaganda true? No!

With God's guidance and grace this is a winnable war! You can do it!

Parents' Conviction 4: We need to create a home environment that provides love, security, and physical affection for our children.

Remember our discussion in Chapter 3 about the importance of helping teens establish their spiritual, emotional, and sexual identity? In many cases the teens who become snared in the trap of illicit sex are insecure in these areas. Spiritually, they do not have an accurate understanding or a clear picture of who they are in Christ.

They are emotionally needy because they don't live in a loving, supportive home environment with strong standards and encouraging parents. And they do not have a healthy sense of who they are as a boy or a girl becoming a man or a woman. The result? They often use sex to meet their identity needs.

The teenage years are filled with self-doubt. This is your chance to teach him that how he feels about himself is not based on his relationships with the opposite sex; it is based on a growing relationship with God.

Your home needs to be your child's emotional watering hole. An oasis where he learns about trusting Christ. A place of refreshment for his soul, where he goes for love and affection (even when he doesn't seem to want it from you).

As a child grows up and develops physically into a young woman or man, a concern may grow in the parent about how much physical affection should be given if the child is of the opposite sex. The tendency is to think he is grown and doesn't need the affection. *Don't stop lavishing your child with physical affection; he needs those hugs and kisses more than ever!* A mom hugging her son and a dad hugging his daughter will send the message to both—you are a young man or a young woman who is worthy of attention and affection from someone of the opposite sex.

How many times have you heard young women say that they sought affection from boys because they never received it from their fathers? Don't make that mistake with your child.

CONCLUSION

The natural questions at this point would be what are the best ways to help a child avoid activities that Scripture forbids? What boundaries can your family set that will protect your child's sexual innocence? In the following chapter, we will help you create a game plan.

UNFORGETTABLE LESSON: Leaky Balloon

As a parent you always have to be ready to seize a teachable moment with your teenager. You never know when it'll come.

Early one evening, I drove Rebecca, then fourteen, to meet some girlfriends for a bunking party. Her friends were running late. As we sat in the parking lot, somehow the topic turned to boys. Soon we found ourselves in a wonderful conversation about how she was going to relate to the opposite sex. Looking back, it was one of those God-ordained moments that only He could orchestrate for a parent and a child.

That parking lot became a sanctuary for a dad and his daughter. We talked about everything. We discussed her limits and how far she was going to go with a young man prior to marriage. We talked about hugging, kissing, and petting.

I talked to her straight about protecting her purity and innocence. What occurred then was an illustration about sexual purity that was so profound that Rebecca and I still jest about who came up with the idea.

My recollection is that I looked down at the console between us and picked up a water balloon. It was stashed ammo from a huge water balloon fight between us and our teenagers that had been waged at our house a couple of days before. (The parents had won.)

Holding the water balloon up for her to see, I said, "Let's say this water balloon is filled with your sexual purity and innocence. This is all that you have. How much of it would you want to give away before you are married?"

It didn't take her long to answer that question. "I wouldn't want to give away any of it!" she retorted.

Then I put it in teenage terms. "Let's say that a young man

comes to you and just wants a little kiss, your first kiss and just a little bit of your innocence. What would you do?"

At that point I held the balloon up and pretended to pierce it with an imaginary needle. I added, "The young man says to you, 'It's just a little drop. Just an ever-so-teensy drop. You'll never miss it.'" Not giving her time to respond, I went on.

"And then another boy comes along and he just wants a little droplet. And after that, let's say that he liked what he got and wants even more of your innocence, and so now you've lost several drops."

With that I punctured the balloon several times with my imaginary needle. "There's more," I said, seeing a growing frown on her face. "Then let's say you fall in love and really like a guy and decide that it's okay to give even more of your purity and innocence away."

I paused, looking deep into her wide eyes. "What's going to happen to innocence and purity? How much will you have to give to the man you marry and spend the rest of your life with?"

Silence filled that semi-darkened car. Rebecca looked up from the balloon to me.

"It'll all be gone," she said with a tinge of sorrow.

"And how would you have lost your purity and inno-cence—all at once or little by little?"

She was coming to her own conclusions now, "Little by little."

"That's exactly right," I affirmed her. "And that's how young people today are losing one of the most precious gifts that they can give to another human being; and they start by giving it away a drop at a time. Then they give away even more, and the holes get larger and it's no longer drops, but a small stream."

Rebecca understood. That water-filled balloon gave her a wonderful object lesson of what God wants her to protect as she matures and negotiates adolescence.

Looking back on that time with her in the car, there's one final question I would have asked her: "Rebecca, knowing what you now know about losing your purity and innocence, where would you draw the line about how far you are going to go with the opposite sex prior to marriage?"

By asking her to verbalize her convictions, I would call her to accountability and create a future opportunity to talk further.

Now what you need to do as a parent is either read this story with your son or daughter and discuss it or create your own demonstration. We suggest the latter. And if you get your own water balloons, fill three of them.

Get a balloon that's strong and large enough so that when you fill it with water and actually prick it with a needle, it won't burst but will dribble out a drop or two, and if you squeeze it, it will shoot a stream of water out. Both the droplet and stream illustrate how sexual involvement can progress in our teenagers' lives.

A second balloon should be a small balloon that is filled as tight as you can and still be able to tie it in a knot. Sticking a pin in this one will illustrate that one small pin can cause the loss of every bit of it—purity, innocence, and virginity—all at once.

The last balloon could be a large balloon with just a little bit of water in it to illustrate a person who doesn't have intercourse but who regularly experiments with sex prior to marriage.

Allow your child to interact with you as long as he or she wants to talk. Be sure to ask, "Okay, now, as a result of this lesson, how far do you intend to go with the opposite sex prior to marriage?"

WHEN TO SAY WHAT ABOUT SEX

The following checklist will encourage healthy discussions about sex with your child.

Note: These are *recommended* ages only. Each child matures at his or her own rate, so a parent needs to use discretion in sharing all material.

Also, specific issues (like modesty, language, movies, etc.) need to be reviewed a number of times, not just when the child is younger.

PARENTS' CHECKLIST OF TOPICS

Birth–5 years
- ❏ Properly identify body parts: penis, vagina, vulva, and breasts
- ❏ God created them male and female (Genesis 1:27)

6–10 Years
- ❏ "The talk"—basics of sex education
- ❏ Modest dress
- ❏ Manners
- ❏ Language/swearing
- ❏ Eyes–movies/television
- ❏ Terms–sperm, egg, ovulation, and intercourse

11–12 Years
- ❏ Puberty—physical, emotional, and relational changes
- ❏ Wet dreams/erection/menstruation (This possibly should be addressed at an earlier age, depending on family history.)
- ❏ Romance and puppy love
- ❏ Girls calling boys and boys calling girls
- ❏ Prerequisites for dating or courtship
- ❏ Age of dating/whom to date

❑ Principles for dating—
    ❑ Date Christians who are growing spiritually
    ❑ Stay away from romance
    ❑ Keep physical distance
    ❑ Acquire certain character qualities for dating
    ❑ Have a plan for dating
❑ Virginity, abstinence, and innocence
❑ Purity, innocence, and blamelessness
❑ Male and female sexual identity
❑ Masturbation
❑ Eyes–pornography, movies, and romance novels

13–15 years
❑ Sexual attraction
❑ Dancing
❑ Music
❑ How to say no to sexual advances
❑ Decide in advance how far he/she will go
❑ Reinforce physical limits
❑ Guidelines with opposite sex—
    ❑ Not going into the opposite sex's bedroom
    ❑ Not going into the opposite sex's home if the parents are not there
    ❑ Present the idea of accountability for dating (interviews/contracts)
    ❑ Convictions about touching, kissing, petting, intercourse

16–18 years
❑ Interview dates (see Chapter 8 for details)
❑ Present dating contracts
❑ Give a purity locket/ring for Sweet 16 birthday
❑ Challenge your child to keep innocence intact

CONVICTION BUILDING PLAN

Use the following questions to help solidify your own convictions and to begin developing a game plan to shape convictions in your child. Refer as needed to the content in this and the next chapter.

Part One. Answer the following questions individually

1. What is the purpose for sex?
2. Do you think premarital sex is wrong? Why, or why not?
3. Do your personal media consumption habits, as well as the way you treat your spouse and others of the opposite sex, communicate clearly the principle of sexual purity?
4. What boundaries do you want to set for your teen as he relates to the opposite sex?
5. What goal or standard will you challenge your teen to?
   - kissing?
   - holding hands?
   - hugs?
   - touching the opposite sex?
   - being alone with the opposite sex?
6. How far should your teen go with the opposite sex prior to marriage?

Part Two. Conclusions

1. Meet with your mate to review your answers to the preceding questions. If you are single, meet with a friend who can give you wisdom and insight.
2. Develop a common statement for the standards you will challenge your teen to.
3. Discuss the following question: How much of sex do you think God intended for us to experience outside of the marriage relationship? Put another way: How much sexual response do you think you should experience prior to marriage?

"But I want you to be wise in what is good,
and innocent in what is evil."
—Romans 16:19

7

Trap 2: Sex (Part Two)

Mom and Dad Need to Teach "Sex Ed"

You may be saying under your breath, "Do I really need to talk to my eleven or twelve year old about deciding what boundaries he's going to draw about sex?"

Yes, you do! Some years ago, we, too, would have wondered if this was a good idea. Children seem so young at that age. So incapable of thinking about anything so profound.

Our experience with sixth graders taught us otherwise.

We learned that this is a prime time for parents to *begin* shaping their child's conscience and core convictions when it comes to facing their own sex drive and relationships with the opposite sex. Why? Because the sex drive "wires" aren't connected yet. For most children of this age, puberty hasn't begun, and children can still hear what we say to them without the distraction of hormones, peers, and the culture.

We had tremendous fun in the class with a little object lesson. We were teaching the young people that they needed to trust that God knows what's best for us when He warns us about experiencing sex outside of marriage. I would hold up a paper sack with an electrical cord coming out of the sack and plugged into an outlet in the wall.

83

"How many of you believe me when I tell you that what I have in this sack could be dangerous to you?" I would ask. "If you really believe me, please stand."

Year after year nearly the whole class stood, but there was always at least one who wouldn't stand, one who didn't believe me—always a boy.

"Okay, come on up here, son, and stand here beside me," I would say. "Now let me get this straight, you did not believe me when I said that there was something in this sack that could be harmful to you. Right?"

By now the boy would be looking at how carefully I was holding the sack, and perhaps wondering if he wanted to change his vote. But I wouldn't let him. "Okay, since you chose not to believe me and don't think it's harmful, I want you to put your hand into the sack."

Then I would whisper into his ear, "I want you to know something. I want you to reach in there very slowly, because you're about to learn there really is something dangerous in there."

At that point the boy's eyes would widen and he would ask, "Do I have to?"

"Yes, you do. You said you didn't believe me." Finally, his hand would reach slowly into the sack. Very slowly. Then like a bolt of lightning, it would shoot out, while the class roared with laughter.

Holding the sack there, with the young man now blowing on his fingers, I would turn again to him and say, "Now do you believe me?"

Immediately he would nod yes, because he had just learned that a warm curling iron was in that sack.

Trust me—we were careful and no real damage was done to the boys who "volunteered." And you know what? They listened very attentively to what I said next:

"What's the point of this lesson? God says that sex is reserved for marriage. It's a mystery. *You can't have a little touch here and there without getting burned.* You need to keep your hands off one another. God made sex and He told us to abstain from any form of sexual immorality. When you get married you can experience sex as God intended. You need to trust God and take Him at His Word. And you don't have to get burned to be assured that what God says is the truth."

SHAPING YOUR CHILD'S CONVICTIONS

We are going to assume that by the time your child is eleven or twelve, you have already shared some of the basic information about sex and human reproduction. If you have not yet begun discussing this topic, now is the time. You don't need to be an expert to talk to your preteen. You only need to be a real person, just a mom or a dad. You've experienced sex, at least once! Just talk to your child! *Don't be afraid of what he'll think.* Go toward your child empowered by God, courageously representing His perspective. God will give you the ability to do this.

You need to see yourself as a protector of your child's innocence, guardian of his purity, and gatekeeper to his soul. No one else on the planet cares about your child like you do.

I was reminded of this truth recently when I received a letter from Pat Orton, a wonderful grandmother who worked in our ministry for more than ten years. She told of some boundaries in the area of sex and dating that her own mother set for her many years ago:

I remember my mother drawing the line for me when I began to date. She instructed me about how a guy should and should not touch me with his hands. For example, she said to never let a guy place his hand on my knee. I see so many dating couples with their hands on each other's knee or with his hand in the back pocket of her jeans and I always remember Mother's words.

Because that line was drawn, my husband and I remained pure in our four-year dating relationship before we were married. I can remember forty years ago the pleasure we both experienced when my husband put his hand on my knee as we drove off on our honeymoon—he laughed and said he had been waiting four years to do that!

I am thankful to my mother for helping me draw the line for purity.[1]

What a fresh reminder of the power of a parent who sets boundaries. It takes courage; you certainly won't win any popularity contests with your children. But your children don't need you to be buddies or chums; they need courageous spiritual and moral leaders, parents who love them enough to challenge their thinking.

If you have already talked about sex, then you will probably want to go back and review the basics; don't believe your child when he says he "already knows about all that." He needs to hear it from you anyway.

Once you've talked to your child about the physical facts of sex in light of God's design, it's time to begin communicating your standards and convictions. Use the questions at the end of the last chapter to begin the process of formulating your own convictions if you haven't already. Don't feel you have to have your convictions all decided before you approach your child. More than likely you will develop many as you encounter situations with your child in the future. But do begin the communication process now.

You will probably want to plan out these discussions at least initially. Think through which parent should start the dialogue with your child. You may decide it is appropriate for the father to handle much of the education in this area with a son, and a mother with a daughter, or you may both want to do it together. Each of you has an important role to play with your child, male or female.

However you divide the responsibilities, your discussions should begin with three critical topics: What the Bible says about sex, why God forbids sex outside of marriage, and how to set standards to maintain purity.

The following are some convictions we are training our teens to adopt and some suggestions for how to teach and model these standards. In addition we will share some suggestions for what a mother and father can do with each child.

Child's Conviction 1: I will believe and trust in God's view of sex.

The best way to combat the world is by teaching the truth of the Scripture. Here are some major points you will want to share with your child about God's view of sex.

God created sex. Not Hugh Hefner, not Dr. Ruth. Genesis 1:27 tells us, "And God created man in His own image, in the image of God He created him; male and female He created them." The Creator of the universe stamped and embedded His image within us in a way that is somehow mysteriously tied to our sexuality.

Christians often are portrayed as backward, narrow-minded prudes. But sexual intercourse in marriage glorifies God. God was not embarrassed when Adam and Eve had intercourse in the garden. He didn't put His hand over his eyes and shame them, "Cut it out! I didn't create you to do that!" No, God designed the equipment and He blessed the union. When God made them male and female He said it was "very good" (Gen. 1:31).

Sex is for procreation in marriage. God created sex so that we can reproduce after our own kind. Genesis 1:28 tells us that God blessed the man and the woman and commanded them to be fruitful and multiply and fill the earth.

Sex is for intimacy in marriage. Genesis 4:1 says, "Now the man had relations with his wife Eve, and she conceived." Adam did not shake Eve's hand. He had relations with his wife, and she conceived because they had intercourse. God intended us to become one flesh to draw us together. It's a wonderful aspect of sex.

One night one of our teenagers came into our bedroom and said to us, "You know, it really bugs me that you shut your door to your bedroom at 10:00 or 10:30 at night. I feel like you're shutting us out of your lives."

We replied that this was by design! It gives us a chance to talk and to know each other better.

Neither of us explained *how* we were knowing each other, but it was the idea that we need the opportunity for intimacy—spiritual, relational, and sexual.

Sex is for pleasure in marriage. God approves of appropriate gestures of love, romance, and pleasure within marriage. Look at Proverbs 5:19: "As a loving hind and a graceful doe, / Let her breasts satisfy you at all times; / Be exhilarated always with her love." That is not Playboy 5:19; that's Proverbs 5:19. God said it. He also wrote an entire book of the Bible about sexual love in marriage, The Song of Solomon. God is not down on sexual pleasure in marriage.

One of the best sex education tools you can use is to model a warm, affectionate, honest marriage. Your children need to see their mom and dad hugging; this lets them see healthy expressions of human sexuality in a marriage relationship that is blessed by God.

Sex was created to be enjoyed by a man and a woman in marriage. These days our media bombard us with the idea that God created and blesses other kinds of sex, like that practiced by homosexuals. You will need to share with your child that there is a radical homosexual element in our culture saying, "We're going to be in your face. You're going to see us kissing on television and in movies. We want to become acceptable."

Our children must know that just because some group wants to validate their behavior, that does not make it right in God's eyes. Our children need to learn how to hate the sin (see Rom. 1:26–27) while loving the sinner.

Sex outside of marriage is a sin. God very clearly forbids fornication (see 1 Cor. 6:9, Matt. 15:18–19). Some believe only a cruel God would give teenagers a strong sex drive and then order them not to act upon it until marriage. But when God forbids something, it is for our own good.

Use the following points to develop a clear, well-thought-out explanation on how God uses sexual purity for our good.

- You feel no guilt, no shame, no emotional scars when you hold to a standard of sexual holiness. You don't hear any accusing voices in your own conscience.
- You won't be tempted to compare your future spouse with a past lover.
- You have no risk of sexually transmitted disease.
- You will not face the possibility of bearing a child out of wedlock.
- It gives you much needed training in self-control and self-denial.

Much of this information about God's view of sex can be discussed with your child in a formal setting as you look up Scriptures together. But also look for casual opportunities to communicate these truths.

I was bringing Ashley, who was about thirteen at the time, home from piano practice one evening. She told me about a note being passed around in class about a boy and a girl who had taken their clothes off and messed around.

I remember telling Ashley, "Sex is beautiful in marriage. There is a time that's right, and if you will wait, God will bless it. But what those two young people are doing is shameful and wrong."

I don't really know what Ashley thought of that conversation. But I believe these moments are the building blocks of a godly perspective about sex.

Child's Conviction 2: I will maintain my purity and innocence until I am married.

As we said in the last chapter, purity and innocence are not lost at the time of physical intercourse; they are lost when your child begins to experience the sexual response God designed for marriage.

Now let's get practical.

Assuming you agree with what God says in His Word about

purity, how will you help your children maintain this conviction to remain pure and innocent until marriage?

Kissing

Let's say your thirteen year old comes to you and says, "Mom, Dad, how far should I go (sexually) with the opposite sex?" Do you know what your standard would be? Do you know how you would answer your child?

To get very specific, what standard on *kissing* will you present to your child? We've been challenging our children to set a goal of not kissing anyone until the wedding ceremony. Now, that may sound totally preposterous to you, and that's fine. But if that standard seems *too* high, answer this question: What line *will* you challenge your child to draw? If you do not challenge your child with a specific standard, we can promise you that your child will most definitely turn to his peers to develop his own standard.

We are not legalistic with our children about the "wedding kiss challenge." We have used an individual approach with all of our teenagers, discussing what their own standard will be.

As we were working on this chapter, our son Samuel called from the university. I asked him if I could ask him a gritty question and then if I could use his answer in the book. Always up to the challenge, Samuel said, "Fine, go for it."

Going for the jugular I asked, "Have you ever kissed a girl?"

Samuel's reply was quick and firm, "Nope! I am waiting until I get to the wedding altar."

Probing deeper, I asked, "Have you ever been tempted?"

"Sure," he said. "But I try to stay out of situations where that temptation can occur."

"When were you tempted?" I went on.

I could almost feel him smile over the phone, "Oh, it was before I decided on my standards, in the seventh grade with a girl I liked."

Now the reason I share that story is twofold: First, there are many young men and women today taking a similar stand for personal purity. And second, Samuel was tempted the most before he established his own standards—we weren't challenging our preteens and teens with that standard back then.

Ultimately, of course, our children will choose a standard of their own. But as your child's protector, you can help him think through the standard he will choose.

We occasionally ask our teenage daughters questions so they will form their own conclusions: "Are you going to allow a young man to kiss you? Why? Why not? How will you handle it if a boy tries to kiss you? What are your feelings about that?"

We've talked with teens about the two types of kisses. One is a kiss of pure affection. It's the kiss on the cheek, on the forehead, or the old-fashioned gentleman's kiss on the lady's hand. The other is a kiss that asks for or demands a response. A sexual response. It is a passionate kiss.

Ask your teen, "If you are going to kiss, which kind of kiss are you going to do? What if your date initiates an affectionate kiss and it turns into a passionate kiss? What are you going to do then?" Even a simple first-time kiss on the lips can quickly move to a passionate kiss.

A question every preteen and teenager ought to grapple with is this: "How much of your own sexual passion and responsiveness do you want to experience outside of marriage?" In the end, it really is up to him, but you can build some firebreaks by helping him determine in advance where he is going to draw the line.

Touching

Next, what standard will you present to your child about *touching*? Today, teenagers are so comfortable and friendly with the opposite sex that they don't think anything about giving each other back rubs and frontal hugs or with sitting on each other's laps. This kind of physical contact is common even in most church youth groups. Most teens would think it odd or outdated to be questioned on this type of behavior.

Your child needs to understand how dangerous touching can be and how quickly it sparks passion. He knows that it feels good; that's why he does it. Holding hands can quickly lead to kissing, passionate kissing, caressing, and petting.

THE HIGH GROUND

We believe that the spiritual awakening that is begging to erupt in America may well occur through our youth. And it may be advanced by a band of parents who say to young people, "We want to lead you to the moral high ground." That high ground is there to be taken if we love our teens and develop relationships with them so that these standards can be implanted in their hearts.

We cannot emphasize enough that your home environment must be one of love, encouragement, security, and forgiveness if you are going to challenge your teens to high moral standards. If your home life is characterized by fear and legalism, your children may rebel.

In the last few years, an increasingly popular phrase in some evangelical churches has been, "No kiss until the wedding kiss!" Unfortunately, some parents are holding this rule over their teenagers like a club, proclaiming, "As long as you live in my house, you will not kiss a person of the opposite sex!" Often this approach leads the child to seek out the very activity the parent desperately wants to forbid.

Instead, challenge your teenager to holiness in this area, knowing full well that he may fall short of it. We believe it's better to have the highest of standards in sex and dating, held before our teens with enormous amounts of love, encouragement, and grace, than to conform to the confusing morality of the world. The Scriptures give parents of teens a great reminder: "Love covers a multitude of sins" (1 Peter 4:8).

Parent-Child Topics

In addition there also are specific subjects you will want to discuss with your sons and daughters separately. Think carefully about which parent should talk about each of these topics. Following are some suggestions:

Mother-Daughter

One thing I (Barbara) did was to take each girl on a weekend retreat before she began adolescence. I took some tapes and other resources (see Appendix B) that are available to help initiate some conversation about sexual development. The materials made it easier to begin a conversation.

First, I talked to them about *how their bodies were about to change, and about menstruation.* Most girls begin menstruating between eleven and thirteen, but sometimes it happens earlier. If you have a nine- or ten-year-old daughter who begins developing physically, be sure to have this talk as soon as possible so she will be prepared.

I didn't do anything elaborate; I simply gathered some information for them to read, and then we talked about it. The girls asked me about issues, and I answered their questions.

Most girls look forward to beginning menstruation; they talk about it among themselves all the time. They know who has started and who hasn't. It is a rite of passage for girls.

Next, I talked about the *differences between boys and girls.* A girl needs to understand that boys are stimulated primarily by sight, by how a girl looks, by the way she sits, walks, handles herself, and by touch.

A girl needs to dress modestly and appropriately—a difficult task in today's culture. She needs to learn how to sit correctly in a dress, and to be careful how she moves her body.

Also, a girl must be very cautious about how she touches a boy. Rubbing up against a boy, giving him a full hug, or even sitting too close can send the wrong signals. Even an innocent touch can ignite a boy sexually.

In addition to that weekend retreat, I looked for informal opportunities to talk. I often discuss these topics as they come up or as I notice the girls changing and growing. Although the facts on the physical changes are important, I have been much more concerned about the attitudes the girls have about what they wear, how they act, how they carry themselves, and how they act around boys.

Father-Daughter

What should Dad do to share the instruction when his daughter is experiencing the changes of puberty? The temptation is to avoid the topic, because girls often push their dads out of their lives during this stage.

I felt it was better for Barbara to go over the basic facts about human reproduction with our girls. However, I've had plenty of conversations with our daughters about protecting their purity and establishing moral boundaries. A father needs to be involved in discussions about sexual feelings and character issues, and in helping a young girl understand what's going on inside a young man's mind and body.

When Ashley (our oldest daughter who is now married) was a preteen, I had the father-daughter ABC sex talk on a ski lift. It was scary but bonding. Many additional father-daughter discussions (as well as mother-daughter) followed as she negotiated adolescence.

What a thrill it was on her wedding day to give her to Michael and know that we had helped her protect her gift.

Mother-Son

Like Dad with his daughter, Mom will have to work hard to stay involved in her son's life.

I (Barbara) think it is important to validate the things Dad is saying and encourage a boy in his process of growing up. These are such difficult years for a boy. He is usually around women all the time, from mom at home and in the carpool to the teachers at school who are mostly women.

Validate your son by letting him know you understand a little of what he is feeling as a young man. Praise him any time he does anything kind or sacrificial for someone else. Tell him that someday his wife will need him to help bring in the groceries. Encourage him to open the door for his sisters or other girls in the carpool. Thank him for his manly help any time he gives it.

I also believe that a boy this age, eleven to fifteen, needs to be kept busy. He needs to be working hard or playing hard. As a boy moves into puberty, if he is not distracted by activities and jobs, his changing body will tell him to pursue girls since they will help him feel like a man.

Father-Son

During preadolescence, I believe it is time to go back through the basics with a boy, talking about how babies are made and about what is happening to his body. I talk to him about pubic and facial hair and other changes awaiting him as he becomes a young man. I talk to him about his voice changing and how he will feel about that—the lack of self-confidence, the embarrassment this will cause him from time to time.

Then we begin to talk about some of the issues he will face, or has already experienced, as his sex drive becomes stronger. We discuss erections and wet dreams. We talk about masturbation (see the following) and pornography (see Chapter 18).

I let him know that he can come to me at any time if he has questions. If he doesn't come to me, I will continue to initiate conversations with him all the way through his emergence into adulthood (his late teens and early twenties).

If I could do one thing differently with our boys, I think when they were eleven or twelve, I would not only have reviewed what was taking place in their bodies, but also talked again more specifically about what was happening simultaneously with girls. They need to have insight into what is happening with a sister or the girl who sits next to them in the classroom.

Specifically, boys need to know that some girls are hungering for affection that they never received from their fathers, and they may seek to receive that affection from boys. Boys also need to know that, while men are stimulated by sight and touch, women are generally more stimulated by the emotional bond in a relationship. Just as girls should avoid wearing provocative clothing, boys should avoid leading a girl on emotionally; some boys become experts at sharing enough of their emotions to attract girls.

Overall, I've wanted our sons to know that sexual conquests are not the measure of one's masculinity and manhood. Self-control and discipline are qualities of a real man. Treating a young lady with common courtesy, respect, and dignity as God's finest creation and learning how to love her are the marks of a godly man.

Masturbation

One of the biggest mistakes we can make on masturbation is to be silent and not discuss it. Most young men, especially, will deal with this issue, so the more information and understanding they have the better.

(Obviously, masturbation can also be an issue with girls. As with boys, real relationships—not fantasy—are the goal. Self-stimulation may be increasing among women because of messages from the culture, some of them from extreme feminists like, "Do this yourself. You don't need a man.")

With boys this subject has to be broached by dad and honestly discussed. It's worth mentioning that some highly respected Christian leaders have varied beliefs concerning this subject. I would differ with some on this issue. Let me explain.

Over the years, I have been reticent to take a strong stand on issues that are not clearly spelled out in Scripture. The Bible is silent about the subject of masturbation. However, it is not silent about sex. Nowhere in Scripture do we find God blessing sex done alone.

Four observations are worth noting:

1. Masturbation betrays the natural function of the sex act as God created it. Sex was not created for a solo, but a duet. God gave us sexual urges to move us to deeper intimacy and unity in marriage with the opposite sex.

2. Masturbation is primarily focused on self, while sex in marriage focused on the other (see 1 Cor. 7:3–4). Why would God want us to spend our single years after puberty learning how to use this gift to satisfy ourselves when the nature of sex is to seek to find the way to satisfy your spouse? There's already enough selfishness in this culture that needs to be eradicated. I believe the higher road is to teach our sons to learn discipline and self-control that will have to be practiced as a single and later in marriage when refraining from sexual intercourse (due to illness, separation because of work, mutual agreement, etc.).

3. Masturbation can and often does lead to other forms of behavior—lust, use of pornography, sexual addictions—that are destructive both now and later in the marriage relationship. Marriage isn't a fantasy; it's a real relationship with a real person who won't always measure up to your dreams. Because the fantasy nature of masturbation and other sexual sins are so closely related, I would have grave concern about telling my son (or daughter) that these forms of sexual behavior are okay because I would have no way of knowing where that practice might lead him.

4. The biblical prescription to singles who are struggling with sexual lust and temptation is to marry, not to masturbate (see 1 Cor. 7:8–9). Paul here could have provided physical relief for those who lack self-control and burn with unmet sexual needs, but instead he points them to marriage.

I can't help but wonder if the huge problem of pornography that we have in the Christian community has occurred in part because we haven't trained our sons to develop self-control in their thought lives and passions.

Fathers need to strongly encourage their sons to abstain from masturbation. We also need to be ready to offer generous amounts of grace and forgiveness if our sons fail.

TESTING YOUR CHILD'S CONVICTIONS

As your child emerges into the teenage years, you will have plenty of opportunity to assist him as his convictions are tested. Frankly, this is where it gets very challenging.

A great way to initiate a good conversation about sex is to do the Unforgettable Lesson at the end of this chapter. This is a questionnaire that your child will fill in on his own, then discuss with you. We have used this questionnaire in many situations—at home and with other preadolescents or teens. It's a great tool.

Here are some other ideas on how to test your preadolescent or teenager's convictions related to sex.

Carefully observe your child in different situations and discuss the possible temptations each might pose. Our children have traveled to numerous retreats and Christian conferences on buses. Once, after walking down the aisle of a chartered bus and saying good-bye to one of our daughters, I couldn't help but notice that the guy-girl ratio was heavily weighted in favor of the guys. The thought lodged in my brain that I should initiate another conversation with my daughter about being careful and then ask a few questions after she returned from the conference about her behavior with the boys.

The payoff when she returned was a great discussion about friendships with boys, romance, and how guys like to define relationships physically rather than verbally. The more susceptible your teenager is to romance and attention from the opposite sex, the more important these kinds of checkups will be.

Give other parents the freedom to make observations. Most parents today don't feel free to call another parent about something they've seen another teenager do. We've been the beneficiary of calls that were embarrassing but resulted in further conviction shaping and training.

Don't hesitate to ask pointed questions: "Did you hold his (or her) hand?" "Did you kiss him (or her)?" "Did you just lie to me?" You may find that the truth may be slow in coming, like peeling an onion. You may have to ask several questions to find out everything.

Ask your child to be accountable to you. Pray that God will help you learn information about any form of sexual indiscretion by your teen.

FOR SINGLE PARENTS

I encourage you to recruit a close friend to support you. He or she might be someone with whom you could develop a plan—perhaps another single parent. And for this topic, your friend really needs to be someone of the same sex.

A special word of caution is in order for single parents of preteens or adolescents who are becoming sexually mature. At least one study has shown that early adolescents in one-parent homes are more prone to engage in sexual activity.[2] Stay alert and be extra sure your child has adequate supervision.

CONCLUSION

Most mistakes that we have made in the area of sex have not been because we were too involved. Instead they have come because we were making some dangerous assumptions that our children's convictions and standards were more firmly in place than we thought.

You might read that last paragraph again, just to make sure you heard us.

We once received a letter from a young woman who got pregnant when she was a teenager, gave birth to a baby, then got married. Her husband was also a teen. She wrote us to encourage parents to think of their own young daughters in the same predicament:

> Look at your sixteen year old. It's your baby girl that now has a baby girl. She wants to finish school but can't. She must work but wants to stay home with the baby. Or it's your sixteen-year-old son. How can he finish high school? He has a wife and a child to support.
>
> Parents, talk to your kids. Tell them. Let them get angry. I would rather my children say, "I hate you and your rules"

than say later, "Why didn't you tell me I was headed for
trouble?"

That letter is a compelling challenge to parents not to sit back
and let their children negotiate the sexual traps alone. Teens need
parents.

Your child may fail in this area. He will feel guilt and perhaps
will fear that you might withdraw from him in rejection. Sin,
shame, and embarrassment all make it difficult to truly connect
with your teen, but in spite of the difficulty, he needs to see, feel,
and know your love, grace, and forgiveness.

At those points you become God's arms of love to a child, just
as He loves us no matter what we do. He still disciplines us, and
there is still a consequence for sin, but there is ample grace. Grace
that accepts, cleanses, and motivates to do what is right.

UNFORGETTABLE LESSON: Sex Q & A

Have your child spend time answering the questions. Then
meet with him or her to discuss the answers.

As you interact with your child about these questions,
don't be deceived if the answers are all pretty good. Our children know how to give the answers parents want.

The ultimate purpose of this question-and-answer time is
to get your child to think about convictions and where he's
going to draw the line. In the process, convictions will form
about sex and marriage.

You may want to have your son or daughter eventually
write his or her convictions and standards on paper. This is
taking the whole process one step farther because to commit
to paper is more permanent than just filling out a questionnaire.

SEX QUESTIONNAIRE

1. What do you think is the purpose of sex?
2. What does the Bible say about sex?
3. What is the purpose of a kiss?
4. What is the purpose of holding hands?
5. What is the purpose of making out?
6. What is the purpose of petting? (Your preteen or teen may not know what this is.)
7. Of everything you have learned about sex, what percent did you learn from the following (the total should equal 100 percent):
   Dad
   Mom
   Media (television, books, etc.)
   School
   Brothers/sisters
   Friends
   Church
   Other
8. Do you think premarital sex is wrong? Why or why not?
9. With whom would you prefer to talk about sex?
10. Have you ever kissed a member of the opposite sex?
11. How far do you plan to go with a member of the opposite sex before marriage?
    No physical involvement
    Holding hands, occasional hug
    Occasional light kissing, plus the above
    Passionate kissing, close hugging
    Passionate petting, touching private places
    Sexual intercourse

CONVICTION BUILDING PLAN

Ask your preteen or teenager to interact with you over the contents of the last two chapters and then write out a statement of how far he intends to go with the opposite sex. Challenge your child to standards that will please God. The statement could include such boundaries as:

Being alone in an apartment or home with the opposite sex
Hugging
Hugging and kissing
Passionate hugging and kissing
Lying down while passionately hugging and kissing
Touching below the neck
Touching below the waist
Taking clothes off
Intercourse

8

Trap 3: Dating

Keeping on the Path to Innocence and Purity

In the fading twilight, the headlights of an approaching car reminded Bill to reach for the dashboard and turn on his lights. As the horde of rush-hour cars streamed by, Bill reminisced about the teenage daughter he had just picked up from band practice.

He smiled as he thought about all those after-school trips over the last few years: dance classes, piano practices, the unending cycle of softball games and tournaments. He glanced at her in the seat next to him and thought, *She's starting to look like her mom. Her childhood has passed so quickly.*

Usually Bill and his daughter made small talk on their brief ride home. Not tonight. Bill was concerned about the growing emotional distance between them. Sure, he knew this gap was normal for teenagers and their parents. But he wasn't ready yet to surrender his role as a parent. He hoped the conversation he was about to initiate would help close that gap. He had prayed for an opportunity to talk to her alone—without her three brothers around. This was it.

"Julie, how are you doing with the guys?" he asked, struggling to disguise the wobble he felt in his voice.

"Oh, okay," Julie replied, in cryptic teenage fashion. She looked nonchalantly out her window as their car crossed a small bridge.

Bill smiled and probed: "You know, your mom and I have been talking about you and all those boys who call on the phone."

Julie squirmed uncomfortably in her seat. Realizing now where this conversation was headed, she rolled her eyes.

"Your mom and I just want to make sure you know what you stand for as you get old enough to date. You know what I mean, Pudd'n?"

Pudd'n was Bill's pet name for his daughter. He hoped it might soften her heart.

She smiled faintly.

"I would like to ask you a very personal question and give you the freedom not to answer if you don't want to." He paused, waiting for her reply.

"Sure, Dad. Why not?" she said flatly.

Bill gripped the steering wheel and shot a glance into her eyes. "Have you thought through how far you are going to go, physically, with the opposite sex?"

Whew. There—there he'd done it! Bill and his wife had talked before with Julie about God's standards about sex, but soon she would be dating and making moral choices on her own. They wanted to encourage her to make the right ones.

"Uh, well, I guess," she replied. She was obviously feeling even more ill at ease.

They were just a block from home, so gently but firmly, Bill pressed the final question: "Well then, would you mind telling me how far you intend to go? Where are you going to draw your boundaries?"

He stopped the car a few feet short of the driveway and feigned a look into the mailbox. He knew his wife always got the mail, but Julie was acting like a basketball team ahead by one point in the fourth quarter, hoping the clock would run out. She was stalling.

Bill faced Julie and waited for her response. If he had waited for a month, he wouldn't have been ready for what she said.

"No, I don't want to tell you" she said firmly.

Decision time for this dad. He deliberated, *What if I press the issue and she gets angry? Do I probe further now or double back later?*

"Okay," he replied, "I'll take that for an answer . . . for now."

A tense silence filled the car as it eased forward and stopped in the driveway.[1]

Bill is definitely a courageous dad, pressing into a relational hot spot where most parents fear to tread. Although it's uncomfortable, he's definitely on the right track.

Just what role should parents play to steer a child away from the traps in the most popular sport for many teens—the dating game?

Let's begin by defining dating in broad terms.

For us, dating or courting is a small part of the overall process of determining God's will for discovering your life partner in marriage. In our family the focus has not been on dating, but more on training our teens in their character and in how to develop a relationship with the opposite sex.

Understanding the Problems Associated with Dating

See if you can recognize this story:

A teenager looks across the room and spots a beautiful young girl. He catches her eye . . . they are entranced . . . they've got to meet each other.

When they first talk, incredible sparks fly between them, and they resolve to meet again. Over the next few days, they spend more and more time together. Their parents and friends are against the match, but they fall in love anyway, and before long they cement their love by sleeping together.

Sound familiar? It should; it's the plot for *Romeo and Juliet* and countless takeoffs ever since. Even the movie *Titanic* is the same old story, with minor variations.

We've all grown up hearing and watching stories like these, which are part of what we like to call the myth of fantasy love. It's a phantom fueled by popular music, television, books, and movies.

The dating game, as currently played by most people, is a dangerous trap for teenagers because it encourages them to pursue this type of romantic, fantasy love at an age when they lack maturity, character, and wisdom. And that, in turn, results in a number of problems:

- One-on-one dating leads couples to spend too much time alone at the peak of the sex drive for a young man.
- Teens make poor choices about whom to date and are negatively influenced by those who do not share their values.
- Teens develop emotional attachments that cause them to desire a physical relationship of the same intensity.
- Acting either from peer pressure or from a need that is not met at home, teens begin pairing off as boyfriend and girlfriend when they are too young and immature to make good decisions.
- Eventually the dating game sets up young people to move from one short-term relationship to another. They seek romance, security, self-fulfillment, and physical gratification. But when the initial infatuation begins to fade, they either move on to another person or form a close, emotional attachment at an age when they are unable to make long-term commitments. And while there are many causes for divorce, it's interesting to note that this pattern of short-term relationships leaves many people unable to fulfill the long-term commitment required of a married couple.

We think it's time for parents to take a long, hard look at the dating game.

There's no doubt that adolescents need to begin learning how to relate to the opposite sex. But that doesn't mean we need to let them follow the same path we did when we were young. It's time to provide some alternatives.

A young man named Josh Harris has written an enlightening book entitled *I Kissed Dating Goodbye*, in which he writes: "I believe the time has come for Christians, male and female, to own up to the mess we've left behind in our selfish pursuit of short-term romance. Dating may seem an innocent game, but as I see it, we are sinning against each other. What excuse will we have when God asks us to account for our actions and attitudes in relationships? If God sees a sparrow fall (Matt. 10:29), do you think He could possibly overlook the broken hearts and scarred emotions we cause in relationships based on selfishness?"[2]

It's heartening to see Christian families seriously thinking this topic through and not just accepting what the culture hands them. Parents need to study, read, pray, and establish their own convictions about dating and its surrounding issues.

The truth is that we didn't have our convictions in place when dating caught us by surprise as our oldest daughter, Ashley, turned twelve. Like so many parents, we thought we had plenty of time to talk about this—later. But then Ashley took a walk with a boy at a Christian conference to go get a Coke. Harmless as it was, it was something of a date. They liked each other and were alone.

We panicked! We didn't want our daughter starting a dating career at age twelve. It was time for some focused attention on dating. So we talked with her and had several healthy discussions. But it occurred around something Ashley was already experiencing. It would have been much better if we had discussed these issues with her prior to her encounter with the young man. It would have made it easier on her . . . and us!

DETERMINING YOUR CONVICTIONS

In forming our own convictions as parents about dating, it's not good enough for us just to back off a step or two from what the world says is acceptable. Too many teenagers are being permanently scarred by the dating game. We want to challenge you to develop a fresh approach, prayerfully determine your limits, and train your child to hold fast to them.

Parents' Conviction 1: Our teenagers need our training, guidance, and ongoing involvement as they approach the issue of guy–girl relationships and dating.

Because our culture tells parents to stay out of the dating lives of our teenagers, we realize this may not be an easy conviction to embrace. We're told that our teens are old enough to begin making their own decisions, that parents who do get involved are old-fashioned, intrusive, and "patriarchal."

To us, it seems, very few parents of teens are involved enough in their children's dating relationships. That's why you need to be involved—other parents aren't! What we have is a youth culture with far too many liberties and not nearly enough parental involvement and boundaries. The result is the moral meltdown of our youth.

Parents' Conviction 2: We must set rules and boundaries for our child.

Perhaps the best way to help corral your ideas on what to do about your child's interaction with the opposite sex is to write out your family's dating policy.

This will require some extended conversation between mom and dad.

What are your standards going to be? What about dating—are you going to let them date or not? At what age? Who will they be able to date? Will you allow them to date another person exclusively?

Be proactive. Too many parents today allow their children to develop exclusive guy–girl relationships at thirteen or fourteen because "that's what everyone else does." Parents tend to think, "What harm can they do? They can't go out in a car alone." But the pattern of romance and emotional involvement gets established.

As Ashley and then Benjamin and Samuel began adolescence, we looked more closely at this issue and over the years developed the following family guidelines:

When a Child Can Date

First of all, we do not think of dating in our culture's definition of the term. Our teens do not go out on a date every Friday and Saturday night. Our junior high and high school age teens don't date anyone exclusively.

Instead, we are encouraging our girls who are still home to focus on the friendship side of their relationships with boys. When our girls do spend time with a boy, it's in a group, not one on one. We're trying to train them to protect their emotions and not to send romantic signals to boys. And when a young man sends romantic signals to one of our daughters, we've talked with him and tried to keep the relationship on a friendship level.

Giving a child the privilege of spending time with a member of the opposite sex is a freedom that is based upon our judgment of how responsible we deem this child to be. Can we trust him to stick with his standards? Is he strong enough to withstand peer pressure in a boy–girl situation?

In light of our reformatted definition of dating, we have the following very general age guidelines for spending time with someone of the opposite sex. (These are for our children still living at home.)

- Doing things together with an approved mixed group of teens away from our home: We have allowed this to begin sometime after age fifteen.
- Double dates or group dates: Usually at age seventeen, maybe earlier.
- Single dates: These are generally discouraged but allowed in certain circumstances.

However, even with these guidelines, three out of four of our teens had their first real date to the school prom in their junior year at age seventeen. And those first dates were all with friends, not with someone with whom they were romantically involved. It's not that our teens were not interested in dates beyond a friendship, but we had talked through the few pros and the many cons of exclusive dating enough that they felt changing the relationship from friendship to romance might ruin the friendship.

Our teenagers would all say that their prom dates were a lot of fun. They spent the whole evening in groups. Many of the parents were involved with before-dance dinners, chaperoning the dance, and hosting after-dance activities at homes or rented facilities. And it was a good opportunity for them to practice their manners and learn how to behave in formal clothes.

Our guidelines might sound repressive to some. A teenager going on a first date at seventeen is certainly not the norm in our culture. But many experts agree that early dating is not a good idea.

It is easy to see why there is a movement of parents to replace traditional dating with a formal courtship between a young man and a woman. These parents are involved in their children's lives, seeking to protect their innocence and purity for marriage.

Whom They Should Date

As a starting point, we believe our teens should develop friendships with and eventually date only other Christians (see 2 Cor. 6:14–16). Why go out with someone who does not have your values? Also, parents need to evaluate the vitality of the Christian walk of the person who may date one of their children. Specifically, is this young man or young woman a *growing* Christian?

In junior high, teens don't have the discernment to know if a friend really is a Christian. They believe that if the child says he is a Christian, then he is. It takes far more maturity than most twelve to sixteen year olds have to see that words and actions need to match.

Train your teen to look for outward qualities that indicate inner character, like a good reputation at school, a self-controlled mouth, wise driving habits to name just a few. These external behaviors can be a reflection of good parental training. It takes time to discover those qualities about a person and even more time to see if they are enduring or just a pretense. Inner character can't be seen "at first sight," "across a crowded room," "when you say your first hello."

Our teens need to be taught that the ultimate purpose of dating or courting is to find someone to marry. They need to be very choosy about who they spend time with in light of that definition. Help them write down the qualities they want to look for in the person they marry. What values really matter? That list then becomes the criteria by which all potential dates are measured.

That's why it's so important for our teens to wait to date. Spiritual and emotional maturity can only come with time. It's also why we want our teens to spend time with the opposite sex in groups. They can learn so much more about each other by observing behavior in a group, as opposed to getting to know someone in the perfectly preened, best behaved, tension-filled environment of a one-on-one date.

Acceptable Kinds of Dates

Specific boundaries need to be established. Even group dates can go awry if the group makes a poor choice on its plans.

Since it would be difficult to list all the potential problems of a particular proposed date, the best policy is to maintain your right to approve any type of date while your teen is living at home. And be careful about making assumptions about Christian activities.

Telephone Use

We believe moms and dads need to determine how their pre-teens and teens spend their time at home. Who do you want to influence your child the most? After spending eight or more hours at school with friends and teachers, are you willing for him to spend one or two more hours on the phone every night with a boy

111

friend or a girl friend? With homework, lessons, practices, and all, will you have any time with your teen to influence him?

Be wise about your child's emotions. Even if your daughter, for example, is not dating, she can still become emotionally attached to a boy over the phone. We've seen it happen. Teens begin to share their feelings, their disappointments, their hopes, their troubles at home, and pretty soon they feel attached.

Even girl talk can create romantic longings as girls chat and dream and ooh and aah about boys. If they can't date for several years, why let them spend hours stirring their emotions and imaginations?

Internet Communications

If your child spends time sending e-mails to people, or participates in chat rooms, you need to monitor what's going on. The subject line of a recent e-mail to one of our daughters was "Sexy Thang." We knew who it was from and, frankly, we didn't like it. We decided I needed to write him to say it was improper for a young man to address a young lady as a "sexy thang." And I asked him to keep the relationship on a friendship level. No gifts. No love letters. Just occasional communication.

Parents' Conviction 3: We (especially dads) need to interview our daughter's dates.

A number of years ago a friend of ours, Jerry Wunder, shared with us the benefits of interviewing your daughter's dates. We've been doing it ever since and found the benefits to be enormous.

First, if your daughter knows in advance what you will be asking and is prepared for what it will be like, she will usually feel honored, protected, and loved. All our girls know this is normal procedure at our house. They expect and, yes, they like it.

Second, because the interview takes place well before the date, dad can evaluate the young man's character in advance. Should you feel it would be unwise for your daughter to spend time with this boy, you can intervene.

Third, we've found that knowing he will have to meet with a dad before he can date our daughter has automatically weeded out a number of unacceptable prospects. It takes a courageous young man or an arrogant one to go through the interview for a date with our daughter. We've met with both kinds!

If you begin talking about interviewing her dates before your daughter begins adolescence, this should not become an issue when you actually begin doing it later on.

I started conducting these interviews when Ashley was seventeen and was mature enough to go on a date. Ultimately I came up with an eight-point checklist that I reviewed with the guys who wanted to go on a date with her. What follows is a condensed composite of the interviews I've had over the years with young men interested in our daughters. Let's call the young man Tom. (The eight points are shown in italics.)

"Tom, the first thing I want to say is that *a woman is God's creation, a beautiful creation, a fine creation.* My daughter is not only a fine young woman, but she is also attractive and pretty, isn't she, Tom?" Tom nods and grins. (Hey, what can he say at that point, she's my daughter!)

"Second, *the attraction of a young man to a young lady is both normal and good. God created it to be that way.* I want you to know that this is okay for you to be attracted to her and want to go out with her.

"Third, *I understand and remember what the sex drive of a young man is like.*" We talk for a bit, and I tell him that I have done informal research on how often a young man thinks about sex (about every seven seconds). I say, "Tom, you and I both know they were lying about the other six seconds!" At this point Tom's eyes are dilating; he is clearing his throat and squirming. We try to laugh to ease the awkwardness.

"Fourth, Tom, *I'm going to hold you accountable for your relationship with my daughter.* I am going to ask you if you are dealing uprightly with my daughter.

"Fifth, *I'm going to challenge you to purity*—not just virginity,

113

since I want you to guard your own innocence as well as my daughter's innocence.

"Sixth, *I want you to respect and uphold the dignity of my daughter by keeping your hands off of her.* Will you keep your hands off my daughter? (I think that's a fair question to ask the young man—if he doesn't faint at this point, then he may be okay!)

"Seventh, *do you understand all of what I've just said to you, Tom?* Do you have any questions? Do you understand that I am going to look you in the eyes and ask you if you are being a gentleman with my daughter whether you go out once or fifty times?

"Eighth, Tom, *when you are a dad someday, I hope you never forget this conversation, and that you will challenge your own children to abide by these standards. And that someday when you have a daughter, you'll interview her dates."*

Doing these interviews is one of the best things I've ever done for my daughters as a dad. And instead of creating tension and separation between my daughters and myself, it has actually drawn us closer together.

Parents' Conviction 4: We need to teach our children how dating fits into the process of finding a mate.

Barbara and I were good friends for several years before our relationship turned from friendship to dating toward marriage. We have noticed that God often seems to follow this pattern. We've heard countless couples tell basically the same story, including our own daughter Ashley and her husband, Michael. They were good friends at the University of Mississippi when God began to speak to his heart. In the next few months this friendship grew into something much deeper, and they were married in 1997.

The teenage years are not the time to be looking for a mate or to form deep emotional romantic attachments. Children need to learn to use their single years to focus on the Lord and trust in Him rather than basing their hopes and their self-worth upon a relationship with someone of the opposite sex.

To help you clarify your convictions about dating, we've included some challenging questions in the Conviction Building Plan at the end of this chapter.

SHAPING YOUR CHILD'S CONVICTIONS

We try to avoid saying to our teens, "Don't do this, don't do this, and for goodness sakes don't do that!" Instead we constantly share what we've learned from Scripture, and we ask them challenging questions so that they learn to make good choices. We want them to conclude, "You know, I don't think I am going to do that."

Child's Conviction 1: I need to understand that the purpose of dating is to find someone to marry. Therefore until I am much older, I will concentrate on building friendships, not romantic emotional attachments with the opposite sex.

An obvious starting point for training in this conviction is to discuss the *purpose of a date.* (We recommend you use the Dating Questionnaire found in the Unforgettable Lesson at the end of this chapter.)

- After you have worked through the Dating Questionnaire, ask your child a few more questions, like: "Why do your peers at your school go out?"
- "What does it mean to *go out*"?
- "What do your friends do who go out?
- "Do they hold hands, kiss, hug?"
- "Why do they do those things?"
- "Do you think it is wise for them to do that?"

Most teens today are drawn to the concept of dating or going out because it makes them feel grown up and popular. It's flattering to be liked by someone, especially in the cruel world of junior high. By high school, these same teens are so accustomed to possessing a boyfriend or girlfriend they feel lost without one.

Unless they are challenged to think otherwise at an early age, they will assume that pairing up in guy–girl romantic relationships is normal. That is why dating is such a trap for teens, especially during the early years of adolescence. Without any restraints, they can be led by their emotions and hormones into a multitude of mistakes.

As parents we need to wisely steer our teens to a higher calling, that of waiting to date until much older. In the meantime, parents need to build the protective boundaries and provide healthy alternatives.

As we've mentioned before, make your home the place to be. Help your son or daughter build several strong same-sex friendships. Encourage those relationships. Let these groups of girls or groups of guys do fun things together. Then, when they are old enough to begin doing mixed group activities, be involved in planning those, emphasizing the friendships.

Try not to let the groups be evenly matched with boys and girls so they think they are to pair off. Another good protective measure is to include siblings. Plan something for your seventh and ninth grader together for instance. It's healthy, more family oriented, and less likely to lead to pairing off.

Also, begin to tell your teens about the process of trusting God to give you a mate. Share how God brought you together. Talk about the benefits of the single years, and how they need to commit themselves to growing in Christ until God leads them to someone. Give them the goal of *becoming* the right person rather than *finding* the right person. In addition, talk about the qualities they should look for in a mate.

Child's Conviction 2: I need to accept my parents' involvement and heed their judgment when it comes to issues surrounding time spent with the opposite sex.

This involvement can take several different forms:

Help your child learn to avoid compromising situations. The Scriptures tell us to "flee immorality." Train your teen to keep his distance from situations that could tempt him to make wrong choices.

Our teens, for example, have had a hard time understanding why we will not allow them to take someone of the opposite sex to their upstairs bedrooms. In their minds, why is taking a friend who is a boy upstairs any different than taking a friend who is a girl? One thought we've shared with our children, which refers to many other situations as well, is to avoid any appearance of evil or wrongdoing. It's based on the idea from Scripture that believers are to be above reproach.

Another Rainey family rule is that no one comes to our house when a parent is not home, and our children don't go to another child's home when his parents are gone. This rule has been easy to transfer to boy–girl situations, because for our teens it's nothing new. The rise of two-income families has allowed a lot of teen couples to become intimate because there's no one home after school.

Hold him accountable for what he does on dates. When your teen does go on a date, don't hesitate to find out what the plans are in detail. Know who the teens are, who is driving, where they will be going, and agree clearly on what time they are to be back. Then spend some time the next day debriefing with him.

Play the Decide in Advance game. Even though your child may just be a preteen, start rehearsing different situations he may face later. What should a girl say to a boy who wants to park with her late at night? What should a boy do if a girl starts making moves on *him*? What should your daughter do if her date refuses to let her go unless she gives in to him? (Date rape is a big issue today on college campuses, and is occurring in high schools as well.)

The best time to make these types of decisions is long before they might occur. The worst time is in a car with a boy or girl whispering in your teenager's ear.

When she was thirteen, Ashley found herself in a situation with a boy whom she liked as a friend. He told her he wanted to kiss her.

"Well, I'm not going to let you," she replied.

He was surprised and said, "Well, I'm going to do it anyway."

117

"No, you're not."

"Yes, I am."

Ashley looked sternly at him and said, "You are not going to kiss me because you are like a reed blowing in the wind, and I am like a steel pole set in concrete."

What a line! She held her ground and prevailed.

Finally, *don't be afraid to step in to limit the scope of a dating relationship.*

Far too many parents are backing off when they should be stepping in. Two of our teens began to get involved in a boy–girl relationship that became too exclusive and too serious in their later years of high school. We encouraged them to back off and put some distance in the relationships. We repeatedly sought to help them understand they were becoming too emotionally attached.

Initially, our teens felt defensive about our observations. We had to put some limits on time spent together to help them pull back to more of a friendship. In one of the relationships we insisted they break up and stop all communication. It was most difficult, but it was clearly the right thing to do. Our teen agrees today, but at the time he had a hard time seeing it.

Child's Conviction 3: I need to treat members of the opposite sex wisely and honorably.

We often tell our teenagers, "When you go out with someone, you're going out with either your future mate or someone else's future mate." It helps our children treat the opposite sex with dignity and honor.

There are a few other specifics they need to learn:

What a Girl Needs to Know About Boys

First, *boys are stimulated by sight and by touch.* (We discussed this in the previous chapter, but it's always good to keep reminding them!)

Second, *girls must be prepared to set the physical boundaries in the dating relationship.* Few boys have been taught and trained by their parents to set limits; they are naturally the aggressors. Elisabeth Elliot stridently challenges young women, "A woman holds the key to the situation where a man's passions are involved. He will be as much of a gentleman as she requires and, when the chips are down, probably no more, even if he has strict standards of his own."[3]

Third, *girls should allow a young man to assume the initiative in a relationship.* Yes, this runs counter to the culture, but it is a key lesson to learn if she wants to form a successful marriage union in the future. Your daughter should be supportive as a boy does show initiative and moral leadership in the relationship.

What a Boy Needs to Know About Girls

First, *our sons need to be taught to be moral leaders and draw boundaries for behavior on dates ahead of time.* From the first date, the girl should know what he will do and not do (physically speaking) in the relationship. Daniel 1:8 says, "Daniel made up his mind that he would not defile himself with the king's choice food." His convictions were in place; his courage was solidifying ahead of time. These verbalized convictions keep a young man out of the trap.

He must also be warned and prepared to deal with girls who will come after him sexually and emotionally. The rules of sexual conduct between male and female have changed in our culture from the biblical model. He needs to be on guard and protect his heart as he relates to girls. And he must understand that it is inappropriate to discuss matters of sexual intimacy with a girlfriend.

Second, *he needs to know that girls are stimulated sexually differently than he is.* Sight and touch stimulate men. Relationship, words, or kindness generally stimulate women.

Third, *some girls today are hungering for affection they are not receiving from their fathers.* A young man needs to understand that if a girl is snuggling up to him and being overly affectionate, she may be subconsciously trying to fill some empty gaps in her heart.

Fourth, *a young man must treat a young lady with dignity.* This starts with common courtesies—opening doors, paying for dates, etc. My sons know what I ask another young man who is taking their sister out, and they know they are accountable to me for treating a young lady the same way.

Child's Conviction 4: I need to earn my parents' trust that I will do the right thing when nobody is watching.

It has become increasingly important for our children to develop some very fundamental convictions as they move into junior high and high school. Our children must be in the process of determining where they stand morally on issues related to dating and sex *before* they are given the freedom to attend a party, dance, school function, or go on a double date.

This doesn't mean that their convictions are fully in place, nor does it mean that they have perfectly obeyed us in the process. It just means that they are taking the steps to grapple with and develop their own set of beliefs to live by.

They must demonstrate that they are responsible, teachable, and accountable. We aren't looking for perfection, but for progress and for a desire to do what's right.

TESTING YOUR CHILD'S CONVICTIONS

The real, meaningful testing of your child's convictions on relating to the opposite sex and dating will not begin until some special person begins to show interest.

Ashley dated a young man for a couple of years during high school. He was a wonderful young man and a strong Christian. We approved of their relationship, but we also stayed very involved. We asked a lot of questions and talked frequently to them as a couple. I had some one-on-one conversations with this young man too.

On one occasion we were all in our car driving home from a basketball game and I looked in my rearview mirror and saw Ashley sitting pretty close to the young man. A couple of days later we asked to speak to both of them. We reminded them that they needed to be very careful of becoming too physically "friendly" with one another.

It was really hard for Ashley. She has always been by nature an expressive young lady. Keeping that desire to express affection under control took a lot of effort on her part, but it was so good for her to learn self-control. All in all the relationship turned out to be very healthy. They dated for over two years and never kissed.

Dating contracts can be very useful tools in clarifying parent-child expectations related to dating guidelines in your home. We have used these on several occasions. The purpose of the contract is to enforce the idea of holding to convictions and remaining accountable in a dating relationship. It also alerts the child that the parents are paying attention and have great interest in their son or daughter's involvement with a person of the opposite sex.

Several sample dating contracts are included at the end of this chapter. (See pages 126–128.)

FOR THE SINGLE PARENT

This is one subject in which you need to hammer out your own set of convictions—*for you.* That's right! Decide how you are going to act when you have the opportunity to go out on a date. Then you will have the freedom to challenge your teen with a similar standard.

Remember your child is a better student of you than you are of him. Your model will set the tone for your child's dating relationships. The spiritual maturity of people you date, courtesies, and how you handle it all will speak volumes.

And if your preteen or teenager is the opposite sex from you, please seriously seek support from a mature adult friend of the same sex as your child.

CONCLUSION

A final word of advice: Be careful to not become obsessed with the sex and dating issues. When you are working so hard to go against the flow of the culture, there's a tendency to become so preoccupied with how your child is doing that you are constantly harping at them, asking them questions. Remember that how you handle your relationship with your child is like playing a solo on a fine violin. It's difficult, and much practice is required. Be very careful how you hold the instrument and don't turn the strings too tight!

PRE-DATE INTERVIEW
WITH DAUGHTER'S POSSIBLE SUITOR

When a young man wishes to date your daughter, meet with him and exhort him in the following areas:

1. God's Creation: "A woman is one of the finest and most beautiful of God's creations." (Read Gen. 1:26, 27; 2:18–25.)

2. Natural Attraction: "The attraction of a young man to a young lady is both normal and good. As a parent, I want you to know that I am glad that you are attracted to my daughter and want to spend time with her. Yes, I've noticed that she is not only a young woman, but also attractive. She is pretty, isn't she?"

3. Male Sex Drive: "I understand and remember a young man's sex drive. I've heard estimates of how often a young man thinks about sex . . . about every seven seconds!"

4. Accountability: "Today's adults are giving freedoms without accountability. But I am going to help you. I will hold you personally accountable for your relationship with my daughter.

5. Purity: "I want you to read 1 Corinthians 7:1. It basically says, 'It is good for a man not to touch a woman.' I want you to keep your hands off my daughter."

6. Respect and Dignity: "I would like to ask you to treat her with respect. Whether you go out only once or fifty times, I will ask you if you are messing around with her physically. Remember, I will be asking. I will be involved, because this is my responsibility."

7. Mutual Understanding: "Do you understand what I have just told you?"

8. A Challenge: "I would like to challenge you to interview *your* daughter's dates when you become a father."

(A detailed discussion on how to do a successful pre-date interview is available on audio. See Appendix B for further information.)

UNFORGETTABLE LESSON: Dating Questionnaire

This can be a great tool for discussing the issues surrounding dating. Have your child answer the following questions, and then set a Coke date to discuss them:

1. What is the purpose of dating?

2. What is a date?

3. How old should you be to date?

4. Why?

5. If you were a parent, when would you let your child date?

6. When should you be able to double-date?

7. Would you choose to date only Christians?

8. Why?

CONVICTION BUILDING PLAN

Here are some questions to help shape and clarify your personal convictions and then begin to shape those of your child.

Part One. Answer the following questions individually

1. Describe your own experiences in relating to the opposite sex. What was your experience in junior high, high school, college, after college, etc.?

2. What dating standards did you follow when you were a teenager? Do you think these standards are acceptable for your child? Why or why not?

3. If you regret mistakes you made in your own dating behavior prior to marriage, have you confessed them to God and claimed His forgiveness? If not, do so and do not allow past sins to prevent you from setting standards of holiness and purity for your child.

4. What standards and guidelines do you feel you need to set for the following issues:

    When to date
    Whom to date
    Telephone calling
    Internet communications
    Acceptable kinds of dates

5. What do you need to teach your child about how to treat someone of the opposite sex?

6. What do you need to teach your child about how to find a mate?

7. How do you think your child feels about dating? Does he have any dating experience yet? Has it been positive or negative? Why?

8. Will your child be open to your involvement in his dating life? What do you need to do to improve the relationship?

9. Are you living out some unresolved fantasies of your own by wanting your child to be popular and physically attractive to the opposite sex?

Part Two. Conclusions

1. Meet with your mate (or a friend if you are single) to discuss your answers to the first section.

2. Together as a couple list the good things and the bad things that can happen when a boy and a girl go on a date. Talk about the type of relationship you want for your son or daughter with the opposite sex.

3. Determine the convictions you hold about dating.

4. Determine what you will do over the next few months to begin shaping your child's convictions.

SAMPLE DATING CONTRACTS[4]
(Copy and use as needed.)

Wait-to-Date Contract

Mom and Dad:

Recognizing

that God holds you accountable to raise me in the admonition of the Lord,

that I am under your authority as a child in this home, and

that you love me unconditionally and are committed to my well being,

I agree to wait until you believe I am mature enough to go on a date.

_____(Child's signature)
_____(Date)
_____(Father's signature)
_____(Mother's signature)

Casual Dating Contract

I, _____, recognize that_____ is a beautiful young woman, one of God's finest creations. Furthermore, I realize her parents have a sacred and solemn responsibility to do all they can to preserve and protect her purity. Additionally, she may someday become another man's wife.

Recognizing the above facts, I do solemnly swear to treat _____ with absolute respect and afford her the dignity God created in her as a woman. I will show her such respect by bringing her home on time, treating her to creative dates, and refraining from physical intimacy throughout our entire dating relationship. I realize that a failure to abide by these commitments may result in a very uncomfortable, eyeball-to-eyeball conversation with her father or mother, and the possible loss of dating privileges.

Furthermore, by signing this document I agree to be accountable at any time to a series of probing questions about my behavior. I will be accountable to her parents as long as we date.

Signed this ____date in the month of _____ in the year of our Lord _____.

_____(Potential suitor)
_____(Witness)
_____(Father's signature)
_____(Mother's signature)

Serious Dating Contract

I, _____, because of the deepening relationship between myself and _____, recognize that the temptation to share physical intimacy increases over an extended period of time. I further recognize that the parents of _____ motivated totally out of love for their daughter, have both the responsibility and duty of doing whatever they can to protect her purity and innocence (Rom. 16:19).

Therefore, I hereby submit to follow the biblical mandate to flee youthful lusts (2 Tim. 2:22). I understand that, by avoiding physical intimacy, I am not only preserving this relationship, but also encouraging it to grow in numerous creative ways. I recognize that, although God made passion as a gift to individuals and couples, it must be managed with absolute integrity. I also realize the culture in which we live makes it difficult for couples to maintain purity. However, I pledge to abstain from sexual misconduct because of my desire to please God and to honor _____.

Failure to abide by any of these principles may result in her parents obtaining an unlisted number for their daughter, severely limiting her dating privileges to one thirty-minute date per month after church, or being forced to take her little brother and/or little sister on all future dates for the next twelve months.

Signed this _____ day in the month of _____ in the year of our Lord _____.

_____(Suitor)
_____(Witness)
_____(Father's signature)
_____(Mother's signature)

"There are six things which the LORD hates,
Yes, seven which are an abomination to Him:
Haughty eyes, a lying tongue,
And hands that shed innocent blood,
A heart that devises wicked plans,
Feet that run rapidly to evil,
A false witness who utters lies,
And one who spreads strife among brothers."
—Proverbs 6:16–19

9

Trap 4: "Attitude"

Checking Pride and Rebellion During Adolescence

He's got a 'tude." "He's got a terrible attitude." "He'd better fix his attitude." "His attitude stinks."

We wonder if Samson's parents and friends ever said words like those about him?

You remember Samson—the popular, affable, good-looking man's man who had everything going for him? Samson was dedicated to God before birth and was definitely gifted and talented. Today Samson might have become an Olympic competitor. He had the tools: athletic ability, physical strength, intelligence, courage, leadership qualities, even great hair!

Although he lived long before the arrival of arrogant, trash-talking athletes, he definitely had a 'tude. Arrogant and proud, Samson thought that all he needed in life were his own strength and abilities. Weren't the rules only designed for weaker and less-gifted men?

He found out how wrong he was when he fell for a woman named Delilah. She plotted with Samson's enemies against him, and when Samson betrayed his lifelong covenant with his Lord, he was left to survive on his own. His life collapsed.

God has some words of His own for what today we call attitude: *rebellion* and *pride*. He despises them both. "Everyone who is proud in heart is an abomination to the LORD" (Prov. 16:5). Jesus said, "And whoever exalts himself shall be humbled; and whoever humbles himself shall be exalted" (Matt. 23:12).

It is a rare adolescent who does not fall victim to the trap of attitude. Regularly, teens will display an attitude of self-conceit or arrogance: "I can do it myself!" "Leave me alone!" "What do *you* know anyway?"

Just this morning, as we said good-bye to three teens heading off to school, one of them was struggling with her attitude. Her countenance was sullen. No one could help her fix her school lunch. Her back was turned ever so slightly away as we read devotions. It was a classic case of "I want *my* way."

At the very core of adolescent behavior is pride, rebellion, and undisguised self-centeredness. It is the root disease of the human heart. Because teens are trying to figure out who they are, what they are supposed to do, what's expected of them, all of these issues focus on the big *me*.

Even if your child doesn't display a boisterous, angry brand of attitude, be aware of passive pride and rebellion, too. Some teens are quieter and do not push against the limits with brass-band gusto. In fact, their pride may be in being the "good" child, always pleasing mom and dad. This child may subtly develop an I'm-better-than-most attitude. Do not be deceived into thinking this type of child is any less prone to sin and does not struggle with pride and selfishness issues.

Passive rebellion manifests itself in failing to do chores, homework, and what's expected. This teen may choose to selectively hear what he wants to hear and then hide behind a statement like, "I'm sorry, I guess I didn't hear you." The parent of this more laid-back child must be very committed to pushing beyond appearances and to discerning the child's heart and mind.

Since genuine satisfaction and success in life involve self-denial and humility, young people are headed for certain trouble if they stay focused on self. Pride is the most important issue that you will ever deal with in your teenager. Ever. At its core is the question of who will be the Master and Lord of your teen's life. Spiritually speaking, this is a life-and-death issue.

Humble Pie and the Teen Years

I didn't eat much humble pie myself during the teen years. I remember how my dad became very dumb and I became pretty smart. Then upon graduation from college, that process started reversing itself. Dad suddenly became a genius. I was finally growing up and realizing how wise he really was.

The tragedy was that it took me nearly eight years to emerge from my self-centered cocoon. That's a long time. No wonder so many parents lose heart with their children during their teen years.

As we know so well, pride and rebellion do not disappear after adolescence. We grapple with them for a lifetime. But we parents have some unique opportunities to advance the cause of humility when our children are adolescents. They need to learn Kingdom rules, which include humbling yourself, putting God first, and not seeking your own interests. All of life's pursuits, whether they be in marriage, raising children, or success in the marketplace, depend upon renouncing the foolish attitudes of youth and attaining godly humility. If you miss humility, you miss life.

DETERMINING YOUR CONVICTIONS

Our house is on a ridge overlooking a distant lake, but a number of years ago our view had become obstructed by several trees. My son Benjamin and I were out doing a little lumberjacking to improve the view. We came upon a big oak that stood just inches across my property line, in a forest owned by the city. When I started up my chain saw, Benjamin asked, "Isn't that tree on city property?"

"No," I shouted over the buzz of the saw. "Property lines are never that exact." The chain saw sliced through the oak in a few seconds, and down it crashed. And as it fell I saw some little orange markers, clearly showing it was a city tree!

At its core, my act was one of selfishness and arrogance.

Afterward, I didn't want to admit my sin to myself or to Benjamin. But over the next few weeks, the Lord began to make noises like a chain saw in the back of my mind. Every time I read the Bible I saw trees. I finally realized I needed to go to the city officials and confess my sin.

When I finally made the call, Benjamin was standing next to me. I told the official who I was, that I had cut down the tree, and that I wanted to make restitution. He said he appreciated my call, but restitution wasn't necessary since "the property lines out there aren't that exact anyway." I thanked him.

Benjamin didn't say much when I told him what the man said, but I could tell he was soaking it all in. Afterward, I put my arm around my son and told him that he didn't have a perfect dad. But he did have a dad who would humble himself and ultimately do what is right, regardless of what it cost him.

Parents' Conviction 1: At the core of the Christian life is death to self, a continual relinquishment of pride and rebellion, and a full surrender to Jesus Christ.

We all agree intellectually that pride, rebellion, and selfishness are deadly. But we adults often are clever at hiding these sins, especially when dealing with our offspring. It is humbling to have to admit character flaws, failures, and sins (like cutting down trees that aren't ours) to our children.

But if we are not admitting our weaknesses and seeking to humble ourselves, there's little chance that pride and rebellion will be flushed from the hearts and minds of our children.

A good way to put flesh on the words *surrender to Jesus Christ* is to encourage a servant's attitude in your family. If necessary, manufacture situations where sharing and teamwork are required: family yard projects, helping each other clean rooms, sharing responsibility for household chores, and so on. Designate certain items, such as games or recreational equipment, that will have to be shared by family members. Obviously, you may create additional conflict, but all of this will help break down the fortresses of me-centered, arrogant selfishness.

Several years ago, I wanted to demonstrate visibly this same attitude that Christ embodies, so I seated our children at a table. One by one I washed their feet, just as Jesus did. I wanted to make a point with our children that a servant spirit is at the heart of true leadership.

Parents' Conviction 2: As parents we must model humility by being teachable, admitting mistakes, and asking for forgiveness.

One of the best admissions you'll ever make to your child is, "I was wrong; I'm sorry; will you forgive me?" You'll have a very attentive audience.

Truthfully, we grow weary of making mistakes. But how we respond to our mistakes is a measure of whether we truly have a humble and teachable spirit. Our children have heard us repeatedly admit fault and ask for forgiveness. When our children see that we are truly humble, it is a lot easier for their hearts to be receptive and shaped by convictions that we share with them.

SHAPING YOUR CHILD'S CONVICTIONS

Sometimes a child's self-oriented actions are just ridiculous.

I (Barbara) was in the kitchen one morning, helping one of our girls finish making her lunch. A teenage mutiny erupted because we had no potato chips.

I told her I was sorry that we were out and suggested some other options, to no avail. She whined, "There's *nothing* in this house to eat. *Nothing* for my lunch!"

In fact, there was enough food in the house to feed a platoon of Marines. I tried to point this out. "We've got yogurt, fruit . . ." But we didn't have the one thing she wanted.

She got so bent out of shape over the potato chips deficit that I had to warn her, "You need to gain control of your attitude; this isn't that big of a deal. I'm going to the store this afternoon. I'll have potato chips tomorrow, but not today."

Our daughter's hysteria escalated even more. "You'll need to come to school and take me and *buy* my lunch!" she said.

I tried to help her gain perspective and relax, but she refused to hear. She was so out of bounds that, to sting her selfishness, I grounded her from the phone for a week. Her disrespect and demanding attitude were inappropriate.

The punishment cooled her whining but did not completely extinguish it. Finally, I said, "You know, honey, I am going to go buy potato chips, but you're not going to take any in your lunch for a week, because you were so demanding."

Our daughter frowned and finally quieted down. What a way to begin a day!

This is the kind of petty and selfish attitude you will sometimes encounter and need to correct. Rewarding such behavior is out of the question. Resist the temptation to give in to some irrational demand just to calm the waters and ease the migraine headache. Take the aspirin. Don't capitulate.

Here are some convictions that will combat attitude problems in your family.

Child's Conviction 1: If I am to grow up and become a true disciple of Jesus Christ, I must submit my will to my God.

Challenging our children to submit their will to God requires formal and informal training. The years between ten and twelve are crucial because you can teach them many basic principles of walking with God before they start displaying too much pride and rebellion.

One of the best tools we've found to shape a child's convictions is to take him through the book of Proverbs, which is a child-rearing manual loaded with real answers to life's traps and issues—its pages repeatedly warn against pride. It's a book about obedience. A book about wisdom or foolishness. A book about life and death.

If we had it to do all over again, beginning when each child was age twelve or thirteen, we'd discuss Proverbs, chapter by chapter, once a year for the next six years. Twenty to thirty minutes a week of formal instruction from Proverbs will provide adequate warning about what happens to a proud, selfish, and foolish person.

Child's Conviction 2: I realize that how I submit to my parents' standards and requests reveals whether my heart is full of pride and rebellion or is of a teachable spirit.

As our children approached their teenage years, we prepared them by *talking about how their perspective of us would change.* We talked about how the nature of the teenage years is to think that you know more than your mom or dad.

We told them what happened when we became teenagers and how it seemed that our parents started taking these "dumb" pills. "Almost overnight our parents were not cool," we said. "They didn't know what they were talking about. As teens we grew smarter than our parents."

We have used this example on numerous occasions to connect with our teenagers and to let them know that we know what's going on in their heads. This has been very helpful in talking to them about their pride and selfish perspective. Of course, we've talked with our children about the dangers of actually seeing your parents as "stupid" or "dumb." We've shown them from Scripture how pride will cut a young person off from those who love him the most and are looking out for his best.

Arrogance and selfishness in a teenager often provoke emotional outbursts against a parent—often a mom. It's important during these times never to forget who the adult is and who the child is. Patiently guide your child in the direction of a teachable spirit. To calm relational waters and encourage a softer heart, prayerfully direct your teen to take some time to get alone with God in his bedroom and write out what's bothering him.

Some of the bigger mistakes we've made in confronting selfish attitudes in our children have come when we've decided to go toe-to-toe with them in an argument. A much better response is to ask them to get alone with God, gather their thoughts, and deal with their attitude by writing a letter to you.

Discipline Technique in the Preteen and Teenage Years

Just how do you go about administering discipline for a stinky attitude or other problems as your child edges into adolescence?

Admittedly, what follows is just an overview, but you should find these pointers helpful:

1. *Affirm your love.* A child about to be corrected must be reminded that the parent's actions have the right motivations.
2. *Speak the truth.* Be clear in your communication. Explain what has happened, why it is wrong, and make sure the child understands clearly the "offense."
3. *Call for admission of guilt and repentance.* The purpose of your confrontation is to expose the problem and see it rectified. The child needs to acknowledge wrongdoing and appropriately express regret. The purpose of repentance is to take a new direction—not to repeat the same action over and over.
4. *Assess a consequence (if necessary).* Examples of discipline for this age group include withholding of privileges, grounding, delaying the opportunity to double-date or single date, and so on.
5. *Reaffirm commitment and love.* Always end a discussion like this with a final reminder: "I love you; I want the best for you. I'm in your corner."

We had a great opportunity recently to do this in a very visual, memorable way with one of our teenage daughters.

This child had been somewhat devious about some upcoming plans—just exactly what her itinerary was to be one evening and how many stops she planned to make with the car.

The three of us were having a heart-to-heart chat about this issue in our master bedroom. Barbara and I were on one end of the bed, and our teenager was flopped down on an opposite corner.

It was already 11:15 P.M., but we knew we were in the eye of a great teaching opportunity. Our daughter needed to understand that accountability must be total for a teenager; she just wasn't free yet to do everything she wanted do without approval from parents.

We sat on the bed and talked in circles for about thirty minutes. She was not getting our point, and in fact was resisting, refusing to acknowledge her wrong attitude. It was one of those moments when the Spirit of God just plops some insight in your lap. I sensed it was time to forget the "front door" approach; I needed to try a side door.

This illustrates an important concept for parents of teenagers: What worked yesterday with a child may not work today, and you have to be flexible. So instead of persisting in confronting this child with her sin, I sneaked in the side door and said: "You know, you're seated on the corner of the bed over here, and it's like you're in one corner and you're putting us in the opposite corner. I want you to know that this isn't a battle between you and your parents. Honey, we're in your corner! We're not in a boxing match with you! We're for you, and we're trying to help you be successful!"

Her expression softened.

"Don't let the enemy convince you otherwise!" I continued. "We want God's best for you, and we're committed to helping make that happen. A part of that is teaching you some things that will help you mature and grow into the kind of person God made you to be.

"Accountability is not a minor issue! This is a big deal, because if you hide just a little thing, the next time you'll be tempted to hide something bigger. If you can get away with it, before long you'll go down a trail called deceit that can destroy your life as a teenager and as an adult."

At this point the light bulb flashed on. She heard what we were saying and her attitude shifted. And at about midnight—mission accomplished—we all went to bed!

Curfews

Let's face it. Teenagers hate curfews. Establishing a curfew means curbing their freedom. A curfew is an intersection where parental authority and adolescent independence meet.

The word *curfew* originally meant "to cover the fire." People who lived in medieval cities had to cover their fires in the evening by a certain time to prevent going to sleep with a burning fire that might flare up and burn down the entire community.

Setting curfews means we literally help them put the fire out before it gets started in situations that could do them damage.

Growing up I always felt that my parents were more strict than the parents of my buddies. They expected me to be home much earlier than my friends and on time!

Being strict has served our family well.

When our daughter, Ashley, went on her first date, she was told to be home at 10:00. She came in just a few minutes after 10:00.

I looked the young man and Ashley in the eye and said, "You were not in on time. Unfortunately, coming in late will cost you."

Barbara and I had agreed that Ashley would be grounded for a couple of weeks if she was late. We knew that was a severe penalty, but we wanted to make a memorable point—not only for her but for her brothers and sisters.

"But, Daddy," she said, "we were home. We were in the driveway before 10:00!"

"Sweetheart, home is *here*. The driveway is out there. You were not in the house at 10:00. When we say 10:00, that means being in the house before 10:00, not 10:05, not 10:10. We are giving you freedom. We are trusting you, and we need you to show us that you can be trusted with more freedom by respecting the limits and not pressing those limits to the edge."

She wasn't very happy about that, but she learned a valuable lesson. And later—some time later!—she said, "Thanks, Mom and Dad, for holding fast to curfews."

Standing by our boundaries had ultimately given her the security of knowing that her parents cared about her enough to hold her accountable, ultimately for her own safety and good.

Since then there have been times when a child was late for a valid reason, and we have extended grace. There are circumstances that occur where your child makes a judgment call that you need to reward, not punish. Your child may be late some night because he chose not to ride home with someone who had been drinking. You always have to make sure as a parent you're getting the rest of the story before you make your judgment.

We have had a lot of dialogue with our children around curfews. We don't just lay the law down. We listen. We talk it out. Together. There's give and take. We help them understand the "why" behind the boundaries and that curfews are for their protection.

Teens need to know exactly what is expected of them. We have found with our teenagers that it is very important to write down and post times and boundaries, as well as what the penalty will be if a curfew or other limit is violated.

A good place to start building patterns of accountability is to insist on a call-me-if-you're-late-or-plans-have-changed policy. Expect and demand accountability from your children. If your daughter is normally home after school at 4:00, if she is going to stay late to work on the newspaper and not be home until 4:30, she needs to call and let you know. Make sure your child always carries some quarters and dimes for these phone calls.

What are reasonable curfews? Curfew times actually start related to bedtime when your children are younger. For instance, when our children were ten they had to be in bed by 8:30. By four-teen, the lights-out deadline was 9:30 or 10:00, depending on the child's need for sleep. Even on weekends, we insist that a fourteen year old be home by 10:00, if he goes out at all.

This is sometimes viewed as repressive, oppressive, and depressive by our children. There have been crocodile tears. They have told us that *"everybody* else can stay out later." But these are our family's standards.

Make sure both of you stand together on the boundaries. We have agreed upon the rules and stand as a unified force.

And don't forget when they do come home on time, reinforce that. Applaud them for doing the right thing.

Child's Conviction 3: I will learn how to deny my own interests in order to help and serve others.

One of the best cures for a selfish, me-centered attitude is to give ourselves to others. Jesus modeled this Himself when He said, "And whoever wishes to be first among you shall be your slave, just as the Son of Man did not come to be served, but to serve, and to give His life a ransom for many" (Matt. 20:27–28).

Be on the lookout for situations where you can help the preadolescent or young teen shift from a selfish focus to the needs of others.

We know a mom who regularly took her son and daughter to a rest home just to get them to think of others. Later on, during the height of his teenage turmoil, her son came home from school one day discouraged and announced that he was going to the rest home to minister to one of its residents. A couple of hours later he returned home, fresh and encouraged, because his mom had taught him about giving to others.

Bottom line: Real life is about serving others with humility, whether in our relationship to Christ or with our brother or sister, who may need to borrow shirt, shoes, dress, or stereo. We are training the next generation how to walk humbly with God and to reach out to others with a servant spirit.

Remind yourself that Someone is even more interested in shaping your child's character and dealing with pride, rebellion, and selfishness than you are. God has ways of getting a child's attention that go way beyond any parent's conniving or planning. He can humble a child very quickly. In fact, we have prayed that for our children. "Lord, You know this child has a problem with pride. Would You do what we can't do? Would You in your gentleness and Your love be compassionate and gracious enough to help correct this child in this situation?"

The good news is that most young men and women in the later teen years will begin to outgrow much of the petty selfish behavior. You may not see it until they are about to leave home or even until after they have left the nest. Persevere—there is hope.

TESTING YOUR CHILD'S CONVICTIONS

With issues like attitudes, you need to become an astute observer and interpreter of your child's heart and actions. So much of good parenting takes place when you're in the hanging-around mode—on duty, ready to inject yourself creatively and positively into the shaping of your child by listening, asking a question, giving a hug, offering an observation, lending a hand.

But what if your child is giving you a lip whip and every word that falls from his tongue seems coated with battery acid? Nothing you say or do—even how you look—qualifies you for membership in the human race. Our suggestion is to wait for natural opportunities to let your child know of the possible consequences.

Let's say that, about the time you are enduring verbal humiliation, he mentions that he wants to go to the football game tomorrow night and that "you'll need to drive me there—the game starts at 7:00 P.M."

Try this kind of response: "Your selfish, disrespectful attitude—the way you have been talking to me—is not acceptable. You want to go to the football game and want me to take you? Before I can do that, you need to demonstrate that you are worthy to be trusted. You need to deal with your arrogant attitude. You need to show me that you are teachable, that you are listening respectfully to me."

Dealing with outright, flagrant rebellion is more difficult. From time to time, we have felt like one of our children was bordering on becoming an in-house prodigal—still home, but in total rebellion against us and God.

Pray diligently and keep loving your child, no matter what. Most likely your child feels terribly unlovable, and he desperately needs to be loved.

One of the ultimate dangers of stiff-necked arrogance and selfishness, allowed to run full course, is isolation.

Some friends of ours are still working through the ramifications of a child who chose to withdraw into her own world. The parents, Bill and Jenna, noticed when their daughter Theresa entered the sixth grade that she was walling herself off from people. Theresa holed up in her room for hours and became increasingly self-centered. She became preoccupied with listening to music, writing letters, and organizing her room.

Realizing their daughter was sliding farther and farther away from them, Bill and Jenna prayed and fasted for her one day a week. In addition, Bill purposefully pursued a relationship with her by taking her on dates, playing games with her, and hanging out in her room. Many of these efforts were met with outright rejection. Theresa bristled when Bill tried to hug her, and she even turned away from him when he tried to kiss her good night.

Theresa was gripped by a selfish heart, an attitude that said, "I don't need you. I don't need anybody."

She didn't share her clothes with her sister. She fought repeatedly with her brother. She didn't accept loving discipline or correction from her parents well. Her heart remained cold for most of her early teenage years.

But Bill and Jenna never quit loving Theresa. When she didn't believe in herself, they believed in her. When she ignored rules, they loved her enough to discipline her. When she rebelled even more, they took her in their arms and loved her.

Once at 3:00 A.M. they bailed her out of jail for driving while intoxicated. Still, Bill and Jenna lovingly pointed out to Theresa that her rebellion was not just against her parents but against God.

Theresa is now twenty and is just beginning to realize how pride and rebellion have clutched her in their jaws. Ever so slowly her heart is thawing. God is using the magnetic power of true love to soften her hardened heart.

It's at times like this that we feel like we are in a spiritual tug of war for our child's soul and life. This is not the time to let go of the rope; it is the time to ask God for victory on your child's behalf.

CONCLUSION

Having four teenagers while writing this book on raising them has some advantages. Recently we were having a nice chat with one of our teens about an issue that demanded teachability and humility. The conversation was sprinkled with statements by our teen saying, "I know. I know. I know. I've heard your lecture already. I know what you're going to say before you say it." This teen was exasperated and unteachable. It wasn't the first time.

Finally, we asked, "Are you going to be teachable? Are you willing to learn and grow? Or are you going to keep resisting the truth and thereby delay your maturity?" Then we reminded our child of something we say quite frequently: "Nothing bad that you do can cause us to love you less, and nothing good that you do can cause us to love you more."[1]

The result was a deeper conversation in which our child's defensive guard began to drop, and we once again challenged this young person to take another step toward adulthood and maturity.

As you face some of life's most challenging issues with your child, do not forget that love ultimately changes a person's life. Your love may be used by God to soften a teen's heart that would otherwise grow hard.

CONVICTION BUILDING PLAN

The following questions will assist you in dealing with "attitude" issues in your home.

Part One. Answer the following questions individually

1. In what ways did you display pride and rebellion when you were a teenager? How did your parents respond to you?
2. In what ways do you still struggle with pride and selfishness?
3. In what ways do you still struggle with rebellious attitudes?
4. How would you rate your mate in the area of pride and selfishness?
5. How do you think your mate would rate you?
6. Pray through all issues where you detect pride and selfishness. Ask for and receive forgiveness. Repent! Claim God's promises and power to change through the Holy Spirit. Ask God to make you a teachable parent. Your life may be the living model that God uses to show your teen what true humility before God and man looks like.
7. In what ways do you see pride and rebellion in your child?

Part Two. Conclusions

1. Meet with your mate and, in a loving way, share your answers from the first section. If you are single, do this with a wise friend.
2. In what ways do you feel your marriage relationship is marked by pride and selfishness? Pray together that you would allow God to root these sins out of your lives.
3. Come up with a game plan for how you can begin to address this issue in the life of your child during the next few weeks.

"I will give heed to the blameless way.
When wilt Thou come to me?
I will walk within my house in the integrity of my heart.
I will set no worthless thing before my eyes."
—Psalm 101:2–3

10

Trap 5: Media

Plucking Pearls from a Mountain of Garbage

Has a tsunami hit your house?

"What's that?" you say!

Another term for tsunami is tidal wave. A tsunami is a series of traveling ocean waves usually triggered by an earthquake. In deep water, a tsunami may reach speeds exceeding six hundred miles per hour. And when all that force hits land, the wave may be a hundred feet or higher.

One of the worst recorded tsunamis occurred in 1970. About 260,000 people were killed when a monstrous wave crashed ashore in what is now Bangladesh.[1]

Although the Raineys live far inland in Arkansas, there's a kind of tsunami that threatens to crash into our house on a daily basis. It's the tidal wave of media.

The human race has never had so much to read, view, experience, or listen to. Just think of the choices you and your children have with a spare hour or two: books, magazines, newspaper, mail, radio, audio cassettes, videotapes, television, cable television, e-mail, computer software, computer games, video games, the Internet. Does this feel like a tidal wave threatening to sweep you away?

Since we live in a media-driven world, how can we stay on top of the media? This is a mammoth parenting issue during adolescence.

The media trap is multifaceted: It's not only what your child chooses to consume, but in what quantity—and what other important life experiences are shortchanged when he's involved with media.

The best advice we can offer on supervising your preadolescent or teen's exposure to media is to stay involved. Media and entertainment issues will provide many opportunities for you to dialogue with your child about your convictions. This will take considerable time and effort, but you need to know the content of the media your child is consuming—music, computer, print, video, TV—all of it.

An often overlooked ramification of media use is that some things that might be appropriate for an older child are not acceptable for a younger one. If you have an older sibling, challenge him to be a good example. An older teen in a family who is making the right choices can help you establish the right standards and help you parent a younger brother or sister.

I (Barbara) remember when our older children were at home. I once told our boys about some of the music they enjoyed, "I don't want you to listen to that stuff because you have little sisters who don't need to hear it. I'm sorry, but what you are doing affects everyone else in the family." They grumbled, but I think they realized deep down inside that they were models.

Although everyone has personal tastes in media, parents need to take responsibility for setting and maintaining media boundaries that are for the good of the entire family.

The apostle Paul gives us a great media filter: "Whatever is true, whatever is honorable, whatever is right, whatever is pure, whatever is lovely, whatever is of good repute, if there is any excellence and if anything worthy of praise, let your mind dwell on these things" (Phil. 4:8).

DETERMINING YOUR CONVICTIONS

It really doesn't matter what the media culprits are.

Men often struggle with the sports monster and, increasingly, the personal computer. Just how many great match-up basketball games do we need to watch between Small Potatoes U and Obscurity Tech? Are we surfing the Internet so much that our hand is looking like a claw from gripping the mouse?

Women may be more inclined to invest too much time in TV dramas, entertainment talk shows, novels, and special-interest magazines.

We need convictions and a personal, proactive plan for handling media wisely. Then we can move on to help our teens make their own solid choices.

Parents' Conviction 1: We have the responsibility and right to screen and set limits to all forms of media consumed by our family.

Here's a suggestion: Make it clear that as long as your child resides in your home, the parents will have the right to screen— and bar—all media consumed by anyone in the family. Ideally, you will be involved in helping choose the media in the first place. As your child gets older, however, he will begin making many of his own decisions. Brace yourself. Some of those decisions will not be good ones. That's why if some media item that violates the family's standards sneaks into your home, you should retain the right to eliminate its use.

Such a stand will not be easy. But if you have a baseline policy like this, you will have a chance to keep your head above water when the waves of media hit.

Parents' Conviction 2: Use of media by parents must set a high standard for media use by children.

If we sit on the couch watching so much TV that our nickname is Spud, we can't expect to easily confine our twelve year old's viewing to a few selected PBS specials each week.

It would be good if every family in America adopted its own media use policy. Ask, "Just what and how much media are we going to devour inside the four walls of our home?"

Americans devote, on average, 15 of 40 free time hours per week watching television. That compares to 6.7 hours socializing, 2.8 hours reading, and 2.2 hours engaging in outdoor recreation.[2] That's a lot of time spent in a passive activity. Important, meaningful activities, such as physical exercise, prayer and Bible study, hobbies, volunteer work at church or in the community, and so on, will never be enjoyed while we vegetate.

Parents' Conviction 3: Media consumption must not replace relationship building.

Perhaps the saddest outcome of having your time eroded by waves of media is that key relationships are shortchanged.

Although sitting next to your spouse or child while watching one TV sitcom after another may seem like an intimate encounter, normally this is just communal "couch potatoing." Not much relating occurs while the mesmerizing tube does most of the talking.

SHAPING YOUR CHILD'S CONVICTIONS

Although similar issues are present in all media, there are unique concerns as well. We'll discuss the media types separately first. Then we'll offer a list of suggested convictions to build into your child.

You may not agree with where we have drawn our lines as a family. The issue isn't what we believe; it's what you and your family stand for and are holding as a conviction.

Television

TV has always had its critics, but in the past, although much programming may have been a waste of time, it was at least innocuous. No more. In addition to the unrealistic view of life that most TV programming presents, now we face increasing doses of violence, sex and sexual perversions, off-color jokes, cynicism, bad language, and the glamorization of sinful and perverse behavior. And it's not just the programming that is offensive: Much advertising glamorizes horrible attitudes and is downright lewd. Unfortunately, disgusting advertisements often air in the middle of "family shows."

Yes, there are some wholesome programs. We repeat, not all TV is bad.

But the garbage spewing from the screen is increasingly foul. TV has become so repulsive that even the federal government has become more involved by requiring warning labels on all programs. The ratings may be of some help to you, but stay on guard. You can be confident that the world view supporting the ratings is not biblically based. And not all shows, such as documentaries and news programs, have ratings. How you and the person rating a program establish standards may be miles apart.

The bottom line with TV is that we parents have to be incredibly involved in determining what we will allow our children to watch and in what quantity.

If you can pull it off, consider pulling the plug—don't watch TV. You and your children really won't miss much, and the benefits could be enormous. You may want to give this serious consideration.

But if TV remains a viewing option in your home, consider:

- Not allowing TV viewing by children without prior approval by a parent.
- Limiting TV viewing to no more than 30 to 60 minutes per day or a certain number of hours per week.
- Videotaping favorite shows. Then you can choose the ideal time for viewing, and by skipping over commercials, save time.

Sometimes, though, no matter how careful you are, something slips by. A number of times, we will see something flash on the

149

screen and we'll say, "Turn it off." Our children will complain, "It's not that bad," or "It's almost over." In spite of their complaints, they are seeing our convictions lived out.

Cable TV

Cable TV provides a plethora of special-interest channels, including religious broadcasting, that offer outstanding information and entertainment. But also on cable, some movie channels show feature-length films uncut.

If you have subscribed to some of the movie channels on cable TV, you may need to reconsider that choice because you may not know what your child is seeing at 3:30 in the afternoon. The cable movie networks avoid showing R-rated movies until after 7:00 at night, but these days it doesn't take an R-rated movie for your children to see things they shouldn't.

And at night when the babysitter is watching or after you have gone to bed and a child sneaks back downstairs, he could be exposed to something graphic.

For these reasons we have drawn a line in the sand in the Rainey home: We don't subscribe to cable. As a result we don't enjoy some of the advantages, but more important, we don't have the distractions and temptations. And we have the opportunity to enjoy more time together.

Movies/Videos

The first thing to do is to stop making movie decisions based on the movie ratings system. The best approach is to see a movie before you decide whether or not your child should see it. However, in previewing movies for your child, you may have to endure something you don't want to file in your brain, either.

Until Hollywood cleans up its act, you might want to adopt the policy of curtailing this form of entertainment.

Nearly every movie is released in video within a few months of its initial release. Resist the urge to see the newest movie within a week of its release. This gives you time to collect reviews, seek out other information on just what a movie contains, and carefully listen to what others you respect have to say about the movie.

Related to bad language in movies, sometimes one of our teenagers will say, "I hear those words at school all the time. What's the difference?"

We respond: "You hear it enough at school. You don't need to hear it here too." Here are some resources that will help you evaluate the suitability of movies:

- *Screen It! Entertainment Reviews for Parents*, <http://www.screenit.com>. A first-rate Web site that will tell you everything you want to know about the quality, morality, and specific language of any film being released. This is the best resource of this type we've seen. Caution: You—not your child—should read the reviews since they are often graphic.
- *Movie Guide*. Ted Baehr has years of experience in evaluating movie content from a Christian perspective. Write him at 3554 Strait Street, Atlanta, GA 30340.

The Internet

Just a few years ago most of us would have thought the Internet was just an information highway. Today we know that you can find almost anything along that highway, and it's not a safe road for an unprepared, novice teenage driver.

Because the material is so easily accessible, we are even more concerned about the Internet than we are about TV viewing. The Internet offers a vast array of educational information on virtually every subject. But it is also an enormous clearinghouse for hard-core pornography. Supposedly the word *sex* is the most searched for word on the Internet.

All it takes is a couple of mouse clicks and your child indicating he is age twenty-one, and the pornographic images will be downloading on your computer.

As a result we control our children's access to the Internet through various means. We also strongly recommend some type of screening software, such as Cybersitter (for information, see Appendix B). Such software will deny visitation to certain categories of Web sites.

One of the largest subscription services recently took a stand against pornography by being the first to offer a porn-free Internet service. (For more information, contact FlashNet Communications, telephone 1-888-FLASHNET. Their web page address is <http://www.flash.net>).

We also encourage you to make sure your home computer is in a very public room of your house. If that's not possible, insist on a no-computer-use-with-the-door-closed policy, and no Internet use when the parents are gone or later at night when you may be asleep. This is not child's play; the Internet is a very dangerous trap.

We have not allowed our teens to have computers in their rooms, except our son Samuel during his senior year because he was editor of the school newspaper.

Stay involved in your children's lives in this area by asking them if they are visiting any Web sites that they shouldn't be. It never hurts to ask. And it never hurts to look and see what sites they have been visiting. Every computer has a memory that logs every step taken. Be careful about assuming your child would never drive down the information highway to the wrong part of town.

Computer and Video Games

Boys in particular are attracted to the large assortment of computer games now on the market. Estimates are that more than 80 percent of the entertainment and learning software sold today is purchased by or for boys.[3]

Many of the games are harmless, involving sports and good-guy-versus-bad-guy story lines. But others are tasteless or decidedly evil in tone. James Oppenheim, an editor of a publication devoted to evaluating media for children, said about such products: "There's this constant chipping away at decency."[4]

Our suggestion on games is similar to that given on most media: Stay involved in what your child borrows or buys. Since such games often are nonreturnable, make sure your child understands that if you later decide the game's content is unacceptable, it's his loss.

We enforced this rule once with one of our children over a computer game that we deemed unacceptable. It was a difficult confrontation because the child felt he could buy what he wanted with his money. He argued long and hard, but we didn't give in. It made a lasting impression about getting prior approval in choices he made.

Reviews of games are available in computer magazines (check the library or the Internet), and demo disks often can be obtained that show a game's features. Of assistance is a rating system for video and computer games.

All of this involvement takes time, but it's well worth the effort. Do you want your preadolescent to spend hours perfecting his effectiveness at blowing people away in software or video games? You must decide

It's difficult to always be on the offensive. Occasionally you'll find yourself in the uncomfortable position of evaluating one of these games after it's been purchased. Pray. God will guide.

Music/Radio

We've lumped these together because most radio usage by teens is listening to music (although the new shock-talk radio is undoubtedly attracting its share of teenagers).

In their early adolescence, we work on helping our teens understand the overt and subtle messages communicated through the music they listen to. We try to convince them how important it is to put good things into their heads, because what goes in stays in and shapes their thinking and their feelings.

Since music is an area more dictated by personal tastes, parents should approach the topic shrewdly and wisely. Particularly as your child gets older, your ability to understand his tastes and why he likes certain kinds of music is critical. You are a coach; you want him to understand for himself how different types of music will affect his emotions and moods, especially how music can play a significant role in romantic relationships with the opposite sex.

With our current young adolescents (they are thirteen and fifteen), we are quite aggressive in monitoring what they listen to. In fact, except for classical music we do not let them listen to stations playing secular music. As our thirteen year old goes to sleep at night, she listens to instrumental praise music.

Again, as with all media they consume, our children know that we will be examining the lyrics of any tapes or CDs they listen to.

Regardless of lyrics, are there types of music that you should ban?

Later in adolescence, when our children have more freedom to choose what they will listen to, we have always encouraged balance in the music. We have concluded that this means that even some types of Christian rock music should not be listened to solely or excessively. We keep going back to the notion that what you put in your brain is what is going to come out in your thoughts, moods, actions. Again, we want our teens to have balance in their lives in all areas, including the music they listen to.

So that we don't leave the wrong impression, each of our older teenagers has done some experimenting with types of secular music that we found questionable. They were not dabbling with extreme, damaging, hard, harsh, vulgar, way-out-there stuff with garbage lyrics. But they have done some exploring. Eventually they have all come back to Christian or acceptable secular music.

The important thing is to engage your child in ongoing discussions.

When one of our daughters was sixteen or so, I (Barbara) observed she was alternately listening to secular and Christian music. The secular music was on a radio station that played Top 40 Pop from the 1980s and the 1990s.

I would walk into her room when she was studying and sit down on her bed. Sometimes I was surprised by the suggestive lyrics in the songs. I would ask our daughter, "Do you know what that is saying?"

"I turn it off when the bad stuff comes on," she'd answer.

"So, you've listened to it long enough to know the song well enough to know the bad parts so you can turn it off?" I would ask. "By then it is already in your head."

We talked this through a number of times over a period of a few months. Our daughter is no longer listening to that secular music. I never told her she couldn't listen to that music; I just asked questions that made her think about what she was doing.

Books and Magazines

Unfortunately, you can't blindly expect publications you may have enjoyed as a teenager to be acceptable for your child.

When I (Barbara) was a teenager in the sixties, I loved looking at *Teen* magazine and *Seventeen* magazine. When Ashley became a teenager I thought it would be so cool to get her a subscription to *Seventeen* magazine. But when I saw the content—with its emphasis on the body, sex, romance, and externals—I was appalled. In all of Ashley's teenage years, she probably only had one or two copies.

About the only teen magazines we've been comfortable with are the excellent publications *Brio* (for girls) and *Breakaway* (for boys) from Focus on the Family. Another good one is *Campus Life*.

Parents need to keep an eye out for adolescent girls reading romances, which can stir up romantic or even sexual emotions. Boys need to be steered away from books that are overly violent or have explicit sexual content.

A magazine that would appear relatively harmless that comes with some unfortunate baggage is *Sports Illustrated*.

When my dad died in 1976, I learned he had a prepaid four-year subscription to *Sports Illustrated*. Since my mom didn't want the magazine, the subscription was switched to me. I'll never forget the first annual swimsuit issue I received. Our children were

155

still little, but I remember thinking, *This is not right. I don't want the children seeing this.* And that was in the late 1970s—back when the swimsuit special was relatively tame. I canceled the magazine.

A decision like that may not seem too substantial, but all of the choices we make about bringing media into our homes and protecting our families add up to a high standard that can rub off on our preadolescents and teenagers.

Taking into consideration all of the information we've presented in this section, we suggest that the following list of convictions on media be shaped in every child:

Child's Conviction 1: I need to allow Jesus Christ to be Lord over all forms of media that I allow in my life. "What would Jesus do, listen to, read, and watch?" is a great question to ask.

Child's Conviction 2: I need to understand that what I allow to come into my mind can affect the way I think and live.

Child's Conviction 3: I need to stand firm and turn away from media temptations quickly.

TESTING YOUR CHILD'S CONVICTIONS

With media issues, you will have a daily opportunity to observe and be involved in your child's choices and habits. Since you share involvement in a certain amount of media use (watching TV, going to a concert, viewing a video, etc.), this gives you an ongoing opportunity to ask questions and discuss content. Make good use of these training times.

And don't forget to ask our favorite question: "Have you been looking at or listening to something that's not good for you?"

Here are some ideas for testing your child's convictions on the media trap:

Listen to his music. On a regular basis, ask your child to play you a song or two from a favorite music group. Keep tuned in to not only what your child enjoys in music but form your own impressions of the group and the lyrics of their songs

Be proactive in selecting reading material. Visit a public library. Explain to a librarian your standards for books your child might read, then have the librarian suggest possible authors and types of books. Check out two titles. Give your child some things to be looking for that might signal objectionable content. Each of you read one of the books and report back. Discuss what you found.

Do some interactive media together. Get on the Internet with your child and do some surfing (exploring). Show your child how to navigate toward acceptable materials and away from questionable Web sites. While still on the computer, *play with your child some of the computer or video games that he enjoys.* Discuss any messages or themes that are portrayed as you play the game.

Play the media Decide in Advance game. You can play some great Decide in Advance games related to media. Try some of these:

- You are watching TV at a neighbor's house when a bad video or cable show comes on. Your friend says his parents don't mind. What would you do?
- You are watching one of your favorite TV shows at home when the story becomes dirty. What would you do?
- You are in a friend's room listening to music. The radio is tuned to a popular music station and a song about sex comes on. What would you do?
- You've just downloaded your e-mail from your browser and you notice a message that mentions something about sex in the title. What would you do?

FOR SINGLE PARENTS

If you share custody of your child, you will need to do all in your power to influence media choices when the child is with your ex-spouse. This may be difficult, but it is certainly worth your effort.

If the media choices allowed by the other spouse do not reflect your standards, don't give up and give in. Keep the bar high and press on, bathing the situation in prayer.

Without tearing down your former spouse, talk about why you have the established certain standards. Your child may never say it, but he will respect you for your standards even though he may resist them.

Another issue for many single parents (it certainly happens in other types of homes too) is the tendency to allow TV and the VCR to be a live-in child-sitter. Although it's understandable why this happens, it's not a good idea. Do everything you can to minimize tube time. We've actually paid our children to read good books.

CONCLUSION

Even as we have been writing these words, there's a rap group playing on the CD upstairs. Laura is trying out for cheerleader. We have not yet listened to the words of that song.

Deborah was on the computer doing a report on the Holocaust and was downloading files left and right. Neither of us was there inspecting her work to make sure that what she was collecting was appropriate.

And one of the children viewed a made-for-TV movie after school that Barbara said hadn't passed muster.

Little House on the Prairie has been replaced by "Little House on the Information Highway" and we realize again that we can't let down our guard.

UNFORGETTABLE LESSON: Boot the Tube

One of the best lessons your child can learn is how tube time robs time from other enjoyable activities. Try this:

1. Make an appointment with your child for a two-hour block of time—ideally on a weekend.
2. Ahead of time, without the child's knowledge, plan a fun-packed two hours of activities. Perhaps having lunch with one of your child's friends, shooting baskets, working on a hobby, twenty minutes reading a book, listening to a CD, playing a board game, giving the dog a bath.
3. When it's time for the two-hour date, before you start in on the fun, say something like this: "To help you understand how time can be used in different ways, you and I could have made a choice today to spend the next two hours watching TV (list some show or shows you might have watched) or doing what we're going to do. I think you'll see how TV often robs us of some really fun ways to use our time."
4. Be sure to get your child's reactions after the two hours are over. Talk about the importance of relationships in your family.

Another Unforgettable Lesson:

Unplug your television for a month and watch what effect it has on your family.

CONVICTION BUILDING PLAN

Answering these questions will help identify and solidify your convictions about media use in your family.

Part One. Answer the following questions individually

1. Make a list of the media you consumed in the last seven days and estimate the amount of time devoted to each type. What surprises you about your answers? Do you see patterns that need changing?

2. How much of your media consumption is intentional, as opposed to media use that "just happens" as a part of your daily schedule?

3. Do you think you are donating too much of your time to media consumption? How might you change?

4. How can you go about making your media use more proactive—better planned and controlled?

5. Concerning your personal tastes in media, are you watching, listening to, or reading any material that you would be ashamed to consume with your preadolescent or teenager? If yes, what are you going to do about it?

Part Two. Conclusions

1. Compare answers from questions in *Part One* with your spouse. If you are single, meet with a friend who can offer wisdom and insight.

2. In what areas of individual media use do each of you need to be held accountable? Prayerfully devise a plan to help one or both of you deal with inappropriate or excessive use of media.

3. If you haven't already done so, have a thorough discussion of media use in your family. Together, create a written policy that covers all media and all family members. For example, what is your family's policy related to PG, PG-13, and R movies? Do you have two separate standards for adults and children? If so, what's your reasoning—and will it hold up if you are asking your child not to put impure images and ideas in his mind, but you are?

*"But let everyone be quick to hear,
slow to speak and slow to anger."*
—James 1:19

11

Trap 6: Unresolved Anger

Harmony and Peace Sure Beat the Alternatives

Have you ever had a scene like this in your home?

Two of our teenagers were asked to clean the kitchen together. Over the next forty-five minutes, I came back in to inspect their work three times.

The first time they were arguing about who had done the most. I asked them kindly to keep on working. The next time they were bickering about who had to sweep the floor. I calmed their emotions and encouraged them to finish the job.

Finally, after I had inspected their halfhearted work, the two gave me the lame excuse that they didn't know what a clean kitchen should look like!

That did it. This normally unflappable dad flipped. The anger that I had controlled during the prior visits erupted and spewed out like lava. I went on a tirade about how they were disrespectful and disobedient. I picked up a box of Kleenex and, in unsanctified rage, flung the box near their feet. Hard!

I whirled around, stormed out of the kitchen, and stomped out the front door, slamming it shut.

Standing there on our front porch, with my blood pressure

higher than the stock market, two profound thoughts dawned on me. First, *It's very cold out here. Why am I standing here freezing and they are inside warm as toast? I'm the father, the one who is paying for this house and supposedly in charge!*

The second thought settled in like the cold and pierced me to the bone. *My anger got the best of me, and I'm acting like a foolish child.*

I don't recall how long I stayed outside, nor do I recall the exact words of the apology to my children that followed. I do recall coming to an important realization: *If I am going to help these children grow up emotionally and know how to appropriately express their anger, then I've got to finish the process of growing up, too.*

God never said we shouldn't get angry. God did say to not let anger spoil and turn into sin—a trap. The Bible cautions, "He who is slow to anger has great understanding, / But he who is quick-tempered exalts folly" (Prov. 14:29). And, "Do not be eager in your heart to be angry, / For anger resides in the bosom of fools" (Eccl. 7:9).

Anger was never intended to be an emotion that we hold onto for more than minutes or at most hours. That's why the Scriptures warn us, "Be angry, and yet do not sin; do not let the sun go down on your anger" (Eph. 4:26). It's nearly impossible to rest with an anger alarm ringing, as all of us have found out more often than we like to admit.

Ross Campbell wrote in *How to Really Love Your Teenager*, "We are instructed in Scripture to 'train up a child in the way he should go,' to educate him 'according to his life requirements' (Proverbs 22:6, KJV and MLB). One of the most important areas in which a teenager needs training is in how to handle anger . . . Anger is normal and occurs in every human being. The problem is not the anger itself but in managing it. This is where most people have problems."[1]

DETERMINING YOUR CONVICTIONS

We must admit there is no subject or emotion in our family that has perplexed us more or made us feel more like novice parents (and failures, at times) than helping our children deal with their anger. And part of the reason is that often when they are angry we get angry too.

It's so important in a family to get a handle on anger. H. Paul Gabriel, M.D., wrote in *Anticipating Adolescence*: "It becomes critical in adolescence that your children have the feeling that you, too, will listen to them carefully, that they can trust you to think about what they have to say, that you might have a true disagreement with them without getting angry with them. Without that feeling, they simply won't have the necessary trust to turn to you with the serious issues of adolescence."[2]

Reaching clear convictions on this topic is a crucial step in achieving a spiritually and emotionally healthy family.

Parents' Conviction 1: Anger is a God-given emotion.

Every family needs a plentiful supply of *good* anger. Note the emphasis on *good*. By that, I mean that when anger inevitably comes, we should recognize it, understand the cause, and deal with it properly. We shouldn't stuff it inside ourselves like a sleeping bag tightly packed into a knapsack. And we shouldn't fling it on others like confetti.

God created anger to be an asset, but it gets misused and twisted in a fallen world. In basic terms, anger is an emotional alarm that sounds a warning when something is wrong. Only a fool would hear a smoke alarm clanging in the middle of the night and stay in bed to enjoy the interesting tones of the alarm. No, the wise man gets out of bed to see what's wrong. Yet when the anger alarm sounds, too often we sit and stew instead of turning it off and finding out what's wrong.

Unfortunately, most families—dad, mom, and children—don't know how to keep good anger from fermenting into spoiled anger. And then when a family has an adolescent or two, the anger issue can take on new dimensions.

We need look no farther than Jesus to see that anger is an acceptable emotion. A number of times Jesus showed strong feelings of anger. Perhaps the most memorable was the day he tipped over the tables of the money changers and chased them out of the temple (see Mark 11:15). Additionally, throughout the Scripture we find that God is described as an angry God who exhibits a righteous anger at man's rebelliousness. The problem is that most of us don't know what to do with appropriate anger when we feel it. We need to grow up and become mature in our expression of this Divine emotion.

Parents' Conviction 2: We must model godly expressions of our anger.

Since most of us adults are still learning how to handle our own anger properly, we often end up getting angry inappropriately with our inappropriately angry child. So an incident that probably started out as a child sinning ends up with two "children" sinning—one of them an adult.

Correcting wrong ideas and habits related to the expression of anger takes time, humility, and the work of the Holy Spirit. In some of us the saved-up anger is buried so deep that we may have to dig awhile to uncover the source. Or we may have labeled our rotting anger with words like *frustration* or *stressed out*.

We need to work at modeling appropriate expressions of anger:

- Not acting or speaking unless emotions are under control (being "quick to hear, slow to speak and slow to anger," as James 1:19 directs us).
- Directing anger at the specific cause rather than spraying anger at our spouse or other people with a long list of complaints.
- Seeking resolution and reconciliation, not payback.

Remember: Children are like little radar units watching how we will react.

Parents' Conviction 3: We will work to avoid provoking our child to anger.

The apostle Paul highlighted the role we parents play in train-

164

ing our children to stay out of the unresolved anger trap. Speaking straightforwardly to dads, he said: "And fathers, do not provoke your children to anger, but bring them up in the discipline and instruction of the Lord" (Eph. 6:4). In another letter Paul wrote, "Fathers, do not exasperate your children, that they may not lose heart" (Col. 3:21).

Often during the preadolescent and teenage years, dads have a tendency to be a bit harsh and clumsy, especially with sons. Perhaps we dads are not as well equipped to handle the nuances of communication and relational maintenance so critical with adolescents. Or perhaps their independent thinking and behavior catches us off guard or feels a bit threatening.

From our experience with teens and work with families, we've established a list of the things parents do to provoke anger in their children. Many more could be listed, but here are our top five:

1. An authoritarian, dictatorial style of relating to a child. (Parental rules without a relationship of love, affection, and fun times together.)
2. A critical spirit. Parents who consistently tear down their teen with a tone of voice.
3. Outright neglect of a child.
4. Not knowing what to expect from parents in terms of boundaries, limits, and rules.
5. A parent who rejects or withdraws from a relationship with his child.

The emotional tone of your family is important. Crawl inside your child's perspective. As you look at yourself as a parent, are there areas where you are provoking your child's anger?

Parents' Conviction 4: We will teach our child about the nature of anger and how to resolve conflict.

Anger is actually a secondary emotion, the result of something else that has happened to us—like smashing your thumb with a

165

hammer; it hurts, you get angry, and you yell. Anger manifests itself in your child when:

- He does something right to please you and you fail to notice. The child is hurt that he was not appreciated for his good effort and expresses that hurt with anger.
- He gets left out of a group at school and experiences rejection, loneliness, and disappointment. He may not take that anger out on friends, but when he gets home, guess who is the recipient of his blowup? Mom, Dad, sister, brother, dog, cat.
- A sibling uses a cutting remark to get back at him for borrowing a shirt without asking. The remark hurts, so the child lashes back with a verbal barrage at the sibling and it escalates into a shouting match. The angry words are the result of the cutting comments.

Anger is almost always a response. When your child is angry you can help him understand what hurt him and work through that issue.

In some ways the most devastating type of anger results in behavior that doesn't even look like anger.

Ross Campbell writes, "Passive-aggressive (PA) behavior causes most problems with today's teenagers, from poor grades to drugs on to suicide . . . Tragically, if a teenager does not learn to handle anger maturely and grow out of the PA stage by the age of sixteen or seventeen, this PA trait will harden and become a permanent part of his or her personality for life."[3]

If you are to choose between allowing your preadolescent or teenager to express anger openly and loudly or to stuff it, it seems preferable to err on the side of letting your child release too much anger. As Campbell notes, young people who do not express their anger are in far greater jeopardy than those who express it.

Passive anger is deceptive, because it seems easier to tolerate than the behavior of a child who screams and throws a fit. But it's a pay-now-or-pay-later proposition. All anger that is not identi-

fied and addressed will bear bitter fruit later in obstinate attitudes, irrational behavior to punish parents or other authority figures, physical symptoms, or depression.

If your child seldom expresses anger openly, pay close attention
to how he responds in situations that would normally provoke disappointment, anger, or frustration.

The time to address anger in a child is *not* in the midst of an
argument or heated words. You may need to give your teenager
some time to cool off or to remind him to choose his words carefully. "A gentle answer turns away wrath, / But a harsh word stirs
up anger" (Prov. 15:1).

A child who is full of anger and expressing it wrongly is like a
mud wrestler. A parent must stay outside the ring, remaining as
objective and loving as possible. When a parent joins the child in
slinging mud emotionally and irrationally, he has stepped into the
mud puddle and become a mud wrestler too.

Resolving Conflict

We have concluded that God must want us parents to repeatedly
train our children in conflict management, because a good bit of the
New Testament speaks of maintaining relationships. Additionally,
most people, regardless of age, do not seem to know how to manage
anger and resolve conflict skillfully with another person.

If the red oil-light starts blinking on your car's dashboard, you
don't pull out a sledgehammer and beat the light to pieces. You pull
off the side of the road and deal with the core issue by adding oil.

That's how anger should be handled in a conflict. Anger should
wisely be seen as the red light telling you that something is
wrong—unmet expectations, hurt, disappointment, and so on. We
need to train our children to pull off to the side and clearly ascer-
tain the problem and then address the core issue.

Parents' Conviction 5: Our home must be a safe haven to express all emotions and especially anger.

Dr. Ross Campbell, whom we quoted earlier in this chapter, has been our guest on the radio broadcast *FamilyLife Today*. Ross has years of experience in dealing with issues between parents and children and has said more than once during interviews that he believes strongly that one of the most mismanaged, misunderstood emotions in young people today is anger. He believes that most parents are squelching their children and not letting them express it appropriately.

Parents need to talk about anger as a couple and discuss what will be considered good and bad anger in their home. (In our family, inappropriate expressions of anger include physically harming another child, using words that threaten to bring emotional damage to another child, or showing disrespect to a parent.)

Hammer out your boundaries by grappling with these questions:

- Can anger be expressed in your home?
- Are children allowed to be angry? If so, what is your definition of appropriate anger? When has that expression of anger gone too far?
- Will children be allowed to withdraw from conflicts and never deal with their anger and the conflict?
- Will children be allowed to express anger by passively ignoring the commands of a parent or the request of a sibling?

As your children step too far and go beyond your boundaries, use these opportunities to teach them how they should have handled their anger in the situation. This repetitious training is tiresome at times, but as your teenager moves into adulthood, he will be able to express himself honestly in relationships.

SHAPING YOUR CHILD'S CONVICTIONS

If you haven't picked up on this yet, the Rainey family is far from perfect. We are amazed at how quickly we can find ourselves in a verbal rhubarb, coming unraveled by anger.

In fits of inappropriate anger our children have slammed doors and thrown pillows and the TV remote control. Our sons have ripped doors off of hinges. Starting as little boys and on through their mid-teens, our boys slugged and tripped and inflicted physical pain and torture on each other innumerable times. Even our "sweet" girls have exchanged a few blows.

Occasionally when they lose it, they just scream at each other. And of course the verbal abuse is oftentimes worse because the pain of the harmful words lasts much longer than the pain of a physical wound.

Even our children's parents have been angry. We've disciplined them in anger, yelled and screamed at an obstinate teenager, slammed a fist down on the table, peeled out of the driveway, and resigned at least 1,029 times as a parent.

Here are some solid convictions we are obviously still working on in the Rainey family.

Child's Conviction 1: I need to be able to understand what causes me to feel angry.

A significant task of adolescence is to learn how to express and deal with anger profitably. Preadolescents and teenagers want to be heard and understood by their parents, but often ideas clash or communication goes awry and anger roars to the surface.

Why? Because some kind of pain or hurt or disappointment or fear or insecurity is fueling that anger in either the teenager or the parent or both.

Our goal as parents is to seek to understand what our children are feeling and to help them identify the emotion and understand how to deal with it themselves. Practically, we want them to know how to "not let the sun go down on your anger." We want our children to be able to say, "I'm angry because of what you said that hurt my feelings," or "I think I yelled at you because I'm so worried that I won't make the squad or team."

169

Child's Conviction 2: I must learn to express anger appropriately and not let it become sin.

Most teenage boys are angry. They don't know what they are angry about; they are just frustrated with themselves, their siblings, and their parents. Occasionally even the parent does not fully know what's going on with his child. Let me illustrate.

When Samuel was fourteen he was a top-rated tennis player, but he struggled at times with getting angry with himself. We had warned him that we wouldn't hesitate to pull him from a match if he couldn't control his anger. He tested our limits a couple of times, but always seemed to get control before we stepped onto the court.

Except at one of his last tournaments. Samuel was well ahead of his opponent, but he was still missing shots he thought he should have made. He beat the air with his racquet, and I looked at him. He slammed a ball into the fence, and I stood up. Finally, he angrily whacked the chain-link fence with his racquet.

That did it. I walked out on the court and declared, "This match is over. My son forfeits for poor sportsmanship."

There was a look of shock on Samuel's face that I'll never forget. But it didn't matter. It was character training time.

The ride home was very quiet. Only near the end did I turn to him and challenge him to deal with his frustration in a more constructive way.

Samuel needed training in learning how to express his anger properly. (At that time, we did not yet know that Samuel was battling muscular dystrophy. Later, after we learned what was going on, I told Samuel I was sorry that we had just assumed that all of his actions were because he had an anger problem. You do the best you know how to do as a parent, but even that isn't enough sometimes.)

As you teach your child to stay out of the anger trap, you must embrace two critical principles:

First, *every person is made in the image of God, and you must not tear at or rip away the image of God in another person*—even if it's *just* mom, dad, sister, or brother. Anger is to be taken care of quickly and efficiently before it deteriorates into bitterness, revenge, or even violence.

Second, *a fruit of the Spirit is self-control.* Since self-control acts like a ten-foot-high hedge in surrounding anger, we need to encourage the growth of this godly fruit in our child. In Ephesians 5:18, Paul exhorts us to be filled with the Holy Spirit. Our children need to learn that, as we surrender the control of our lives to the Holy Spirit, He produces in us the self-control that is needed in dealing with anger.

Child's Conviction 3: I must know how to resolve conflict when I have been hurt or when I have hurt another person.

If anger is the spark, then conflict is the fire. As you go through the process of building and maintaining a relationship with your youngster, you must tell him that you will hurt and disappoint each other. There will be breaches of trust that demand that you know how to resolve conflict.

Let's pretend that you and your daughter are having a conflict. You told her she could not stay later than 4:00 P.M. to get a Coke with her friends. At 6:00 P.M. she came in and hurried past you. When you asked her why she was late, she said angrily, "I was with my friends. What's so bad about that? We weren't out doing drugs or something. You are just too strict."

Here's how you might work through this conflict using three key ideas: communication, forgiveness, and reconciliation.

Communication: Assuming your own feelings are under control, you might say something like this to your daughter: "No, the truth is that you are late, and your behavior, your attitude, is not acceptable, and your words have hurt me."

What if your daughter rejects this olive branch and looks back to you, steely eyed, and says, "Good. That's what I wanted to do."

You can't force someone to have a good attitude. At this point you will have to manage your feelings, step back, and say: "Well,

I just want you to know I love you, and when you're ready to ask for forgiveness and reconciliation in this relationship, I'm here. The door is always open; you may not like it being open; you may not want to come back in; you may choose to go another direction. But the door to this relationship from my end is wide open. You are welcome at any point to come back and talk with the right attitude."

Forgiveness: When your child calms down and is ready to move to the next step, model forgiveness in action. (Younger adolescents may need you to move toward them to resolve the relational break; they may be so self-absorbed that they can't properly manage their emotions.)

In this incident, if the daughter says, "I'm really sorry, Mom," you need to warmly, sincerely reply, "I forgive you, honey." Since the conflict is not fully resolved at this point, before the relationship can begin to heal, forgiveness must be liberally applied like a soothing ointment.

Reconciliation: If you've disobeyed or hurt another person, just because you've said "I'm sorry" doesn't mean you're totally off the hook. What will be necessary to make things right in the relationship?

In this conflict your daughter will need to show by her humble acceptance of consequences that she is truly sorry and eager to restore warmth to the relationship through actions and attitudes that rebuild trust. And next time, she will need to be home ahead of time.

TESTING YOUR CHILD'S CONVICTIONS

The person who pays the highest price in raising teenagers is a mom.

During part of his early teen years, Benjamin persecuted his siblings in the daytime and prosecuted Barbara at night. He was a fine young man, but he was in a struggle with his parents in general, and he had his mom worn-out and exasperated.

172

I had used every weapon in my arsenal to get his attention, but none worked. Finally, one night after he had fought another round with his mom, I said, "Benjamin, come on, we're going out for a drive."

We went to a restaurant and I sat across from him. Taking a saltshaker in one hand and a pepper shaker in the other and placing the two side-by-side on the table, I said, "This saltshaker is your mom, and the pepper is you." I moved the pepper shaker ahead of the saltshaker and said, "Here's what is happening. You escalate matters emotionally, and for your mom to be able to feel like she is in control, what does she do?"

Benjamin nodded his head as he slid the saltshaker ahead of the pepper shaker. "Right. She escalates the emotions even further," I said. "Then what do you do?" He didn't have to answer. I moved the pepper shaker ahead of the saltshaker. "And then what does your mom feel like she has to do?"

He was getting the point.

Looking him intensely in the eyes, I went on, "Son, you are *not* going to win at this, because in the end you are going to have to deal with me. You are dealing wrongly with your mom, and you need to continue the process of growing up and learn how to express anger appropriately without taking it out on your mom."

That conversation was a turning point—not an immediate, complete change—but a slow turn, like making a 180-degree course correction with an aircraft carrier.

Benjamin finally understood he would not win and that he was going to have to change or face his dad. He knew that he was mugging his mother. He needed to be called to godly, responsible behavior and then held accountable to express his anger appropriately.

Here are some other situations that illustrate how to test your child's convictions and maturity in dealing with anger.

When a child storms off in anger. Depends on the situation.

Should you make the child come back and deal with it? Do you allow some time for a cool down?

One time Rebecca told Barbara that she was frustrated that her younger sister Laura was not paying attention to something important that Rebecca was sharing. Rebecca felt disrespected.

She said, "I left the room and went upstairs. I was so mad! I cleaned my room. Can you believe I cleaned my room because I was mad?"

"That was a lot better than other things you could have done with your anger," Barbara said.

"Yes, it really is," Rebecca said.

I realized again that there are times when a child needs to be able to just let off steam. We both went and talked to Laura, and she apologized.

But whether you force resolution or just let matters cool depends on the situation. If you feel like your child is running away from a conflict into denial and is not making an effort to resolve the issue, then you need to bring him back.

When a child experiences conflict in his relationships. Look for opportunities to coach your child through conflict situations. Role-play how to handle anger and confess inappropriate anger.

Ashley had a best friend during her teen years. They became exclusive friends, bosom buddies. Then her friend started dating a young man, and Ashley was left standing alone by her locker at school. Disappointed and dejected, she was hurt and became angry.

Rather than sit back and wait for an emotional scene between the two, we talked to Ashley about what she was feeling and what she needed to do. A healthy but difficult conversation between the two girls occurred, and we applauded Ashley for handling her anger constructively.

FOR THE SINGLE PARENT

One thing that makes children really angry is hearing their parents cut each other down. Single parents who find themselves raising preteens and teens because of a divorce will be tempted to express plenty of inappropriate anger aimed at the ex-spouse.

May we encourage you to resist that temptation, regardless of who made what mistakes in the past? Remember that you are a family and must set the tone for your family by not allowing anger to gain a foothold in your life.

Commit from this day forward to:

- Speak well of your spouse, or say nothing at all—unless your former spouse is engaged in wrong behavior or encouraging it in your child.
- Process any anger you experience for your spouse with the Lord in prayer and with a godly friend, not your child.
- Pray and ask God to enable you to model how to handle your anger as daily situations arise that will challenge your emotional responses.

CONCLUSION

Mom, Dad, brace yourself. Dealing with this trap of unresolved anger in your home is one of the most challenging assignments you'll ever take on as an adult. It demands that you be above the fray and know what's going on in your child and yourself and not lose sight of your objective—what it is you are trying to build into the character of your child.

It will take most of us years and many angry incidents to train our children to stay out of the trap and learn how to resolve anger.

There's hope, though. We have found that a more peaceful period will arrive in your relationship with your child in his late teens. But in the meantime, you must steel yourself to endure considerable emotional intensity, hurt, disappointment, discouragement, and even feelings of failure as a parent.

UNFORGETTABLE LESSON:
The Case of the Two Cubes

After an incident when your preadolescent or young teen has been angry, do some teaching on anger with this short demonstration.

Place two ice cubes in separate cups. Explain that with anger we have two choices, (a) deal with anger, or (b) lock it away, stuff it.

At this point, put one cup and cube in the refrigerator freezer; leave the other cup out.

Ask your child to comment on what's going to happen to the two cubes?

The one left out will melt. It will not be ice for long—only a matter of hours at most. It will be long gone by bedtime. "Do not let the sun go down on your wrath."

The ice cube stuffed away in the freezer will stay frozen, hard, cold—for as long as it stays put away.

Thereafter, when anger visits your home, remind each other of the two ice cubes and the two choices we all have in dealing with our anger.

CONVICTION BUILDING PLAN

Building a family plan to deal with anger in both adults and children is a great idea. Use these questions to help complete the task.

Part One: Answer the following questions individually

1. What are some of the incidents of anger you recall in your family during your childhood?
2. Was the anger expressed properly or improperly? How did you feel about it as a child?
3. What's your track record on handling anger? What situations

176

cause problems for you? How are other people affected by the way you handle anger?

4. Do others have to point out that you are angry or are you aware of your anger as it occurs?

5. Would you pray with your spouse that God would heal areas of your heart that deal with anger and need His healing touch?

6. How does your child handle anger? What patterns are evident in his life? In what situations does he not handle anger well?

Part Two: Conclusions

1. Meet with your mate (a friend if you're single) to share your answers from the first section.

2. Pray together that you would become better models to your child on this issue.

3. Discuss what you can do during the next month to begin addressing this issue with your child.

"For God sees not as man sees,
for man looks at the outward appearance,
but the LORD *looks at the heart."*
—*1 Samuel 16:7*

12

Trap 7: Appearance

The State of the Heart, Not the Haircut, Is the Goal

Many parents don't think too much about thorny appearance issues until they find themselves picking out a party dress with their fifteen-year-old daughter or deciding if it's okay for a fourteen-year-old son to buy a pair of baggy pants that look large enough to house triplets.

I'll never forget the time Barbara and Ashley came home from their first prom shopping trip as mother and daughter. Ashley was so excited. She had found *the* dress.

Since we had already agreed that both mom and dad would approve the dress, the next thing I knew I was standing in this small shop jammed with prom dresses. Soon Ashley came out of the dressing room, beaming like a bride. One look, and I knew I was in trouble. By my standards as a dad, there were two problems with the dress: It was cut too low in the front and nonexistent in the back.

Ashley tried valiantly to allay my fears. "The straps can be shortened in the front, and that'll pull it up," she assured me. But no amount of strap-shortening was going to rescue a dress that was a good half-yard short of material!

As I did my best to break the news to her, her face took on a "I'm not a happy camper" look. She said she had tried on so many dresses and this was the only one she really liked.

I was flooded with self-doubt: Was I being too prudish? I wished the prom would never happen. It was probably going to cost me my relationship with my daughter. *She'll leave here hating me, I thought. She will never talk to me again. And she'll probably elope after the prom is over just to get away from me!*

As we left that dress shop with our arms empty, I put my arm around Ashley and sought to comfort her, telling her that I'd take her to every shop in town until we found the right dress. It did take a couple of trips and a little time, but we finally found a good, modest one.

Interestingly enough, years later I asked Ashley if she recalled that incident. She couldn't even remember it! She had no recollection of this heartbreaking, life-scarring moment when I said no to the perfect prom dress.

LOOKING ON THE OUTSIDE OR INSIDE

We know from Scripture that God views appearances much differently than the world does. He once told Samuel, "Do not look at his appearance or at the height of his stature . . . for God sees not as man sees, for man looks at the outward appearance, but the LORD looks at the heart" (1 Sam. 16:7).

Society, however, is almost totally sold out to image and appearance. This presents an incredible trap for young people seeking to establish who they are and what they should stand for. If we are to combat this pressure to conform to the superficial, we need to draw upon our reservoir of relational goodwill with our children to guide them toward grooming the heart instead of conforming to popular appearance.

How good is the heart-to-heart part of your relationship with your child? If it's in good shape, and the two of you can have honest, civil discussions about things like the length of a skirt, chances are very good that some acceptable combination of parental wisdom and youthful tastes can be achieved.

But if hearts are cold and the relationship has gone in the ditch, it probably isn't a haircut that's responsible for the real clash anyway. And if as a parent you try to drive your convictions into a youngster's life without a flourishing relationship, rebellion will certainly bloom. Instead of hair being merely green, it will be three different shades of green. Or instead of having two holes in earlobes, there will be twelve.

Of course, how we care for and present ourselves as followers of Christ does matter. It's just that externals are not nearly as important as how we are on the inside. We do want our teens to have an appearance that honors God: "Or do you not know that your body is a temple of the Holy Spirit who is in you, whom you have from God, and that you are not your own? For you have been bought with a price: therefore glorify God in your body" (1 Cor. 6:19–20).

Teenagers can do some strange things because they want to defy parents, identify with the culture, or look like friends. Some young people just want to do things that will solidify their emerging identity. But more often than not, there's peer pressure involved— i.e., someone else is providing acceptance and exerting influence.

Know the Lay of the Land

You need to know the range of styles in haircuts, jewelry, makeup, clothes, and shoes that exist in your child's world. It can be very difficult, but out of this diversity of options you and your child should be able to agree on a look that will not embarrass him but also meet your standards.

Although there certainly is a wide latitude in appearance, it seems to most parents that a child should at least keep himself groomed and avoid sloppiness. If your child's appearance-related issues are really more about taste than substance, we advise backing off on this issue.

Perhaps the most dangerous appearance trap for preadolescents and teenagers is body image—attempting to conform physically to some cultural ideal of attractiveness.

Young girls will punish themselves with diets—even starvation—to try to look as thin as popular models. The body-image scam is particularly cruel because the photos of most models are retouched and are often altered through computer re-imaging. Some of the models themselves are unhealthy or battling eating disorders. (If you have a child who is constantly saying "I'm too fat" when she's not, stay alert. For further information, see our section on Eating Disorders at the end of this chapter.)

As we write on this topic of appearance, we fear that some of what we share may sound like a refurbished version of 1940s Christian legalism. We think not. In our unbridled freedom and liberty, isn't it possible we have gone so far today that there is almost no standard or conscience on appearance issues? Have we lost our saltiness, the preservative nature of what Christianity is to be in a culture? We are not advocating that parents adopt some I'm-right-take-it-or-leave-it approach. We *are* advocating careful, probing thought by parents, a prayerful critique of what the culture does and not just blind acceptance nor extreme outright rejection.

DETERMINING YOUR CONVICTIONS

Coming home from work one day, I happened to walk down the hall behind my teenage son. Something was precariously wrong with his jeans. From my vantage point they were ready to slide off his behind at any time. I kept my mouth shut.

Later, I found out from a more learned mother that my son was being fashionable by "sagging" his britches. After I had thought it through, I went to my son and chatted with him about the sagging fad. We talked about the pressure to conform and discussed what he ought to do. Over the coming weeks, with additional conversations, his jeans crawled back up to a more decent elevation.

Little did I know that my son's jeans would prove to be only the first of many discussions about our teenager's appearance. This is not an easy process for even the most "in" parent. Like the other traps, it demands that you hammer out what you really believe is important.

Parents' Conviction 1: Our appearance will model the right blend of biblical values to our children.

Some couples underestimate how their outward appearance influences their children. A mother's appearance, for example, is a statement of her character and of her values as a woman.

I (Barbara) believe moms especially need to be careful. Daughters are watching what we wear, how we act, and how we present the body. Does our clothing adequately reflect the femininity we possess? Is our clothing style too masculine, too provocative, too trendy, too dowdy, too flashy? Are we cultivating the inner person so that our daughters and our sons will see what's really important in our life? Do our actions back up our words or contradict them?

Parents' Conviction 2: We will focus on the heart of our child, not just exterior appearance.

The words written by the apostle Peter are on target: "Let not your adornment be merely external—braiding the hair, and wearing gold jewelry, or putting on dresses; but let it be the hidden person of the heart, with the imperishable quality of a gentle and quiet spirit, which is precious in the sight of God" (1 Peter 3:3–4).

Both moms and dads need to do a self-check on some attitudes that can be subtly dangerous: Is your child extremely attractive? If so, are you deriving some unhealthy satisfaction and pride by catering to this natural beauty and indulging him or her in a closet bulging with the latest styles? Are you allowing your daughter to wear body-emphasizing outfits, thinking to yourself, *She's only twelve, and she looks so cute in that outfit.* These are all value-driven statements that come from the heart about what is ultimately important.

Be careful about the value system to which you would expose your child if, for example, you decide to enroll her in modeling classes because of her external good looks. Would this subtly create some wrong perspectives in your child about herself and others?

Or perhaps you have a child who is not particularly attractive or is overweight. How do you feel about your child's appearance? Are you disappointed? Are you wondering if you should put your child on a program of diet and exercise? If so, what attitudes are you conveying? Are you showing a lack of acceptance and love based on this child's outward appearance?

Since the next two convictions are so similar, we will present and comment on them as a unit:

Parents' Conviction 3: Our daughter must emphasize her femininity while being modest and tasteful.

Parents' Conviction 4: Our son must emphasize his masculinity while being modest and tasteful.

Verbally affirm masculine dress and appearance in your sons and feminine dress and appearance in your daughters.

One thing we fear is being lost in this culture is distinctive male and female dress. Encourage your son or your daughter to cultivate unique gender qualities by rejecting unisex clothing; affirm them verbally for their wisdom and attractiveness.

We compliment our sons when they dress up and wear a tie. And we rave about our daughters when they wear a dress.

Formal teaching opportunities can be used to build these values into a child's life. In a Bible study I had with one of our daughters, I pointed out how the book of Proverbs paints a picture of the harlot who used her sexual powers to trap, seduce, and ultimately destroy a young man. I shared honestly with my daughter how every woman has been given the potential of a unique, God-given power over men—a mystical intrigue and a sexual power. For a young lady, that sexual power needs to be saved and appropriately hidden until she is married.

Young men and young women are hungry for affirming words as their sexual identities emerge. Use these struggles around clothing and appearance to challenge them to become God's man and God's woman.

SHAPING YOUR CHILD'S CONVICTIONS

The ultimate goal related to appearance is to help your preadolescent or early teen understand that how he presents himself is a spiritual matter. The way he grooms and dresses his body says much about his values and whether he is seeking to bring attention to himself or to Jesus Christ.

In this section we will list several possible convictions for a child, as well as look at some specific appearance-related issues, including makeup, manners, ear and body piercing, and what if you and your child don't agree?

The process of shaping convictions needs to begin early. Talk with your preteen child in advance about the issues he'll face as he moves into the teenage years. Help him begin to draw some boundaries around the issues that matter most to you as a parent. Here's a checklist of what we talked about with our sons and daughters.

Our sons:
- Modesty
- Masculinity
- Saggy, sloppy, or grunge clothing
- T-shirts with inappropriate messages
- Clothing with holes in it, especially in inappropriate places

Our daughters:
- Modesty
- Femininity
- Swimsuits
- Ear piercing

- Halter tops and other skimpy clothing
- Length of dresses, skirts, and shorts

In each of these areas, we pressed our children to tell us what their convictions were. If necessary, we would gently attempt to steer them in a direction we wanted them to go. This was never accomplished in a single conversation, but over months and years of hammering away on some of these topics.

Dads can help their daughters by teaching them how a young man thinks when he sees a young lady who is dressed immodestly. One practical way of doing this is taking your daughter on a date and going shopping with her. It will help you appreciate the challenge that a young lady faces when she wants to dress modestly. As you walk around you can talk frankly about why it's important for a girl to dress modestly and cultivate the inner person of the heart. Talk about why some young women want the attention that dressing immodestly brings. Discuss what type of young man a young lady is likely to attract when she inappropriately flaunts her sexual beauty.

A mom could take her son on a similar date. She might point out why girls appreciate boys who know how to dress appropriately and attractively. Boys often only want to wear T-shirts—and some carry repulsive or suggestive messages. Is this an image he wants to present? He doesn't need to use his chest as a billboard for something that violates good values and standards. We've even drawn the line at vulgar T-shirts by sending neighborhood boys home who have come over to see our sons.

Child's Conviction 1: My appearance and dress need to emphasize my heart's loyalty to Christ, not my body.

An obvious issue is whether overall appearance should be sloppy or neat. Explain to your child that being sloppy projects an image that he may not want. For example, it may communicate to a teacher that he doesn't care about learning.

At the same time, remember that dressing sloppy is not uncommon for teens, especially boys. If you determine it is just a passing stage, try to help him see what his image communicates, what is unacceptable attire for school, what is appropriate attire for church, and then let the rest go. We've learned to flex a lot. You have to know where and when to draw the line.

If his affection for the grunge look is a reflection of his feelings about life, ask God for ways to encourage him, to help him succeed, and to communicate love and acceptance.

Child's Conviction 2: When in doubt, modesty is the best policy.

We believe it's time for a modesty revolution. A return to what the apostle Paul instructed Timothy: "I want women to adorn themselves with proper clothing, modestly and discreetly, not with braided hair and gold or pearls or costly garments; but rather by means of good works, as befits women making a claim to godliness" (1 Tim. 2:9–10).

Although boys need to learn how to present themselves appropriately, modesty in clothing is a particularly critical issue for girls. Some girls naturally seem to have more modest tastes, while others gravitate toward more immodest types of clothing. Especially when young, they don't understand consciously how accentuating certain parts of the body affects boys and men. Boys do pay more attention to a more enticing appearance. That's enjoyable for girls, so they may lean even more toward this kind of dress to attract even more attention. They don't fully realize the values they are portraying and what type of boys they're wooing.

The earlier our young women begin learning modesty, the better. It is very hard for teenage girls to cover up more when they've not been trained in modesty from an early age, especially when they are living in a culture that encourages females to flaunt their bodies.

Take bathing suits, for example. If you start allowing your daughter to wear a little two-piece bikini when she's four, you may have a battle on your hands when her figure blossoms and you want to switch her to a one-piece suit at fourteen.

And it isn't good enough anymore to breathe a sigh of relief if your daughter does go shopping for a one-piece bathing suit. Most are very provocative. With girls especially, finding a consistently modest wardrobe is an unending task. Wearing a T-shirt over a bathing suit may not be such a bad idea.

Depending on the child, you have to be ready for at least two scenarios related to fashionable clothes. First, the girl with the great figure will be able to wear everything in the store and look good in almost everything. The store clerks will be applauding, saying how great she looks. She may look fabulous, but a particular garment may not meet your standards for modesty. It's best to have your hardest conversations about these issues *before* she starts trying on clothes.

Perhaps, however, your daughter does not have the "perfect" body type. She is probably more normal or average than the model types, but that is no consolation to her when you go shopping. Instead of being able to wear everything in every store, she may have difficulty finding anything that fits attractively.

She may want to cover up or camouflage her "flaws." She may go for items like short shorts or a tank top that accentuate her good qualities. Or she may go for a distinctly unfeminine baggy or grunge look.

As a mom you need to help each daughter appreciate her blossoming femininity—to seek a modest balanced approach by not flaunting her body with skimpy, skin-tight outfits or by burying her body in layers of big, baggy, shapeless items.

Following are some thoughts on other appearance-related topics.

Makeup

This is one area where the cultural trend has moved back to a more acceptable position. Heavy makeup for teenagers is passé— no more painted lady look of the 1950s and 1960s. We allow our girls, starting at about age thirteen or so, to wear a little bit of blush and mascara and just a touch of light lipstick.

Just to illustrate how hard parents can be to please, I (Barbara) have sometimes wished our older teenage girls would wear a little *more* makeup. The style now is so plain and almost colorless that

I have wanted to say, "Why don't you go put on a little blush or mascara? You look pale and washed out." But I've kept my mouth shut, deciding I'd rather they be plain and natural than excessively painted.

Manners

Boys need to learn how to treat girls with dignity and respect, as women who are created in the image of God. And then girls need to learn how to let boys treat them that way.

Barbara has devoted some of our family nights to this. Once we had a "manners week," because our children needed a little training. We taught them some proper things about table manners: how girls should be seated by the boys, how boys should open the doors for the girls, and so on.

The children thought it was corny at times, but at least they got some practice. We had some rules on a poster hanging on the wall, and it ended up being a fun week of learning for all of us. Knowing manners builds confidence in a person, regardless of the age.

On one occasion, as our older children were just approaching their teenage years, we celebrated some manners training by going out to eat at a nice restaurant. In this fast-food culture, it felt quite civilized to observe our children seated around an elegant table, knowing which fork, spoon, and knife was to be used.

Ear and Body Piercing—or the Next Fad?

One of the rites of passage in our family was for our girls to have the privilege of getting their ears pierced when they were in the sixth grade. At that point they would only wear silver balls in their ears. They waited until they were thirteen and had earned the right to wear the fancier hoops, hearts, and pearls. We always made that a big deal at our home.

Our girls have asked more than once, "Can we get our ears double-pierced or triple-pierced?

I (Barbara) have responded, "No, at age eighteen, or when you are on your own at twenty-one, you can do whatever you want.

You can punch holes all over the place. But as long as you are living at home, no."

How about pierced ears for boys? This has never been an issue with us, but had we been asked, we probably would have said the same thing: "No, if you want to get them pierced, you can do that when you get in college. But not as long as you are at home."

If either had asked why, we would have said, "This is something that we have agreed upon as parents. And we've decided that you'll have to wait a little while longer and be on your own before you are allowed to deface your body."

What about the next fad? If we updated this book every month, we probably could not keep up with some new way to "look cool." As a parent you must prayerfully decide which fads are truly sinful or just choices on appearance your child can make on his own. Where are you going to draw the line and where you are willing to negotiate? The answers to those questions will vary for each family. But a good appearance bottom line: The "look" must be modest and God-honoring.

What If You and Your Child Disagree?

Fortunately, none of our preadolescents or teenagers have had an all-out rebellion against our standards on appearance. But we have had a lot of disagreements. Loads of tears. Tons of emotions. And hours of discussion, especially with the girls, while buying clothes.

Listen carefully to your child. Love him enough to say no. Hold your ground, because most teens don't really know what's best for themselves. It's good to remember that these turbulent disagreements will pass and that your child most likely won't remember that they even occurred.

Every parent needs to consider asking four questions in a standoff with his child:

1. Have I prayed about this issue and asked God for wisdom in how to handle it?

189

2. Are we in agreement as a couple? God will often use your spouse to balance you in an area where you might be extreme.
3. Is the issue a clear matter of right and wrong or is it a preference? If the issue is something on which your child is clearly wrong, then you know what you need to do. But if it's in the gray area, go slow before drawing your sword.
4. Is the issue really worth its cost? We've erred at times because we made marginal issues too large.

It hasn't happened frequently, but on occasion we have crossed swords with one of our daughters. This happened with one of our teenage daughters when she outgrew a dress that had fit her fine at the beginning of adolescence. Suddenly what had been a cute black dress was now pretty short (she had grown three or four inches) and very tight (her figure had filled out nicely).

It was a Sunday morning right before church, but that didn't matter. We told her she couldn't wear that dress any longer. It was clearly no longer modest.

This was not a popular decision. We held our ground, even though she launched a pretty good verbal counterattack and a barrage of tears. (Being a parent can be so ugly at times.)

She never knew it, but as I stood there in the midst of all those female tears I was questioning my convictions. I was waffling inside, but playing poker on the outside. In the end we stood our ground and she wore another dress.

If you see that an important boundary is about to be crossed, don't second-guess yourself. Don't be afraid. Go ahead and stand strong. But be prepared to withstand the battle that follows.

TESTING YOUR CHILD'S CONVICTIONS

Here are some ways to test your preadolescent or teenager on his journey through the appearance traps.

Ask questions. Ask your child what he thinks about his appearance. Is he satisfied with his clothes, haircut, etc.? Why or why not?

Encourage your child to observe others. Without becoming critical, help your child or teen observe what others wear and the impression that clothing styles give. A good place to do this would be while you're at a mall or a sporting event where there's a large crowd of people. Make an observation or two and involve your child in the thinking process by asking him questions.

Organize a panel discussion. If you are involved in your child's Sunday school class or youth group, suggest a panel discussion on the subject of dress. You will need a strong person to moderate the questions and discussion to keep it focused. Hand select the panelists who are three or four years older than the class— those who have standards that will represent what you are trying to teach your children. Have the guys talk about what they feel when girls wear clothing that calls attention to their bodies. Ask them to tell the girls how they should dress to help them avoid temptation.

Likewise, have the girls tell the guys what they find attractive in the way a guy dresses. Our teens need to hear the truth on this subject, and usually hearing it from someone other than mom and dad is very effective.

Always be ready to applaud. On the issue of appearance, the big deal is to applaud and compliment like crazy when your child makes good choices, especially on his own.

FOR THE SINGLE PARENT

One of the downsides of being a single parent, as you know, is that you don't have a backup in the midst of a true fire fight with a teenager over some appearance issue. Find a same-sex, mature Christian friend from church whom you respect and who would be willing to help you in the middle of a heated disagreement with your teen.

Ideally, this friend would have already raised his or her teens past the stage that you find yourself in. Call and bounce your problem off your friend and get a fresh perspective. And if you aren't making headway with your teen in terms of persuading him, ask the friend to come to your home and see if he can help bring some understanding to the situation.

The bottom line: At times you will need help in standing your ground. A standard-bearing soul mate can help you stand firm when your child is tempting you to drop your convictions.

CONCLUSION

Appearance issues can be incredibly serious, but they also can provide some humor and opportunities to expand our horizons.

I remember when our boys wanted to wear necklaces. For me this was a bit hard to take. Where I come from, real men don't wear necklaces.

How far is this going to go? I thought. But then wisdom triumphed over emotions: *You'd better keep your mouth shut*, I decided.

As it turned out, their neck items were pretty masculine looking—a nice leather necklace with a pewter ichthys (a fish and the symbol for Christianity). My fears were unfounded. It's kind of grown on me. In fact I wouldn't have minded owning one myself!

A WORD ABOUT EATING DISORDERS[1]

Two of the more disturbing and potentially dangerous behaviors found among teenagers is the gorging-purging pattern of bulimia or the starvation pattern of anorexia nervosa.

No doubt the incredible pressure to be thin, felt in particular by young girls, is partly the culprit for the rise of eating disorders.

Both of these problems are found predominantly among girls. A recent study found that one million teenagers are affected by some symptoms of bulimia or anorexia. Anorexia is estimated to affect as many as one out of every one hundred females aged twelve to eighteen.

Anorexia and bulimia often are triggered by disturbing life situations: puberty, ridicule over weight, first sexual contact, death of a loved one, separation from family due to college or some other reason, or other trauma.

The two disorders may intermingle in an individual. Bulimia symptoms are found in 40 to 50 percent of individuals suffering with anorexia.

Anorexia

Anorexia is by far the more dangerous of the two disorders. About 18 percent of anorexics die from self-inflicted starvation.

Anorexia most commonly begins in adolescence, but it can show up in a child as young as eight years old. Often the problem is kicked off by an innocent comment: "You're looking a little chubby, dear."

Although anorexia often involves a pattern of excessive dieting over a long period of time, it may be a single, limited episode—a child may lose a significant amount of weight within a few months but then recover, begin eating more normally, and not repeat the self-destructive behavior.

Symptoms of anorexia include:

- Extreme weight loss
- Unusually high desire to please parents or others
- Dry, pale skin; brittle hair
- Cessation of menstruation in females
- Anemia
- Refusal to maintain a weight higher than the *minimal* normal weight for a given age and height.
- Intense fear of gaining weight or becoming fat, even though underweight
- Denial and defensiveness about the problem

Bulimia

Bulimia occurs about twice as often as anorexia. This eating disorder often begins in conjunction with a diet and starts in adolescence or the early twenties. A binge incident normally lasts less than two hours during which as many as 3,400 calories of soft, sweet foods are easily consumed. (Ice cream is often a favorite.) To lose the weight, a bulimic then turns to some method of purging.

Much health damage can result from a persistent binge-purge cycle because of the upsetting of the body's balance of nutrients. Problems can include fatigue, seizures, muscle cramps, and decreased bone density. Repeated vomiting can harm the esophagus and stomach, make the gums recede, and erode tooth enamel.

Symptoms of bulimia include:

- Preoccupation with body shape and weight
- Recurrent episodes of binge eating (rapid consumption of a large amount of food in a short period of time)
- Regularly engaging in either self-induced vomiting, use of laxatives or diuretics, strict dieting or excessive fasting, or vigorous exercise in order to prevent weight gain.
- Persistent over-concern with body size and weight
- Low self-esteem
- Depression (may not be a symptom of bulimia, but often occurs with it)

What should you do if you suspect either anorexic or bulimic tendencies in your child?

Of the two disorders, anorexia is more difficult to confront and treat because the child will vigorously deny the problem. *If you feel your child is obsessed with dieting and is looking overly thin, talk to your pediatrician immediately.*

In the more *extreme* cases, where the child is suffering from starvation, hospitalization and intravenous feeding may be required until the immediate crisis passes. Extensive evaluation and counseling may be required, including the possibility of treatment at a residential care facility.

Above all, do not delay in obtaining help. Early, effective treatment is often avoided because parents deny the problem or attempt to "fix" it themselves. A team approach that includes a nutritionist, pediatrician, and psychologist is particularly beneficial. Find professional helpers who have extensive experience in dealing with eating disorders.[2]

CONVICTION BUILDING PLAN

Answer the following questions to determine your own convictions about appearance and to begin shaping the convictions of your child.

Part One. Answer the following questions individually

1. Did you have any conflicts with your parents about appearance when you were a teenager?
2. What type of example do you set for your child on this issue?
   - Are you too preoccupied with your own appearance?
   - Are there any issues of sloppiness or immodesty in your own appearance that need correction?
3. Does your child follow your example in any way? Are you comfortable with that?
4. Are you comfortable that your child, as he grows, will probably have different tastes from you in clothing and in other issues of appearance?
5. As you look at your child, what issues come to mind when you think of the trap of appearance?
6. What type of pressure is your child receiving on this issue from peers, from the media?
7. How will you apply the scriptural principle of looking beyond outward appearances to the heart in dealing with your child on these issues?
8. What are the nonnegotiable boundaries that you will estab-

lish for your children? On what issues of dress or appearance will you flex and on which will you draw a line in the sand?

- Neckwear
- Multicolored fingernail polish
- Baggy pants
- Freaky hair styles—including neon-colored or multicolored hair
- Body piercing—ears, nose, belly button
- Immodest clothing
- Feminine clothing for boys
- Masculine clothing for girls
- Swimsuits (There are several types—where will you draw the line?)
- Grunge dressing
- Tattoos
- Toe rings
- Other

Part Two. Conclusions

1. Meet with your mate and share your answers from the first section. If you are single, do this with a trusted friend.
2. What appearance issues are you most concerned about with your child?
3. Write down three things you will do over the next month to begin addressing this issue with your child.

*"Put away from you a deceitful mouth,
And put devious lips far from you."*
—Proverbs 4:24

13

Trap 8: Deceit

There's No Substitute for Integrity

One of the trapper's tricks is to place his trap not far from where the animal lives, on the paths where the animal regularly moves in finding food and water. In other words, he places the trap fairly close to the animal's home.

We fool ourselves if we think the traps set for our children are only set along the paths teenagers take in our increasingly dangerous culture. In reality, the worst traps of all may be those set close to home—very close—in their own hearts and minds.

The Bible dashes any foolish notions about our inherent integrity. The prophet Jeremiah paints an ugly picture of a man's heart: "The heart is more deceitful than all else / And is desperately sick; / Who can understand it?" (Jer. 17:9).

That truth applies to our preteens and teens too. A tendency toward lying and other types of deception—cheating in school, breaking promises, fudging on the truth—usually resurfaces during adolescence. The child who is developing more complex thinking abilities now has a better set of tools to use in being deceitful. Also, teenagers have more freedom and independence than they enjoyed before, which means more opportunity to make choices they might want to hide. Peers also have more direct, unobstructed influence and say things like, "Nobody will ever know" or "You don't have to tell your parents."

As we train our children, sometimes we forget what we are up against: A child's heart is deceitful.

It's intriguing that God identified seven things He really hates (Prov. 6:16–19) and that two of the seven concern outright deceit—"a lying tongue" and "a false witness who utters lies." If God took the time to make this list, we parents had better do a good job of training and disciplining our children away from His hated seven.

Deceit seems to fall into two major types. The first being *lying*. The child is tempted to misrepresent the truth, but gets caught in the lie. This is serious, but relatively easy to deal with. The guilt is obvious; the guilty party can do little but admit wrong and seek mercy.

The second type of deceit is a subtle pattern of *habitual craftiness*. This murky, constant shading of the truth can create exhaustion plus a sense of hopelessness in the parent. A parent may feel that the teaching and training of his child is ineffective and that he is raising a cheating riverboat gambler.

But wherever the deception falls on the deceit scale really doesn't matter. It's all deceit. And God will have none of it: "He who practices deceit shall not dwell within my house; / He who speaks falsehood shall not maintain his position before me" (Ps. 101:7). As we shape our children's convictions about deceit we need to be careful to give them God's perspective of lies, false appearances, and misrepresentations of the truth.

The Case of the Missing Money

Deceit has crept inside the walls of the Rainey home and led to great discouragement for us as parents. But we've had major spiritual and character breakthroughs primarily because we prayed. One such incident is particularly memorable.

I keep my money in a money clip. One day on my way home from work I stopped at an ATM for some cash. I knew exactly the amount of money in my possession—twelve five-dollar bills.

I came home and put the clip on my desk where one of our children (who was about fourteen at the time) was studying. For some reason (there are these divinely inspired moments in parenting) before I went to bed that night, I decided I would check my money clip. (I had not set it next to this child as a temptation. I just left it where I always did.)

I found eleven five-dollar bills. One of them had mysteriously evaporated.

I went to the child who had been studying at my desk and who was now in bed and said, "You know, I had my money clip on the desk. The Lord just prompted me to go down and look at my money clip to see if all the money was there. I had twelve five-dollar bills in there, and now I only have eleven. Did you take that money?"

"Oh no, Dad. I would *never* do that."

I paused. Looking the child deeply in the eyes, I said, "Well, if I am wrong and somebody else did it, then I want to pray to God that He enables me to catch that particular child. But you are the only one I know who has been near that money clip since I left it there. You know what I am going to do? I am going to pray that if you took that money that the Lord would go to work on you. And if you didn't take it, then you'll be okay."

I got down on my knees next to the child's bed and put my hands on the child. I said, "Lord, you know all things, and we do not pull anything over on you. If I am wrong on this, Lord, I pray that you will help me find out and apologize to this child later. But if this child stole that five-dollar bill, Father, I pray that you would make this child miserable."

Two nights later the child walked in to our bedroom, and it was grim. With a shame-filled, guilt-ridden face, the child admitted, "I took that money. And furthermore, I have been stealing money out of your pants pocket for some time."

As a consequence, we got some serious hard labor out of this child—painting the ceiling of a large screened-in porch that required many hours.

199

We also had some long, hard conversations. We look back now and see that event as a turning point in the spiritual development of that child.

DETERMINING YOUR CONVICTIONS

A life of integrity is a life you can trust.

The psalmist speaks of the power of purity and of a life of integrity: "I will give heed to the blameless way. / When wilt Thou come to me? / I will walk within my house in the integrity of my heart. / I will set no worthless thing before my eyes; / I hate the work of those who fall away; / It shall not fasten its grip on me. / A perverse heart shall depart from me; / I will know no evil . . . He who walks in a blameless way is the one who will minister to me" (Ps. 101:2–4, 6).

The message of Scripture is simply this: How we live in private does matter because God sees all. A life of integrity is the powerful basis from which to build character into another person's life.

There are several core convictions you will need to hold if you desire to keep your child from building a pattern of deceit in his life.

Parents' Conviction 1: It is the nature of every person's heart to be deceitful.

The bad news is that all of us have deceitful hearts. The good news is that God is at work, hammering us into shape—to resemble Jesus, "who gave Himself for us, that He might redeem us from every lawless deed and purify for Himself a people for His own possession, zealous for good deeds" (Titus 2:14).

Look at your life to see if there is any persistent deceit. If so, you will not make much headway in challenging deceit in your child. Watch for the subtle deceptions we adults are so prone to—giving phony reasons for not taking phone calls, failing to keep promises to our children, offering excuses to get out of commitments and to

200

change plans, and so on. You need to face up to these areas where you're failing and ask God to work in your heart so that you model a life of integrity for your child.

Deceit can be one of the more difficult sins to attack in our hearts because we can be deceived by our own deceit! Completing the Conviction Building Plan at the end of this chapter will help give you and your spouse the opportunity to assist each other in identifying deceitful patterns in your lives.

Parents' Conviction 2: We must model integrity to our child.

I have enjoyed hunting with all our children. In the process we've hunted with other fathers who have ignored and broken game laws while their children were watching. I've often wondered what must be going on in those young people's lives as they watch their father habitually break the law. Are they concluding that cheating must be okay if Dad does it?

Remember, your life is like a door. You can open it to deceit, lies, and misrepresentations of the truth. Or you can open it to truth, the pathway through which integrity gains entrance into your family and your child's life.

SHAPING YOUR CHILD'S CONVICTIONS

In their heart of hearts, preadolescents and teenagers want to be trusted, and they long for more responsibility and freedom. But trust must be earned.

We have made a statement repeatedly to our children: "You're about to move into a period of your life where you want more responsibility and freedom. As your parents we want to give that to you, but we will not give you more than you are mature enough to handle.

"If you want more responsibility, you must be trustworthy. Likewise, if you want more freedom, you must be responsible. To be trustworthy means you need to do what's right when no one is looking."

Child's Conviction 1: I know deceit is dangerous and will lead me down an evil path.

Shaping your child's convictions about deceit begins as you *teach him to fear God.* Proverbs 14:27 encourages us, "The fear of the LORD is a fountain of life, / That one may avoid the snares of death." And Proverbs 16:6, "And by the fear of the LORD one keeps away from evil."

Teach your child to fear God by teaching him who He really is. He is truth. Love. Holy. Sovereign. Omnipotent. Omnipresent. And more. As our children see us practicing the presence of God in our lives, they too will grow in the understanding that God sees all and that He is to be feared.

In addition, *teach your child about his own tendency to deceive and to lie.* We are all just one step away from being ensnared by this trap.

You can do this by sharing situations from your life where you stepped into a deceitful snare. Talk about the consequences of those choices.

One of our teens wasn't being 100 percent truthful, and I took him out and talked about a lie that I had told as an adult early in my ministry. I talked about how I rationalized and how I justified my deception. And I talked about its impact on my life. I warned him that I saw a pattern in his life that could, if not unchecked, cost him for a lifetime. I appealed to this particular teenager to firm up his convictions and become a person of integrity.

Child's Conviction 2: I need to speak the truth because it is the right thing to do.

Teach your child the truth in two ways:

First, *teach him about Jesus Christ.* Jesus said, "I am the truth." You expose your child to the truth as you teach about Jesus Christ's life, His mission, and His teachings. He is the incarnation of the truth. And as your child understands what a straight line looks like, he'll be able to spot the deceitful line.

Second, *teach him the Scripture.* Diligently teach the truth of God's Word through Scripture-memory programs, family Bible study, and Bible-verse reminders of what it looks like to obey God when life and truth collide.

Help your child develop his convictions by contrasting the results of being deceitful with the result of telling the truth. There's no better book in the Bible for doing this than Proverbs. For example:

My son, give attention to my words;
Incline your ear to my sayings.
Do not let them depart from your sight;
Keep them in the midst of your heart.
For they are life to those who find them,
And health to all their whole body.
Watch over your heart with all diligence,
For from it flow the springs of life.
Put away from you a deceitful mouth,
And put devious lips far from you.
Let your eyes look directly ahead,
And let your gaze be fixed straight in front of you.
Watch the path of your feet,
And all your ways will be established.
Do not turn to the right nor to the left;
Turn your foot from evil." (4:20–27)

When we train our children to know and ponder the truth of God's Word, that Scripture will help them guard their hearts from deceit, evil, and destruction.

Child's Conviction 3: I will tell the truth regardless of what consequences I may face.

Why do people lie and deceive? In many cases, they may be attempting to avoid responsibility for their mistakes or misjudgments. Or they may be attempting to manipulate others to do what they want them to. Or they may be desperately trying to stay in control of their lives.

- The man who misrepresents his income when he fills out his tax forms is selfishly trying to keep his money.
- The woman who lies to her friends about her alcohol problem is trying to maintain a favorable impression.
- The child who steals money and then lies about it to his parents is trying to avoid punishment.
- The child who cheats on a test is trying to avoid the consequences of not studying properly.

One reason lying is an affront to God is that it displays a lack of trust in Him. Your child must be taught that it's better to tell the truth and trust in God's control of his life.

As we all know too well, it's often not easy to live lives unmarred by deceit. Our children feel the same way. So when they do make the right choices—like admitting a mistake or telling the truth when it might get them in trouble—make sure you let them know what a great thing they have done.

Parents often reward their children for good things that are not eternal things—like good grades on a report card. But how about rewards for progress in living honestly?

Dealing with Sneaky Deceit

Often, a child will take advantage of you in any way he can to get to do what he wants. Just when you think you've told him what is expected of him, he comes back with statements like:

"I didn't understand what you were saying. I thought you meant . . ."

"I forgot."

"I didn't hear you."

"You didn't say that."

The solid ground you thought you were standing on starts to

shift, and as a parent you wind up thinking, *Was I unclear? What did I tell them, anyway?*

The first step in solving this problem is to *write things down.* With six children, I (Barbara) really can't remember everything I say. When you're giving directions to so many, you do forget. I don't write down everything, but I have started a section in my notebook where I record penalties, disciplines, and rules on the issues that are very important.

All chores, for example, are written out and posted in the kitchen. I spell out what a clean kitchen looks like. This prevents our children from taking advantage of any fuzziness in our directions.

After establishing that foundation, *challenge your teens when you think they are not being truthful:* "Now, I *know* you heard me" or "I think you selectively chose not to hear me. And I want you to know that's a lie; that's not the truth." Discipline may be appropriate. You may also want to warn them that persisting in this behavior will lead to bad consequences in the future: "When you are an adult, you can pretend not to hear, but it will get you fired from a job."

Disciplining Deceit

So what happens if you catch your child red-handed in a lie?

Let's say your daughter spent the night with a friend and told you the next day that they watched a clean family movie. Then you learn that the movie was anything but clean and that she knew it all along.

After uncovering the lie, one of your assets as a parent is to delay punishment—not too long, but long enough to let the child's imagination run a bit wild. Take a few hours or even wait overnight. Set your game plan. Stick your heads together and pray over your options.

When you meet with your child, first *find out why he felt the need to lie to you.* Is there something amiss in your relationship? Does he feel overly restricted?

Don't let your child rationalize the deceit. He may try to take the offense back into that gray area.

Then, *choose a consequence that involves restricting something your child loves to do.* On one occasion, we disciplined one of our boys by telling him he couldn't be part of his baseball team for a game; he had to sit on the sidelines and watch, and he was their top pitcher. That was a memorable punishment for him. For our girls, grounding them from the phone, their favorite source of social interaction, is a painful penalty. Recently we've added e-mail to the list of privileges to remove as a discipline.

Your discipline needs to match the level of deceit. If it really has been a crafty deceit, perhaps a con job perpetrated over a long period of time, the discipline needs to be more severe. It needs to imprint the lesson on your teen's character.

Finally, let your child know that *he will need to earn back your trust.* When you deceive another person, it takes time for that relationship to be healed and for trust to be reestablished.

TESTING YOUR CHILD'S CONVICTIONS

Here are some ways to test how well your child is handling the deceit trap:

Watch for cheating at school. This may not be the easiest type of deceit to detect. Observe your child's study habits, homework, grades, and general demeanor related to school. Does it appear he is depending too heavily on others to get answers or help with homework? Are you helping more than you should? Stay in close touch with all of your child's teachers. Make sure grades on the report card seem to match up with effort related to schoolwork. Tell your child's teacher that you want to know if your child *ever* attempts to cheat.

If your child is caught cheating, gather all the facts. A trip to the school to talk with the teacher is best. Was it a one-time occurrence or are there suspicions of a pattern? Talk with your child. Sometimes teachers make mistakes or treat students unfairly. If cheating is confirmed, talk with your child. If the child admits to cheating and has not lied further about the incident, make sure you affirm him for telling the truth. However, consequences are definitely in order—both at school and at home. You must treat this as a very serious matter.

Have the child apologize to you, to the teacher, and to any child whose work he may have copied. Have him say, "I cheated. I was wrong. Will you forgive me?"

In most cases the teacher will give your child a zero or an *F* for cheating. Discuss with your child the consequences. He will need to study even harder to bring his grade up to offset the poor mark.

Finally, decide on an appropriate discipline for the offense. Grounding and/or hard labor around the house are often good choices.

The cheating issue has hit our family. A teacher called us, and we went through the shame. We met with the teacher. Our child was embarrassed.

As we talked to the child, we let him know that we were disappointed that he felt he had to cheat. We let him feel our shame. (Later the child told us that that had hurt worse than the penalty.) Then we asked our child to go to the teacher and ask his forgiveness. This child has never forgotten that lesson.

Stay alert. Keep your eyes and ears wide open. What are you observing about your child's behavior and attitudes? What is being said to you? Are you buying it? Watch for subtleties such as repeatedly "forgetting" to bring home a grade report from school.

Work with the child who is struggling with tardiness. A firstborn child generally is very prompt, but a sibling who follows may use tardiness as a way to demonstrate his emerging independence.

If a child consistently is late, one of the best ways to approach this (not in the heat of the moment) is to explain the natural consequences of what will happen if this continues. We make the tardy one clean the kitchen, a big job at our house.

Play the Decide in Advance game. Practically help your child decide in advance what he would do with a few of the many deceit-filled traps he will face as he grows up:

- You know you are not to ride your bike on the highway, but you're with a group of friends who turn onto the highway. When you stop, they all come back and say, "C'mon. Your parents will never find out." There are eight of them, and you are about to be left behind. What would you do?
- You make a bad grade at the end of the first nine weeks and decide to hide the report card, hoping you can pull your grade up by semester. A week later your mom asks why you haven't brought home a report card. How do you answer?
- An envelope containing all of your sister's savings was left out on her dresser. There's over eighty dollars in small bills, and you decide she'll probably never miss a ten-dollar bill. You take one. But that night there is a family meeting and your dad asks, "Did anyone happen to see an extra ten dollars that's missing from sister's savings?" What would you say?
- Your mom asks you to clean the kitchen while she's running your brother to a soccer match. You don't do it. She comes back and asks you why you didn't clean the kitchen. You say "I forgot." Is that the truth? What should you have said and done?

Do not surrender access to your child's room. Teenagers love to assert control over their own space, and to a fairly significant extent, a child's room should be his enclave of individuality and private peace. But it's still your house, and you are still the parent. Let your child know through your actions that you feel perfectly free to drop into the room frequently—both when your child is home (knock, of course) or away.

Sometime when the child is away, take inventory of the room— yes, do some discreet snooping. There's a war going on for the mind and heart of your child. Don't let the enemy slip some live hand grenades into your child's life—bad music, pornography, alcohol, drugs. And consider carefully whether to let a private phone line or phone extension be placed in that room, especially with a preadolescent or younger teen. Do you want him to have unlimited and unsupervised access to his peers?

Recruit a "spy" network. From now until your child leaves home and moves on to adulthood, you will slowly relinquish control, and the child will increasingly not be at home. In the interest of keeping tabs on how your child is handling new challenges, you need a network of parents, teachers, youth workers, coaches, employers, and other observers who will feel comfortable in sharing information with you occasionally. If they see your child going into a movie that they know you do not approve of, they should feel free to call and tell you.

My mom had these spies all over town when I was growing up. The effect was that I felt she was omnipresent; I always felt accountable for my actions.

This intelligence gathering should be extremely discreet and certainly not overdone. Your child deserves the opportunity to build trust. But other parents may spot things about your children that may be hidden from you, such as how they drive when you are not with them. Friends who feel free to call you may prevent your child from going too far down the wrong path.

Ask probing questions. Even if you don't learn much each time you do your quizzing, it's good for a son or daughter to know you are going to be asking lots of questions. If a child is lying and trying to get away with something, you will catch him. Most children are just not that good at fibbing.

One of our girls went to a conference alone for a couple of days. When she came back home, I sat on the edge of the bed and asked how things went.

"Great."

"How about your relationship with boys?"

"That's okay. No big deal."

"There were no romances?"

"No, none of that."

"Did you hold a boy's hand?" Silence.

"Yes, but we went to this park, and, see, we were supposed to hold hands because there were a lot of people at the park and it was for security purposes." Laughter.

I call this "peeling the onion." And I peeled the onion one more layer and said, "Did you hold his hand at any other point?"

"W-e-l-l, as a matter of fact, I did on the bus on the way back."

"Security needed then?"

"Ha, ha, Dad"

"Did he try to kiss you?"

"No."

"Did you try to kiss him?"

"No."

"Good for you. I just wanted to make sure everything was okay."

We don't carry on this type quizzing on a daily basis, but it's good for a child to know that you have a healthy curiosity and know how to ask some probing questions.

Pray for wisdom and opportunities to uncover deceit. God wants to help us with our children more than we can imagine. Perhaps your son is hanging around with some new friends and you feel unsettled. There's nothing outwardly wrong; you're just bothered. Ask God for wisdom and insight into the situation. He loves to respond to the prayers of helpless parents. Let us assure you, God *will* orchestrate circumstances to enable you to catch your child if he is deceiving you.

CONCLUSION

King David told us why we should passionately long to banish deceit from ourselves and our children. He posed the question, "O Lord, who may abide in Thy tent? / Who may dwell on Thy holy hill?"

In other words, "Who gets the privilege of being near you, Lord?"

David's answer: "He who walks with integrity, and works righteousness, / And speaks truth in his heart" (Ps. 15:1–2).

Honesty is important to God. May we together raise a generation of young people who turn away from lies, who dwell near God, and who pursue righteousness all their days.

FOR THE SINGLE PARENT

Being single-handed as a parent means that you need an even better network of spies and eyes looking out for the best interests of your child. Prayerfully consider a number of parents who have children the same age as yours and commission them to help you catch your child doing things right or wrong.

Ask these friends to step into your child's life occasionally just to see how he is doing. And if your child is going through a period where he is being deceptive, you might want to consider using these friends to intervene in your child's life, to confront and rescue him from the trap of deception. Ask them to join you in praying and fasting for you and your child.

UNFORGETTABLE LESSON: BATTER UP

Get together with your preteen or teenager and read the following story by Bill Cosby. Then finish by doing the exercise that follows. Get ready to share some laughs together and to talk about an unforgettable lesson!

Let me repeat: *nothing* is harder for a parent than getting your children to do the right thing. There is such a rich variety of ways for you to fail: by using threats, by using bribery, by using reason, by using example, by using blackmail, or by pleading for mercy. Walk into any bus terminal in America and you will see men on benches poignantly staring into space with the looks of generals who have just surrendered. They are fathers who have run out of ways to get their children to do the right thing, for such a feat is even harder than getting my daughter to remember her own telephone number.

I succeeded once. It happened after my son, who was twelve at the time, had sent me on a trip to the end of my rope. He had taken up a new hobby: lying; and he was doing it so well that he was raising it to an art. Disturbing letters were coming from school—disturbing to me, not to him, for he was full of the feeling that he could get away with anything; and he was right.

"No longer are we going to *ask* you to do something," I told him one day, "we're going to *tell* you that you'd better do it. This is the law of our house: you do what we *tell* you to do. Thomas Jefferson will pardon me, but you're the one American who isn't ready for freedom. You don't function well with it. Do you understand?"

"Yes, Dad," he said.

A few days later, I called from Las Vegas and learned from my wife that this law of the house had been broken. I was hardly taken by surprise to learn that the outlaw was my son.

"Why didn't you do what you were told?" I said to him on the phone. "This is the second time I've had to tell you, and your mother's very upset. The school also says you're not coming in with the work."

"Well, I just don't feel like doing it," he said.

"Very well. How does this idea strike you? When I come home on Thursday, I'm going to kick your butt."

Now I know that many distinguished psychologists feel that kicking butt is a reversion to the Stone Age. But children may have paid more attention in the Stone Age. When a father said, "No shrinking heads this week," his boy may have listened.

On Thursday, I came home, but I couldn't find the boy. He didn't make an appearance at dinner, and when I awoke the next morning, he still wasn't there. So I assembled my staff and solemnly said, "Ladies, where is my son?"

"He's around here *somewhere*," one of my daughters said. They were the French underground hiding one of their heroes from the Nazis.

At last, just before dinner, he entered the house, tired of wandering in the wilderness.

"Young man," I said, "I told you that when I came home, I would kick your behind."

"Yes, Dad," he replied.

"And you know why, don't you?"

"Yes, Dad."

"Then let's go over to the barn."

He may have been slow in his studies, but by now he must have suspected that I wasn't planning a lesson in animal husbandry. When we reached the barn, I said, "Son, we are now going to have a little talk about breaking the law and lying."

As the boy watched me roll up my sleeves, his usual cool gave way to fear, even though I was a father with absolutely no batting average: I have never before hit him or any of the other children. Was I making a mistake now? If so, it would just be mistake number nine thousand, seven hundred, and sixty-three.

"Dad, I know I was wrong," he said, "and I'm really sorry for what I did. I'll never do it again."

"I appreciate your saying that," I said, "and I love you; but I made a promise to you and you wouldn't respect me if I broke it."

"Oh, Dad, *I'd* respect you—I'd respect you like crazy!"

"Son, it's too late."

"It's *never* too late!"

He was reaching heights of legal eloquence, which didn't help him because I've often wanted to hit lawyers, too.

"Just turn around," I said. "I want you to know that this is a form of punishment I truly do not believe in."

"I hate to see you go against your *principles*, Dad."

"I can make an exception. I also won't say that this will hurt me more than it will hurt you. That would be true only if I turned around and let you hit *me*. This is simply a barbaric form of punishment,* but it happens to match your barbaric behavior."

And then I hit him. He rose up on his toes in the point position and the tears began.

"Now do you understand my point about never lying again?" I said.

"Oh *yes*, Dad!" he said. "I've never understood it better."

"Fine. Now you can go."

He turned around to leave and I hit him again. When he turned back to me with a look of having been betrayed, I said, "I'm sorry; I lied. Do you ever want me to lie to you again?"

"No, Dad," he said.

And to this day, he has not lied again to me or my wife. Moreover, we received a letter from his school taking credit for having done a wonderful job on our son. I'm glad I had been able to supplement this work by the school with my own parent-student conference in the barn.[1]

Discuss with your child:

What did Mr. Cosby feel?

What did his son feel?

Why did Mr. Cosby choose to spank his son for lying when he had never spanked him for anything else?

(*By the way, we would take issue with Mr. Cosby's definition of spanking being "hitting." It's not barbaric, it's biblical. Spanking and hitting a child are two completely different things. Spanking is a measured amount of pain, appropriate for the child's age, given in love for the purpose of correction and training. Hitting doesn't have the child's good in mind. It is getting even and is done out of pure anger with no purpose or forethought. Hitting is abuse. Spanking used effectively can correct, instruct, and turn a child away from barbaric behavior.)

CONVICTION BUILDING PLAN

Use the following questions to solidify your own convictions about deceit and integrity and to begin developing a plan to shape your child's convictions.

Part One. Answer the following questions individually

1. In what ways did you deceive your parents when you were young?
2. What patterns of deceit can you identify in your life now?
3. Do you see any patterns of deceit in the life of your mate?
4. What patterns of deceit do you see in your child?

Part Two. Conclusions

1. Without condemning one another, share your answers from the questions you completed individually. If you are single, meet with a friend who can offer wisdom and insight.
2. What types of deceit are your children observing in you? Have they begun manifesting any of these traits and habits in their lives?

3. Talk about how you can hold each other accountable when you fail in these areas.

4. As a couple, go through the main points of Shaping Your Child's Convictions in this chapter and decide upon an action plan of what you will do to begin modeling and teaching these to your child.

5. Decide in advance what the level of penalty is generally going to be for deceit in your family. We have decided that misrepresentations of the truth will be dealt with severely, such as grounding from all communication—no phone, no e-mail, no going to friend's homes for a period of time—depending upon the magnitude of the lie.

"The teaching of the wise is a fountain of life,
To turn aside from the snares of death."
—Proverbs 13:14

14

Trap 9: Substance Abuse

Trying to Find Happiness in All the Wrong Places

After a speaking engagement in a large city, Barbara and I were on our way to the airport with a host couple. As we rode along, getting better acquainted, the couple began telling us about their lives. Both had accomplished much in their careers, and as is true with so many American families, they enjoyed the blessings of ample material success.

The conversation then took a serious turn. Their faces saddened as they related the story of how their only son had begun to pull away from them as he moved into adolescence.

"I should have picked up on the clues that he gave us from the very beginning," the father said. "He began to dress in a counter-cultural fashion. His behavior became that of a recluse, not letting us into his life."

The father admitted that his own scrambled priorities had distracted him from his family and had allowed his son too much freedom. He grimly acknowledged that he had allowed his son to push him out of his life at a time when his son most needed him.

The young man had started using drugs and then became hooked. His drug habit had placed him in a lifestyle and with a crowd that put even his life in jeopardy.

After several failed attempts to extricate their son from this drug culture, finally the mom and dad literally had to steal their son from this harmful peer group and ship him off to a rehabilitation institution on the opposite side of the United States.

As I listened to this chilling story, I thought *Why does this happen?*

The reasons are somewhat unique in every home, but the parents had already verbalized what is often a common theme: A father working hard to provide, but probably too busy; a mom also with a full plate; and a preteen or teenager left operating without enough involvement from his parents, tumbling into a dangerous trap, often with the assistance of an influential peer group.

Substance abuse is frighteningly widespread among our nation's youth. A recent survey of over one hundred thousand students in sixth through twelfth grade found that 29.5 percent of them reported using an illicit drug at least once in the past twelve months. (That compared to 18.6 percent who gave the same response in a study conducted about a decade earlier.)[1]

The survey also reported that among just the twelfth graders, 40.8 percent had used an illicit drug in the past year. Looking at alcohol use alone, 75.6 percent of the seniors in high school reported having at least one drink in the past year.[2]

And do not ignore the issue of smoking. One study found that of students in grades six through eight, 31.1 percent had smoked cigarettes at least once in the past year. Of those in grades nine through twelve, 49.2 percent had lit up at least once in the last twelve months.[3] It has been well-documented that most adult smokers began the habit as teenagers.

That is astounding. Frightening. Why is this stuff, from the hard-core substances—alcohol and drugs—to the soft-core substances—cigarettes, uppers, downers, inhalants, diet pills, and other over-the-counter medications—such a trap to our youth?

We believe there are four primary reasons why teenagers end up as substance abusers:

218

- Rebellion/cry for help
- Stress/seeking escape
- Curiosity/mind expansion
- Peer pressure/mentor craving

Most parents would probably not be surprised that a child's rebellion or emotional hunger might drive a child toward use of alcohol or drugs. But stress?

David Elkind, noted specialist in adolescent psychology, writes: "Young people use drugs for the same reason adults do, to reduce stress . . . Alcohol is the intoxicant of choice among teenagers."[4]

Over the years we have seen pressure escalate on teens to do well in school, be involved in activities, and have a job. This adultlike stress on children who are still growing up may be unprecedented. Should we be surprised that substance abuse has skyrocketed among our youth?

An Emotional Thirst

Parents must stay connected and, if need be, aggressively involved in their child's life to prevent him from quenching an emotional thirst in artificial ways. We believe that one of the primary reasons a child drinks alcohol, for example, is because he does not feel enough love and acceptance at home. Taking a drink or smoking a joint can reduce the pain and stress caused by the insecurities of adolescence.

I'll never forget talking to Benjamin the first fall he attended the university. He made an observation about why his friends drank. "Dad, it's as though they don't like themselves when they are sober."

I agree with him. It's because they may have grown up in a home where they didn't experience love and acceptance and feel good about who God made them to be. In contrast, by not drinking you're saying, "I like who God made me, and I don't need something extra to make me like myself."

DETERMINING YOUR CONVICTIONS

In this section we'll confine our discussion to alcohol and tobacco, assuming all will agree that the use of illegal drugs is wrong. The trickier subject for Christians is to reach biblically informed conclusions on legal substances.

We will not try here to explore these subjects at length. Our goal is to encourage you to form your own convictions that you can hold with integrity as you shape the life of your child. To help you do that we present our own views, which we know some within the family of Christ may not agree with.

The harmful effects of smoking and of secondary smoke are well documented. We sympathize with those who may have developed the habit earlier in life and may have tried to quit repeatedly. A nicotine addiction is serious.

If this is a problem for you, preventing the smoking habit in your child may give you an added incentive to stop smoking. Research has shown that if a parent smokes, it's more likely the child will smoke. The good news is that when a parent stops smoking, the child will also mimic that behavior.[5] Kicking the habit could improve the health of everyone in your family!

Alcohol use is a more challenging issue.

Much has been said in the Christian community about drinking. We don't believe that Scripture teaches that drinking is wrong. Certainly, drunkenness is prohibited in Scripture. Ephesians 5:18 says, "Do not get drunk with wine, for that is dissipation, but be filled with the Spirit." In other words, we are not to be controlled by anything or anyone other than God.

Although the Bible may not prohibit alcohol use, we felt early on with our children that we did not want to give them a potentially confusing message and possible temptation. We decided to abstain from drinking. We reasoned that if they felt it was okay for Mom and Dad to have wine with an occasional meal or to drink a beer now and then, would they know these instances were exceptions? We decided that our children would not have the maturity to conclude, "This is an exception."

Instead we thought they might look at us and say, "Well, if Mom and Dad do this, it must be okay for me too"—long before they were mature enough to form their own rock-solid convictions.

Concerning the use of any substances, here are three convictions that have guided our thinking and behavior.

Parents' Conviction 1: Teaching and modeling a rich love relationship with Jesus Christ will draw our child away from a desire for any false high.

This is *the* key to fending off a host of temptations. Show your child something that he will long for and desire to replicate in his own life.

Our Creator placed within our souls deep longings for happiness and satisfaction that only God can satisfy. In our sinful frailty we are prone to make idols of false gods that seem to promise the happiness we seek.

We parents need to make sure, by what we teach and how we live, that our children understand happiness and deep satisfaction are available from only one Source. As John Piper has written about God: "His people adore him unashamedly for the 'exceeding joy' they find in him (Ps. 43:4). He is the source of complete and unending pleasure: 'In thy presence is fullness of joy; in thy right hand there are pleasures forever' (Ps. 16:11)."[6]

Parents' Conviction 2: We will present a model of personal behavior that minimizes our child's opportunity to have any excuse to use or abuse substances.

The following words of King David express well the desire we have to not cause our children to stumble by what they see us doing: "My eyes shall be upon the faithful of the land, that they may dwell with me; / He who walks in a blameless way is the one who will minister to me" (Ps. 101:6).

This says so clearly that a pure and blameless life is a powerful example. If we have major flaws or compromises in our lives, our children will see them.

This conviction led us to not drink alcohol. We determined to present our children the highest model possible for them to replicate.

A related topic requires comment here. If you or anyone in your home is taking any type of prescription medication, be aware that many children initially begin experimenting with drugs at home.

A friend of mine told me that, as a teenager, his friends jokingly said their drug dealer was his mother. She kept some mood-altering prescription drugs in her medicine cabinet, and the boys pilfered a few capsules at a time to mix with alcohol to provide themselves with a high.

Parents' Conviction 3: We will stay emotionally connected to our child, offering generous attention, acceptance, affection — love.

Research supports the wisdom of this conviction. Robert Blum, reporting on a study done with 90,000 seventh through twelfth graders nationwide, said: "'Kids have less emotional distress' when they feel connected. They experience 'less suicidal thoughts, less suicidal attempts. They are less involved with interpersonal violence. They smoke less, drink less, use marijuana less, have a later onset of the age of intercourse—everything you can think of . . . Connectedness with parents protects adolescents.'"[7]

We could not say it any better; stay very close to your child.

SHAPING YOUR CHILD'S CONVICTIONS

When two of our children, Samuel and Rebecca, were young teenagers, I treated them to probably the most memorable evening we've ever spent together. We attended an Alcoholics Anonymous (AA) meeting.

I had been invited by a friend to go with him to an AA meeting in Little Rock. I decided to take two of our teens along to give them a glimpse of real people who have admitted their addiction to alcohol and other drugs.

We drove to a rugged section of Little Rock on that Tuesday evening and sat down in a pew. Men and women of all ages, several races, and from every economic stratum poured into that meeting hall—people from the street, from downtown businesses, from the suburbs. Some wore tattered clothes; some wore expensive three-piece suits.

That evening made a big impact on Rebecca and Samuel. They watched people stand to give testimonies, often in tears, of how alcohol had destroyed their lives and how much they needed God to release them from the bondage of their addiction.

As we drove home I told my children that many of the men at the meeting were fathers who had seen their marriages and families ripped apart by alcohol. I knew an indelible image had been etched in the minds of my daughter and son.

What other specific actions should you consider to help your child withstand the temptations of substance abuse in junior high, high school, and beyond?

A starting point would be to practice what we have talked about earlier: Your model, your stand, your character are your strongest weapons in helping your child stand strong.

A second point is to build a relationship with your child so that he can know beyond a shadow of a doubt, "I am loved, I am accepted, I am okay, I do not have to depend on my peers for identity and security." Basically, you want to encourage fluid communication and guard against any kind of isolation.

A third point is to be on the offensive. Share your convictions on these topics. Research with teens has shown that it is very helpful for parents to make their values explicit.[8] Your child listens to you more than you may think.

One caution: Some parents allow a child to do some limited drinking at home. The rationale is that if the child is going to drink, they want to see how he handles the beverage in a manageable, safe environment.

223

We need to ask if this really is the best approach in a country where 71.4 million people are directly affected by alcohol abuse or addiction?[9]

Knowing that one in ten people has a predisposition toward alcoholism, why would you want to put a drug in his hands and encourage him in a direction that could destroy his life?

One of our radio program guests, Mary Glynn Peeples, once shared a humorous but insightful story about how she monitored substance issues in her family and dealt with a possible smoking incident with her son, Mark:

> As long as they [her children] were home, I was awake every night when they came in. I was in the living room reading a book, and I always had cake or cookies or ice cream. They sat with me at a small table, and we had a nice midnight snack—so I could smell them . . .
>
> We'd just sit in there, and we'd visit and talk; they thought how wonderful mom was that she always had something good to eat. I did that because I didn't smoke or drink, so I could smell it.
>
> One night I fell asleep, and Mark went to his room. I went down to turn the light out, and when I opened the door it was filled with cigarette smoke [odors] . . . I woke him up and said, "Mark, you've been smoking."
>
> "I have not," he said.
>
> "You have too," I said, "open your mouth." I stuck my nose in his mouth—he had not.
>
> "Are you satisfied?" he said.
>
> "Yes," I said. I picked up his football jacket, and it was filled with smoke.
>
> The next day at church he had his harem around him; he called me over and did a good imitation of me: "You know what she did last night. She told me to open my mouth and she stuck her nose in my mouth to see if I'd been smoking. Mom, how much longer are you going to do that?"

"Well, until you go off to school," I said.

He laughed. And as I walked away I thought, *Why did he laugh?* He did it because he was proud that he had a mother who cared that much.

Finally, you may want to offer an incentive to help motivate your child to stay away from these harmful substances. We have made a promise to all of our children when they turn thirteen: If they complete their high school years without drinking, doing drugs, smoking, or having sex, we will buy them a car. We've not promised them what kind of a car it might be, making clear that it might, in the words of our friend and associate Bob Horner, be a Rolls Canardly: *rolls* down the hill, but *can hardly* make it back up! This reward has given our children added desire to avoid these traps.

Here are two convictions we would recommend be shaped in every child concerning substance use and abuse issues:

Child's Conviction 1: I will honor and protect my own body because it is the temple of the Holy Spirit.

These familiar words from the apostle Paul apply: "Or do you not know that your body is a temple of the Holy Spirit who is in you, whom you have from God, and that you are not your own? For you were bought with a price; therefore glorify God in your body" (1 Cor. 6:19–20).

That is what we are training our youth to do: walk in the power of the Holy Spirit and not be controlled by peer pressure, by alcohol, or by choices that will take them in the wrong direction.

Child's Conviction 2: I will decide in advance what I will do when presented with the opportunity to smoke, drink alcohol, or use other drugs.

In preparing your child for the substance abuse trap, brief him on what he will undoubtedly face. Your child will have an opportunity to smoke, drink, and do drugs in junior high or sooner. Some children are coming to school drunk; others are bringing a bottle with them and drinking during the day. They may be your child's classmates. Sometimes a bottle is passed around, and our children must deal with the temptation.

One thing we have done is role-play with our children what they would do if an alcoholic beverage is put in front of them or someone offers them drugs. Or what would they do if asked to get in a car when everyone else—including the driver—had been drinking?

The tests on these issues come in waves for years.

Some time back I took our son Benjamin to college, and as I was helping him unload his clothing and move his gear into his room, we took a rest on the tailgate of a pickup truck and watched other students coming in. Their arms were loaded with cases of beer and sacks of liquor. It was just 3:00 P.M. and some of them were already completed wasted.

Granted, it was a weekend and classes had not started. But suddenly I was overtaken by fear. I wondered if all of our efforts as parents, all of the hours of discipline, building character, and helping Benjamin face issues in his life had adequately prepared my son. Would he pass the test?

That's the challenge we all face. We have to project ourselves into the future and see ourselves sitting on the back of that pickup with a son or daughter. How will they handle that situation when the time comes? Will they be able to stand firm?

As I sat with Benjamin on that tailgate, I turned to Benjamin and looked him in the eye. "Son, I've got to tell you that watching all these young men get wasted on booze really causes me to question the wisdom of sending you into the midst of all this."

There was only a brief silence and he returned my gaze. "Dad, this is my mission field," he replied. "It's going to be tough, but if it was easy these guys wouldn't need Jesus Christ. This is what you and Mom have trained me for. God has led me and He will protect me."

There I sat, rebuked by my eighteen-year-old son. He was a young man of faith.

Later he told me that when he was initiated, surrounded by the entire fraternity of nearly one hundred guys, they put a bottle of champagne in his hand. The idea was that each pledge was to chug the whole bottle.

At that point there was no dad or mom standing alongside him.

Benjamin shook up the bottle and sprayed the whole fraternity, totally emptying it on the group! Five other guys, out of a group of about forty pledges, did the same thing.

That took courage. But that internal gumption was not developed during that moment when our son was surrounded. It was built in a series of small steps over a period of many years.

Two years later our second son, Samuel, demonstrated similar courage by replicating his brother's champagne shower!

On their own, our children must be prepared to make the choice to be different—not to be pious or religious, but to be a young person who operates on firmly held personal convictions.

What if You Suspect Substance Use or Catch Your Child?

Unfortunately, many parents deny symptoms of drug or alcohol abuse or simply look the other way. Some common signs of such abuse include school difficulties (a sudden drop in grades or attendance), loss of appetite, weight loss, periods of hyperactivity, bloodshot eyes, lethargy, and fatigue,[10] and puzzling behavior.

Our interview with a former drug user helped yield the following list:

- Does your child often take an extra change of clothes when he goes out with friends? This is an old trick to hide the smell of alcohol or smoke. The child changes into the fresh set shortly before arriving back home.
- Does your child use breath fresheners or mints excessively, possibly to hide cigarette or alcohol odors?

- Have you seen a can or bottle of a product called Ozium? This is a chemical used in mortuaries to cover smells. Drug users may use this in their cars or on clothing to conceal smells of alcohol, tobacco smoke, or marijuana.

If you have some suspicions and think you need to know what drug paraphernalia is called or looks like, take a tour on the Internet. All that's needed is a search on key words like *marijuana, reefer, joint* to find the information needed.

If you are suspicious about what may be happening with your child late at night or when you are away from home for an extended period of time, do not hesitate to go to neighbors and tell them to alert you if anything out of the ordinary happens.

A couple once came to a FamilyLife Marriage Conference, and while they were gone, their teenage daughter had her friends in their home for a drug fest. The parents might never have known, but the neighbors told them what had happened.

Never be shy about doing room inspections or engaging in late-night reconnaissance. Waiting up at night to welcome home a child and interact with him is advisable.

If you find out your child is high from alcohol or drugs, when both of you are ready to talk (he's sober, and you have emotions under control), sit down and find out what's going on, then administer appropriate consequences.

If the drinking or other drug use persists, consider drawing up a contract clarifying the behavior you expect from him and what boundaries will apply.

If all else fails, consider calling on others to help with an intervention, perhaps asking another adult such as your youth pastor to help you confront your child's substance abuse.

Above all, never stop praying and trusting God for direction and strength. Two of our friends, Bill and Ann Parkinson, went through a difficult experience with a son who for a while drank and pulled away from them and their values. Talking about this experience, Ann made these comments on a *FamilyLife Today* radio broadcast:

> I can't say God gave me a peace. What God did give me was an inner conviction that He was in this ball game with me, that I was never going to be alone, and that He loved our son even more than I did. Let me tell you how that came about . . .
>
> As a mom, I was feeling defeated, and it was just so painful that this child that I loved and would sacrifice my body for would cause me this much pain. I remember standing out on my front porch . . . I was angry at God. I was angry at my son for putting me in this pain, and I can remember standing out there saying to myself, "You know what? I just need to let this guy go—he is pushing against me—I just need to let him go . . ."
>
> I can remember there was this voice in my head that said, "Who wants you to give up?" And the thought that came to my mind was *Satan*, and I thought, *That's right, and I'm not going to let him win.*
>
> That's when mentally I decided I was not going to give up on my son . . . if a mom gives up, who has he got in his corner? That's when I chose . . . to pray for him—not to pull myself emotionally away, but to love him unconditionally, even when he didn't deserve it.

What a great insight this is for all of us. And in time, Bill and Ann's persistence paid off; God did bring their son back.

TESTING YOUR CHILD'S CONVICTIONS

An excellent way to help test your child's values related to substance use is to have frequent discussions. We have talked on a number of occasions at the dinner table, even when our children were little, about the lives of people we knew whose marriages and families had been ruined by alcohol or drugs. So from a young age our children heard about the dangers of drugs and knew the real life stories behind them.

A great laboratory for these talks is the family room. While watching athletic events on TV, you can count on a beer commercial rolling in about every ten minutes. Ask your child, "How valid is the lifestyle being presented in these ads?" "Is it true that getting high brings happiness and no problems?"

Movies also provide opportunities. Samuel and I were watching a movie, a decent movie, and in the middle of it there was drinking. I said, "Now, why are they throwing that in there, Samuel? They're saying that's the way to have fun, that drinking is respectable. I want you to know that that isn't the way to happiness."

Alcohol and driving. As your child gets older and may be riding in cars with older teens, keep your antenna high and don't assume anything. You must know something about the teenagers your child is riding with. And if you ever suspect anyone is drinking and driving, never hesitate to intervene before it is too late. Each of our children has known that he will lose his privileges to drive for an extended period of time if we ever find him driving and drinking.

FOR THE SINGLE PARENT

If your former spouse drinks, you will want to consider your options for communicating your convictions to your preteen or teen. Asking your former spouse to give up drinking may be out of the question, although we would encourage you to talk with him or her about the issues we've raised in this chapter. Appeal to the need to present a unified front to your teenager and the potential danger that this substance represents.

If you can't reach agreement, spend some time shaping your own convictions and how you are going to talk about them with your child. Anticipate the questions that will come because mom and dad don't believe the same thing. Know how you will respond to the inevitable questions that will come if your child sees your spouse drinking or drunk.

Talk to other single parents who may be facing similar situations and hammer out your strategies and statements together.

As always, resist the urge to speak evil of your former spouse.

CONCLUSION

I recently celebrated my fiftieth birthday, and a special moment during a party held at FamilyLife headquarters was a phone call from our son, Benjamin, who was overseas doing mission work.

During his call, with the FamilyLife staff listening in, Benjamin paid tribute to me, even crying as he talked about how much our relationship means to him.

After the birthday party was over, I went back to my office and on my desk was a note from one of the staff:

> Dennis, happy birthday! I'm glad to see you taking it so well. I don't mind being 54. I see it only as just a number. Good health to me is more an issue than age. God has blessed us both with good health so far. It is a privilege to work with you for families, and I hope the rest of your day is as great as this beginning.
>
> Hearing your son overseas was both special and hard. I couldn't help but feel the contrast.
>
> Today my son goes to court to be sentenced to prison for drugs. Pray for him to come to repentance. I have not seen him in over four years. I know that God has heard my prayers for him, and that God will do what is best for all concerned.

I did pray for that young man and his parents. I also thanked God that, so far, each of our children has developed convictions that have steered him away from lifestyles and choices that could not only hurt his health but destroy his life.

Substance abuse is a killer snare, and ultimately only God can protect our children. But we need to pray hard and work hard to steer them away from this trap's ghastly jaws.

UNFORGETTABLE LESSON: AA Field Trip

As we mentioned earlier in this chapter, we can think of no better way to drive home the consequences of substance use and abuse than to attend an Alcoholics Anonymous meeting.

There are thousands of AA chapters throughout the United States. To obtain information, look up *Alcoholics Anonymous* in the business section of a phone directory. Or you may want to talk to someone on staff at your church (or at your place of work) to find out who might be an AA member and willing to serve as your host for a visit to a meeting. Be sure to make arrangements ahead of time—don't just drop in on an AA meeting.

Combined with this field trip to an AA meeting, we suggest you construct a simple pledge or covenant related to smoking, alcohol, and drug use that you and your child could sign, frame, and hang in your home.

A friend of ours, Bill Elliff, has a framed copy in his office of a commitment he made in Sunday school when he was just twelve years old. In the handwriting that could only belong to a boy that age, it reads:

MY PLEDGE

On this day, the first of March, 1964,
I solemnly pledge that I will never harm my body,

Hurt my influence with others, or displease my God
By drinking an alcoholic beverage or by smoking.

Signed

Bill Elliff

Today, over thirty years later, Bill and wife, Holly, have eight wonderful children, and Bill pastors one of the largest churches in Arkansas. He has fulfilled that pledge 100 percent.

This simple act done as a child continues to bear fruit in Bill's life. The same can be true for your child.

CONVICTION BUILDING PLAN

Working through the following questions will help you firm up convictions on the use of alcohol, tobacco, or other substances.

Part One. Answer the following questions individually

1. Think back to your own childhood. Did your parents drink or smoke? What impact has the example of your parents had on your decision to drink or smoke?
2. If you smoke or drink, do you think you should do either in front of your child? Why or why not?
3. Are there any other substances that you use that might give your child the impression that you need this substance in order to be happy or deal with life? Examples might be excessive consumption of certain foods, use of mood-altering medications, excessive consumption of coffee or soft drinks, etc.?

Part Two. Conclusions

1. Without condemning one another, share your answers to the questions you completed individually. If you are single, meet with a friend who can offer wisdom and insight.
2. Do you and your spouse hold differing views on alcohol and tobacco use? If so, why?

3. For the benefit of your child, seek to agree on a family policy related to alcohol and tobacco use in your home. Make a list of the points in that policy now.
4. Work out a plan as to how you will inform your child of the family's policy on alcohol and tobacco use and how it will be applied to the child. Work through some scenarios that help the child decide in advance how to deal with temptations to smoke, drink, or use drugs.
5. Discuss how both of you will stay emotionally connected to your child, thereby reducing the risk he will seek to have his needs met from a substance.

15

Trap 10: Busyness

Life Is Good When Parents and Children Sl-o-o-o-w Down

A life bulging with activity nearly became a trap for our daughter.

Rebecca had a natural flair for gymnastics, and I (Barbara) loved watching her perform. But as she progressed in her skills, Dennis and I became concerned about the amount of time she was expected to practice. She would go to the gym after school and not get home until 8:30 at night—three days a week.

It seemed like she was spending more time with her coach and team than with us. If she kept moving to higher levels in gymnastics, she would be away from her family even more. We knew we needed to spend more time with her as she approached adolescence. On top of that, our oldest daughter, Ashley, was about to enter her senior year of high school, and we didn't want our family to become fragmented during her final year at home.

When we talked about this with Rebecca, she responded by talking about how much she loved gymnastics and about her dreams and aspirations. But we could also hear the quiver in her voice that said, "I miss you too."

After much prayer, agony, and discussion, Dennis and I decided it was time for Rebecca to quit gymnastics. Few decisions have been more difficult. We know other parents have made the opposite decision, and with a different sport or different circumstances, we might not have asked Rebecca to quit.

The bottom line, though, was that we wanted a relationship with our daughter, and we knew that a strong relationship requires time. We wanted *our* lives and values, not her coaches', to be the major influence in her life. To continue equipping her for life, we needed Rebecca to be an integral part of our family. *Real* values drove our decision.

Busyness is a trap that snares many a child and adult. We are a hurried, exhausted, and weary culture. Too many children today are close to overdosing on activities. The opportunities for them to try new things, explore their interests, and develop their abilities and gifts seem unprecedented in history.

Dr. Paul Gabriel wrote in *Anticipating Adolescence,* "Time is needed in these years for leisure, for playing alone and with friends, for allowing the imagination to expand and life to become fuller and more interesting. Without it, social and emotional growth are stunted."[1]

Many parents, however, fail to give their children this needed leisure time. Instead, the after-school hours are filled with one activity after another. Then, as their oldest child emerges from the golden years, they are unprepared for how this busyness will affect the entire family.

If you don't get on top of this—especially if you have two or more children close in age—your schedules (yours and your children's) are on a collision course. You will crash. You will be heard mumbling, as you make your fifth taxi run some afternoon, "This is crazy. I'm going insane. How did I get myself into this? We're never home anymore. We never sit down and eat dinner together. This is destroying our family." As children proceed through the teenage years, the problem only grows worse, especially after a child earns his driver's license. We know of many families who allow the schedules of their children to control their home life to the point where they rarely ever enjoy a meal together.

There's certainly nothing wrong with an active life, as long as the right perspective is maintained. Idleness is just as bad as being too busy. Solomon warned, "Through indolence the rafters sag, and through slackness the house leaks" (Eccl. 10:18).

But the opposite problem—frenzy—creates a disturbance in our mind and soul that makes it hard for us to "Cease striving and know that I am God" (Ps. 46:10). Do you know how to be still? Does your child? We fear many Christian teens will not be able to hear God speak to them because they've not been taught to rest and to listen. They are addicted to activity and external stimuli.

As parents you need to set the course for your preadolescent child while you still have control of the schedule, knowing there is a time around the corner when the activity monster will barge through your front door and eat your time and resources. We encourage you to formulate an activities mission statement that will set boundaries for the well-being of everyone in your family.

DETERMINING YOUR CONVICTIONS

If your day planner has a blinking NO VACANCY sign hanging on it, chances are good that everyone else in the home is running on turbo too. What does your schedule look like? Overloaded? Does it reflect your higher priorities? What type of lifestyle are you modeling? How often are you at home?

You need to examine every activity that takes you away from your spouse and children and determine if it is worth the cost. This applies even to ministry activities; we need to be involved in our church and to be reaching out to others in our community, but not at the continual expense of our families.

Our observation is that the root of busyness is often found in the values parents adopt from others or from the culture. In addition to ensuring a good education, we often want our children to gain other skills. So we get them involved in one or more of myriad choices of lessons: piano, guitar, voice, art, gymnastics, or drama, to name a few. Then we let them join competitive athletic teams:

soccer, baseball, basketball, football, tennis, and swimming. And don't forget the clubs like Boy Scouts or Girl Scouts or Awana.

What are our motives? Why do we want our children involved in outside activities like sports, cheerleading, or music? Are we simply responding to our child's wishes or trying to match what other parents are doing in our community?

One temptation any parent faces is allowing a child's activities to feed his own self-esteem. We feel an unmistakable pride when a child hits a home run in baseball or performs well in a piano recital. But are we using this experience to relive our own youth? Are we enjoying our child's accomplishments as a substitute for what we may have missed as an adolescent?

How many times have you heard the sad story of a child who years later admits that he participated in a sport only to please a parent but now hates the sport and doesn't want much to do with the parent, either? Some parents don't face their own feelings and are not willing to sacrifice an activity that they love but that might not be best for the child.

In our family we continue to work on refining the following convictions, which we recommend to any harried parent.

Parents' Conviction 1: Sabbath rest and refreshment need to be a priority in our family's schedule.

Christians need to recover God's solution for schedule stress. He thought so much of the idea that He modeled it for us during creation by taking a well-deserved seventh day off. Then He put it in our operating manual (the fourth commandment) and elaborated more on it than on any of the other commandments:

> Remember the Sabbath day, to keep it holy. Six days you shall labor and do all your work, but the seventh day is a sabbath of the LORD your God; in it you shall not do any work, you or your son or your daughter, your male or your female servant or your cattle or your sojourner who stays with you. For in six days the LORD made the heavens and the earth, the

sea and all that is in them, and rested on the seventh day; therefore the LORD blessed the sabbath day and made it holy" (Ex. 20:8–11).

Is Sunday any different around your home from any other day of the week? If not, you are missing out on a great personal and family benefit.

Parents' Conviction 2: Career advancement, personal interests, church involvement, and other activities must not have priority over our personal relationship with God and our commitment to our family.

It's too easy for parents to let the family become consumed by busyness. Activities and accomplishment become the basis for significance. We become activity driven rather than value driven.

To keep life properly focused, you should schedule times that ensure attention to priorities. For example, make sure that the entire family eats breakfast together each day, or schedule a special family night each week. Make it nonnegotiable.

Don't set unreasonable goals. Once your children become teenagers, you will find that it's impossible to eat together every night. But rather than giving up as some parents do, look at your schedule and figure out a way to share a meal at least two or three days a week.

Parents' Conviction 3: Busyness, by its very nature, will cause us to lose focus on the important things in life.

This is the dark side of busyness: We get caught up in the activity or event of the moment and lose perspective on what is really significant in life—relationships, time with the Lord, rest, service to others. The momentary and the temporary grow in importance in our lives because busyness drives us. Consequently, family values take a backseat. What really matters is lost because we just have no time.

Although growing and experiencing life through a variety of activities can be a positive thing, we must guard against allowing

239

these experiences to become counterproductive in preparing a child to walk with Christ, relate to others, and contribute to the Kingdom of God.

SHAPING YOUR CHILD'S CONVICTIONS

Teaching your child how to get a grip on schedules and activities is a gift that will never lose its value. The following are our core convictions in managing busyness.

Child's Conviction 1: I will learn the value of quiet and rest.

I (Barbara) have thought often about the story of how God spoke to young Samuel in the Old Testament. What impresses me is that this young boy knew it was God. I wonder how many of our children would be able to hear God calling their names through all the noise in the background?

Encourage, *insist*, that your child spend time regularly just being still—not watching TV or doing computer games, but reading, listening to soft music, or pursuing calm hobbies. This environment is also necessary for teaching your child how to have a daily time of prayer and Scripture reading.

A child at this age, who is still growing physically, needs sleep. One of our friends, whose daughter is thirteen, noticed that she was staying up later and later at night to finish her homework. Her parents were pleased that she was committed to her schoolwork, but they were concerned that she wasn't getting enough sleep. She wasn't goofing off; it just took a lot of time to practice the piano and basketball, do chores, and then finish schoolwork. She needed to be in bed by about 9:30, but all of these demands on her time were keeping her up until as late as 10:30. The parents directed their daughter to cut back on one of her commitments in order to get the rest she needed.

A few years ago we decided to make the Sabbath a day of rest in our family. We learned that slowing everybody down and changing the routine is not easy.

We try to make sure our children get their homework done by Saturday night so that they don't have long assignments to do on Sunday. We do our best not to shop on Sunday. If they want to listen to music, it has to be Christian. And we try to limit phone calls to family only.

Sunday afternoon at our place is pretty quiet. Lots of naps, reading, and recreation. Relationship building. There's more we could do to make the Sabbath restful, but even these simple things help.

Related to these values of quiet and rest is the surprising side benefit of grounding—showing your child the benefits of lowering stress.

We have found grounding to be a good disciplinary measure for preadolescents and young teens, because it inflicts the pain of separation from peers and enjoyable social activities. And we have been surprised on many occasions how this punishment—which can seem to the child like a life sentence of medieval torture—turns out to be something of a vacation from a too-demanding schedule and even from peer pressure.

After the initial moaning and groaning subsides, the child seems to relax and actually enjoys hanging out at home and catching up on family time. Of course, you probably will not get this message verbally from the child, but you can see it in his attitude.

Child's Conviction 2: I will recognize the value of spending adequate time with my parents, brothers, and sisters.

In our family there is one value that ranks above nearly all others: "Family has priority."

This value has done more than any other to control busyness in our home. Ever since our children were small, they have heard us say over and over, "We are always going to discriminate in favor of our family rather than against our family."

This value does not remove conflict, and it can create signifi-

pain when you have to say no to a child. But it is a chunk of granite to stand on when the winds of schedule insanity start to blow.

One Christmas one of our teenage daughters misunderstood what day the family would leave to visit my mother. On this weekend our daughter had a full slate of parties, concerts, caroling—all that great holiday fun. We had to let her know she was going to miss all of it because we were traveling out of town.

We understood why she got upset and blew a gasket. "Why do we have to go away on a weekend when I have all these opportunities?" she said with tears.

"Because it's Christmas, honey," we said. "That's just life. We wouldn't be going to see Grandma if it wasn't Christmas, and you wouldn't be having all these fun things to do if it wasn't Christmas. But you know we're going to choose family over friends and all these activities."

We really did feel her anguish, but even as she was still so angry she wanted to kick the cat, we were proud to hear her say: "I know. I agree. My family is a priority."

Keeping some schedule sanity in your home might even pit you against the church. For example, our church, which has a fantastic youth program, schedules a New Year's Eve party that goes until 1:00 A.M. for the junior high and 4:00 A.M. for the senior high. Unless you are willing for your child to be driving or be driven by someone else in the dead of night on New Year's Eve, the only way you are going to be assured of his safety is to go to the church and pick him up. For us that would involve two forty-minute round trips in the middle of the night, assuming the parties ended on time.

It's great fun for all the youth, but what can happen is that Mom and Dad pay the price by having to stay up all night. The next day the whole family is cranky—not the most pleasant kickoff for the new year. In addition, we have a traditional family activity we enjoy on New Year's Day. So we've decided that for our family the sacrifice is not worth it. Having a value like "family first" helps clarify decision making when there are two good choices.

Although a preadolescent will increasingly want to do more things on his own, don't totally surrender the opportunity to do some things together—one on one or as a family.

Try to find at least one activity you and your child enjoy doing together. During their adolescent years, I introduced hunting to the boys and now the girls. This has provided many memorable experiences. And there's no reason we won't keep enjoying this shared activity long after the children have left our nest.

Child's Conviction 3: I will not be involved in an activity just because "everyone else" is, but because it is something I enjoy and it helps me grow.

After some experimentation, we have learned that it's best to support the child's strengths with ongoing involvement in just one or two activities. Two of our girls use their gymnastic ability in cheerleading, while our third daughter develops her musical talents with piano lessons and involvement in band. We then limit or say no to involvement in other activities, with the exception that during the spring two of our girls play softball for a couple of months.

In the activities you do choose for your children, take advantage of opportunities to build character. You can teach compelling life lessons through these experiences—for instance, the importance of commitment and loyalty. Too often among adults and children there is a tendency to sign up for some activity but then later to drop out. Don't allow your preadolescent or teen to do this unless he is encountering a serious difficulty, such as an abusive coach or a health-threatening situation. Use the opportunity to show him how he needs to follow through on the commitment made to others.

Child's Conviction 4: I will learn to make decisions and plan so that my schedule is balanced and not overloaded.

As your child grows older, begin teaching him how to make sound, wise decisions. We're not talking here about the mechanics of time management and how to keep a schedule (as good as they are); rather, we are talking about how to operate from a biblical mind-set, how to know important personal values, how to evaluate the cost involved with any choice, and how to analyze options and make a good decision. This may be the best inoculation to prevent chronic busyness.

As our children have moved through the teenage years, they've heard us repeat the phrase, "No one does it all!" so often that they can complete it before we get the first word out of our mouths. But we've tried to teach them that life is full of trade-offs. They have to settle for limited objectives.

As a parent you do need to set some limits. For example, determine ahead of time how often you will let your child spend the night with a friend. How many days can he go home with someone after school? How many nights during the week can he attend school or church activities? How often can he work? (That last question especially applies to young adolescent girls who babysit.) Repeatedly you will hear yourself saying things like, "I don't think it's a good idea for you to go to the roller skating party tonight since you have a dance recital tomorrow."

We've found that if you don't have some kind of boundary, then home becomes little more than a pit stop for fuel (food), new tires (money), and water (a peck on the cheek or a pat on the back by mom or dad).

The child's weekly schedule needs balance. Observing the Sabbath is a good first step. But the concept of appropriate pacing, with ample time to be still and reflect on what life means and where the child is headed, also needs to permeate the regular routine.

This will require your involvement over a significant period of time. For example, at the beginning of a school year you will want to sit down with your child and list all the possible outside activities he could participate in. Talk about the pros and cons of each option—how much time would be required, how it would affect other areas of his life, and so on. Ask questions such as:

"How will this activity benefit you as a person?"

"How will this affect your relationship with the others in your family?"

"Is anyone pressuring you to participate in this?"

"Will this add too much stress?"

"What could suffer as a result of participating in this activity?"

"Do you feel this is something God is leading you to do?"

As your child matures, he will make more choices on his own, stumble through some agonizing mistakes, and continue to learn. Don't be surprised if you are still helping your children in this area as they exit adolescence. This is tough enough for us to regularly pull off as adults.

As a parent, you also need to monitor part-time jobs closely.

Learning how to work for someone other than mom or dad is a positive thing for a young person. Many preadolescents first have such a work experience as babysitters or lawn cutters. Later they often move on to some type of retail or fast-food environment. (We have much more to say about jobs in Chapter 17, page 281).

How busy should teenagers become with work? One of our mistakes may have been letting some of our children work too many hours. During the school year we suggest carefully monitoring anything above ten hours a week. More than that, and they will probably feel a lot of stress.

Don't step back from setting some boundaries. For example, one of our limits is that we don't allow any work on Sundays. That's part of the reason why many of our children have worked for a fast-food restaurant chain located in malls called Chick-fil-A, which is not open on the Sabbath.

Discuss your expectations on study time and grades with your teen. Then prayerfully count what the decision to take the job means. "If you say yes to an employer, son, you are saying yes to being there when he calls and when you are expected to work. That means you may not get to go fishing with your buddies or you won't be able to lie out and get a tan if the weather is nice. Are you willing to give up that pleasure to be able to go to work to earn money?" We have *repeatedly* found that teenagers don't do well in anticipating the true cost of decisions.

Finally, monitor what the commitment and the part-time job is doing to your teen and to your family. Sometimes part-time jobs mean more work for parents—running a child to the place of employment and picking him up later in the evening. It may be too disruptive to your family.

TESTING YOUR CHILD'S CONVICTIONS

The busyness trap will provide daily opportunities to check out how your child is doing in keeping priorities in order and not succumbing to stress. Following are some ways to test the progress of your teenager as he builds his convictions:

Since participation in activities or doing other fun things with friends should be viewed as a privilege and not a right, you should not be afraid to require certain minimum requirements. These might include cleaning his room, maintaining a certain grade point average, finishing chores, or reading a set number of books. These boundaries can be used to instruct your teen in the nature of commitments and real responsibility.

One of our family sayings is, "Work first, play second." We are continually working on instilling this concept in our teens by verbally reminding them and serving consequences when they fail.

Watch your child carefully to make sure he is meeting his top priorities and help him make adjustments if necessary. For example, midweek youth group meetings and discipleship groups can be very important to the spiritual growth of our children. If your teen is too busy with other activities, then it may be time to review all that the child is doing and trim some of the fat from his schedule so he can go to church.

One of our teens became very busy with activities and in the process brought home a grade card well below his capability. Part of our discipline was to remove the privilege of attending youth group for a period of time. However, this decision earned us the reputation among his Christian peers as the parents who "grounded their child from God." That criticism wounded our teen more than us. He had to live with the accusations. Not all decisions that you make need to be understood by everyone. You are your child's parents. Be courageous and do what your teen needs.

Let your child experience the pain of failing to count the cost when making a decision. Resist the urge to rescue him. Use those mistakes to tutor your child for the future.

Remind yourself that your child needs to learn self-denial. Lamentations 3:27 says, "It is good for a man that he should bear / The yoke in his youth." This means that it is good for our children to bear some burdens, to deny themselves, and to pay the price for the overall good of the family. It's not good to cater to their every whim and let them have everything they want. They need to learn how to deny themselves, because suffering and self-denial are central to following Christ. Do we want our children to be genuine disciples of Christ or just comfortable and happy?

Take advantage of natural teaching opportunities. For example, if you and your spouse have a regular time of planning, consider bringing your child along and letting him eavesdrop as you go through the process of making decisions about how you spend your time. You might even want to have a test ready for your teen that helps him apply what he's just seen to his life.

Or let's say your fifteen year old comes home and announces she is considering trying out for the volleyball team. Sit down with her and discuss all that she is presently committed to doing. Look at a calendar and talk about how her schedule will change during different months of the year. Ask her what she is going to eliminate in order to be able to fulfill her commitment to be at all the games and live a life with balance.

Some Words About Driving Privileges

Youth may experience few "rites of passage" in our culture, but one major moment during adolescence comes close: obtaining the "right to pass in a car," the teenager's passport to freedom—the driver's license.

Probably no other single event produces more changes in the relationship with your child than the acquisition of that small picture ID lovingly carried in purse, wallet, pocket, or backpack.

We've included this brief discussion of driving under the Busyness trap because access to a car presents even more opportunities for a teenager to stay on the go. For the first time, the teenager has the opportunity to go where he wants without depending on a parent to take him there. This freedom can be intoxicating. He drives himself to school functions, to extracurricular activities, or to work. Friends drive over to visit—or to pick him up to go somewhere else. He spends less and less time with his family.

It is at this critical juncture that some parents lose control of their child. If you fail to place some sensible limits on his schedule, it may irrevocably change the atmosphere in your home. You will need to work closely with your teenager to help him make good decisions that allow him to get enough rest, to fulfill all his responsibilities, and to spend time with the family.

At the same time, remember that the right to obtain the coveted driver's license and operate a car independently is one of the best trump cards a mom and dad hold in the parenting deck. Most children look forward to the day when they will smoothly back Dad's Oldsmobile out of the garage, wave, and drive off—alone. For a host of reasons, we parents need to be sure they are ready, because the number one killer of teenagers remains death in an automobile accident.[2]

It's not enough that a child have the physical and mental coordination to drive. He also must be emotionally and spiritually mature to understand the responsibility of guiding a 4,000-pound, potentially lethal machine down a highway at 65 miles an hour.

We know that every family must shape its own policies related to driving the family car, but here are some lessons learned by this dad and mom who have maintained and insured a fleet of up to six (very "used") cars for the family.

Don't feel rushed about granting driving privileges: The key words here are "rushed" and "privilege." Driving is not a constitutional right that every parent must grant on the very day a child is eligible for a learner's permit or driver's license. Some children are ready early; others are not. In Arkansas where we live, a fourteen-year-old can obtain a permit. We think that is too young and have not allowed any of our children to start driving at that age. We see no reason for a teenager to start learning to drive until at least fifteen.

Insist on driver's education. If at all possible, send your child through some formal instruction. You also will need to help teach driving skills, but teenagers often listen better to a stranger. A driver's training certificate will reduce your insurance bill too.

Impose meaningful restrictions. Here are some of the rules we instituted for our children:

- When they receive their license, they are not allowed to drive alone without an adult until we feel the child is mature enough to handle the responsibility.
- We also require them to drive 10 miles per hour under the stated speed limit. A 55 mph speedway becomes 45 mph for a limited time. We don't do this for a long period, because driving slower than the traffic flow can be dangerous. But we do ask our teen to start out well under control of his automobile.
- We limit new drivers to specific routes—like to and from school only. Driving in town on busy streets is reserved until the child has demonstrated enough composure to be able to handle the pressure.
- We do not allow our daughters to drive alone after certain hours. We've also insisted with all of our children that they keep plenty of gas in the tank. We do not want them stalled on the highway.

Set up a clear system of penalties. When beginning to drive, we have allowed each of our children to use one of our older, but mechanically safe cars—the kind that only needs minimum insurance coverage. (Prepare yourself—every child will probably have a fender bender. Better to ding up the old Pinto then the newer Taurus, if you catch our drift.) You may want to consider requiring your teenager to pay for all or some of the gas, insurance, and maintenance expenses. At the same time, we have talked to each child about penalties for irresponsible behavior:

- If a child gets a ticket, he will pay for the ticket and any increase in insurance charges that result. (In our family we have paid for insurance; other parents may ask the child to pay some or all of the premium. If you have a son, get ready to put a second mortgage on the house!) If a child gets multiple tickets, in addition to fines and penalties from the state, he loses driving privileges at home.
- If a child ever drinks and drives, the car will be taken away completely—for starters.
- If a child does not maintain a B average in high school and college, the difference in the higher insurance premium will be paid by him.
- If we ever hear from a neighbor or friend that a child has been seen driving recklessly, a loss in driving privileges will result.

The good news about having a new driver in the house is that another significant milepost (ahem!) has been passed in your parenting journey. And it sure is nice to not have to spend quite so much time behind the wheel of the family taxi.

FOR THE SINGLE PARENT

As difficult as it may be at times to arrange, be sure that you have some time in your schedule to rest. This will not only be good for you but will model for your child the healthy perspective of balancing your life.

Additionally, if you do not take a regular planning retreat (at least once every six months), we encourage you to schedule some time just to get away and regain perspective about life, your children, and your calendar. Work out a child-care arrangement with another single parent, if necessary, so that you can get this time alone to refresh and renew your spiritual and emotional batteries.

CONCLUSION

All of this advice is based on a dangerous assumption that we parents are in control of our schedules and that the trap called busyness has not ensnared our feet.

One of the best things we have done to keep out of this trap is a weekly date night when the two of us go out for dinner and discuss our family's schedule related to our convictions.

We show up every Sunday night at a certain restaurant armed with schedulers and notepads. The restaurant workers know us by name; in fact, once when we missed a couple of weeks, a waitress asked if our marriage was okay.

No other single thing that we have done has helped us more than this regular time that is devoted to making certain that our calendar reflects our family's real values.

UNFORGETTABLE LESSON: Busy Body

Have some fun with this one—and make the point that too much activity makes it impossible to really enjoy anything very much.

Start out by having your child hold a table knife. Place five kernels of corn or beans on the knife's blade and ask him to balance them. No problem yet! Now ask the child to keep the knife in place and begin writing a note to someone with the other hand. Now ask the child to begin to tapping his foot while writing the note and balancing the corn. Next the child should start to sing a song.

You can add other activities until your child can't handle all of them at once. After you've both had a good laugh about this, talk through the connection of this activity to living a life that's too busy and unfocused.

CONVICTION BUILDING PLAN

Here are some questions to help you solidify convictions related to too much busyness.

Part One. Answer the following questions individually

1. How do you rate the level of busyness for each person in your family? List each name here, along with your evaluation on a scale of 1 to 10, with 1 being not busy at all and 10 being maxed out.

2. In what ways—positive and negative—are your activities affecting your family? List each major one and perhaps small ones too if there are a number of them.

3. On a 1 to 10 point scale with 1 being poor and 10 being excellent, how would you rate your relationship with each of your children? Ask your mate to give you a rating on these relationships too. Compare your analysis and discuss. Then ask your child to rate your relationship and discuss.

4. List the activities each of your children are involved in. Why do you want each child involved in certain activities?

5. Do you find yourself increasingly frustrated because it seems that you care more about an activity your child is involved in than he does? Does he often not want to go? Why? Is it possible your motives are off base?

6. Make a list of the qualities and talents you have observed in your preadolescent or teenager. Try to focus more on apti-

tudes than specifics—i.e., list "good hand-and-eye coordination" as opposed to "baseball." After making the list, ask yourself, "Am I giving this child enough opportunity to develop these skills in a good variety of situations—so that he can determine what he really wants to do?"

When our boys were around seven or eight, we poured concrete and mounted a basketball hoop next to our garage. We discovered, however, that our son Samuel spent more time hitting a tennis ball against the garage wall with an old racket of ours than he did shooting baskets. It became clear that although he enjoyed basketball, he really preferred tennis.

7. What *family* activities do you feel are essential to build the atmosphere you desire for your home? What type of weekly interaction do you think is critical for your family?

8. Do you have enough time each week to rest and to enjoy one another? Do you observe the Sabbath?

9. What changes do you think you should begin making to ensure that your family's schedule reflects your priorities?

Part Two. Conclusions

1. Discuss the preceding questions with your mate. If you are single, talk about them with a friend who can give you wise input.

2. Write one or two sentences that present your primary convictions about the place outside activities should have in your family.

3. How will your convictions help you make future decisions about your schedule and that of your children?

4. What decisions need to be made right now to begin living according to your priorities?

5. Pull out your calendars and begin making the necessary adjustments to your daily, weekly, and annual schedule.

16

Trap 11: The Tongue

Words Can Hurt or Heal

Wwhat would it be like to share your home with a lion, a cobra, a grizzly bear, and a grumpy pit bull who all suffer from persistent migraine headaches? And just to keep life from getting boring, your backyard pets are a buffalo and a wild boar affectionately called Sublime Swine.

Your pets are all tamed and trained, so they roam unrestrained throughout your home. Would you think of this as a place where you could relax totally and drift off to sleep at night without an anxious thought?

Believe it or not, there's a housing situation that's much worse. The beasts romp freely there too, but the ferocious creatures are neither tame nor trained. Although the greatest of animal trainers have tried to restrain them, these snarling monsters refuse to submit. Leashes and bridles are of no use—they are just tasty snacks to chew up.

In our home we know all about these wild and uncontrollable brutes. We've had as many as eight of them at once prowling through our house. And we must inform you, several of these untamable beasts are lurking in your home too. Don't let down your guard. Stay alert. The deadly tongues are running loose!

James, the brother of Jesus, wrote a description of these venomous vipers: "For every species of beasts and birds, of reptiles and creatures of the sea, is tamed, and has been tamed by the human race. But no one can tame the tongue; it is a restless evil and full of deadly poison" (3:7–8).

James also reported, "The tongue is a fire, the very world of iniquity; the tongue is set among our members as that which defiles the entire body, and sets on fire the course of our life, and is set on fire by hell . . . With it we bless our Lord and Father; and with it we curse men, who have been made in the likeness of God; from the same mouth come both blessing and cursing" (3:6, 9–10).

The Scriptures don't lie. We'll never tame the tongues we live with, ours included. But these wildest of beasts can be corralled and, over time and with diligent, persistent effort, trained to deliver blessing rather than poison.

The tongue is a wild beast in anyone, but it becomes an especially deadly trap for preadolescents and teenagers. The pressure to curse and to make sarcastic, critical comments is enormous, especially for junior high boys. Ask your child about the pressure to swear and to cut others down (called *cut-downs*), and he'll tell you "everyone does it."

Within the family, the tongue trap is dominant in two areas. The first is *disrespect to parents*. We may look back on our generation and see that as parents we gave our children far too much freedom to grumble and speak their mind. Have we as a culture overreacted against that old cliché, that children should be "seen and not heard"? We've swung too far in the opposite direction when we allow our teenagers to show disrespect at the expense of adults without being disciplined and corrected.

The second area in the family where the tongue is dominant is *sibling rivalry*. We wish we had a ten-dollar bill for every sibling skirmish we've seen in the Rainey household. Our children have verbally sparred over such life-changing issues as

- Who gets to sit in the front seat of the car.
- Who got the biggest slice of Mom's homemade apple pie.
- Who has had the most friends over to the house, or who had a friend over to spend the night at the house last.
- Who made the mess and who cleaned it up last.
- Who had permission to wear what: "She never asked to wear my blouse."
- Who got more freedom when he was growing up.

The good news is that a tongue trained and harnessed by the Holy Spirit becomes a powerful beast of blessing. A tamed tongue will sing praises and offer wisdom and encouragement. A trained tongue can comfort those who mourn and offer kindness to a stranger. With such a tongue we can confess Christ and offer words of love to a spouse, a child, a parent, a friend, even an enemy.

DETERMINING YOUR CONVICTIONS

My dad did not use foul language. On a couple of occasions, however, he did drop a word that was totally out of character for him; I remember being so shocked and surprised that it made an impact on me. And I don't ever recall hearing a disrespectful or cross word from Dad aimed at Mom. He was a model of keeping his tongue under control throughout his life, which included nearly forty-six years of marriage. As I grew older, I decided I wanted to give the same gift to my sons and daughters.

While seeking to control the rambunctious tongues on the loose in our home, here are some convictions that have been our guide:

Parents' Conviction 1: Since mutual respect is the foundation of all healthy relationships, how we relate as a couple and speak to our child is the best model of the pleasing use of the tongue.

If you hope to control the wild tongues in your family, first you must clean up your own speech. For example, how Dad speaks to Mom and vice versa—and how both speak to the children—must set the course. If the parents speak respectfully to one another, they can then expect their children to do the same.

Cursing is clearly wrong. But what about slang words that are right on the edge of gutter language? And what of other toxins of the tongue, like gossiping or criticizing people behind their backs? Do our preadolescents and teens hear us using unwholesome speech to describe our neighbors or coworkers? What comments do they hear us making regularly about the boss or the pastor or the governor? What do we say when somebody cuts us off in traffic or dumps trash on our yard? Do we obey God's commandment to honor our own parents (see Ex. 20:12) or do we grumble about the burden they've become?

The book of Proverbs is full of admonitions on the use of the tongue. Here are just two to keep in mind:

"The mouth of the righteous is a fountain of life, / But the mouth of the wicked conceals violence" (10:11).

"With his mouth the godless man destroys his neighbor, / But through knowledge the righteous will be delivered" (11:9).

Parents' Conviction 2: Because life and death are in the power of the tongue, our child's tongue must be trained to bring life.

As a couple you need to determine where you are going to draw the line on your adolescent's use of his tongue. What kind of tone do you want to set in your home? Will you allow a child to speak to another child disrespectfully without being penalized? Will you punish the cut-downs in your family? Will you have boundaries for inappropriate anger? If so, what will those boundaries be?

Will you and your spouse back each other and take the time to train your preteen and teen in the use of this wild beast?

As the author of Proverbs noted, the stakes are large: "Death and life are in the power of the tongue" (18:21).

SHAPING YOUR CHILD'S CONVICTIONS

A child needs to be trained to ask himself whether his words honor or dishonor God. And he needs to know he is accountable for every word that slips from his lips. We often pray out loud in our family that we will remember that God does hear everything we say: "The eyes of the LORD are in every place, / Watching the evil and the good" (Prov. 15:3).

Years ago I was with Benjamin (he was about eight) trout fishing in the Rockies. We were walking across a field on our way to a stream when Ben stumbled and used the Lord's name inappropriately. I stopped him and talked with him about how he should never use God's name in a hateful way or in a way that meant nothing, because that is what it means to take God's name in vain.

Teaching moments like that will help your child develop a proper awe, reverence, and fear of the Lord. Ecclesiastes 12:13–14 says, "Fear God and keep His commandments, because this applies to every person. For God will bring every act to judgment, everything which is hidden, whether it is good or evil."

What principles must your child learn so that the tongue is an instrument for building others up instead of cutting them down? Here are several convictions to consider.

Child's Conviction 1: I must understand how my words impact others—for good or for evil.

As repulsive as cursing may be, the other acidic mayhem caused by the tongue is just as bad. As preadolescents and teenagers develop more refined reasoning skills, their ability to put down and cut down others increases.

Dealing With Cut-Downs

Parents start facing this issue prior to adolescence, and it continues on into the teen years with a vengeance. (Is there any place on earth where more unkind things are said than in the typical junior high school?)

Cut-downs start with seemingly little harmless verbal jabs but often escalate quickly to hateful words crafted to tear the other person apart. The resulting feelings can lead to fights and terribly wounded relationships.

Although cursing may be more of a temptation for boys, girls seem to struggle with gossiping. They are more inclined to talk about one another—and it's easy to let those catty, critical remarks dominate conversations.

If you don't nip this type of talk in the bud, it will take up permanent residence at your house. A child must be taught that cutting others down in any way demeans people and is repulsive because every person is made in the image of God.

Genesis 1:26 tells us, "Then God said, 'Let Us make man in Our image, according to Our likeness.'" God doesn't make losers, nerds, or geeks. He creates people in His image, worthy of respect. At the center of every successful human relationship is respect— for your parent, your neighbor, your friend, your teacher, your spouse, your boss. We are to give people kindness, not derision.

We take cut-downs seriously in our household, and so we impose discipline to stop them. In some cases, we've taken away phone privileges or grounded a child. We know families who have used vinegar or a drop or two of Tabasco sauce on the tongue to teach a child that his words can sting others. Both are harmless when used sparingly and reinforce the point—words can hurt.

Our boys came home from their first couple of days at the junior high (after being home schooled for five years) with a bad case of the cut-downs. When I told them they would be disciplined for these verbal jabs, they responded by saying "No way! Everybody at school does it! We just can't help ourselves!"

They actually were beginning to convince us that they were victims of their circumstances. But we called their bluff and said that they could have one freebie, after that it was going to cost them five dollars per cut-down. Such an outcry went up from their ranks. But they never even used their one gratis cut-down. The habit evaporated.

For us, the bottom line is that we don't allow our children when angry to say certain hurtful things like "I hate you" or "I wish you'd never been born" or "I wish you weren't in our family." Those kinds of statements can inflict wounds of hurt that a sibling might take years to get over. Frankly, our children have said plenty of hurtful things to each other over the years, but this level of verbal vengeance was ruled off-limits long before they reached the teen years. On a couple of occasions children have screamed hate-filled words at one another, but not without severe discipline.

After you draw the line at what is unacceptable in your family, train your children in an acceptable substitute. For instance, instead of "I hate you," you may want to teach your preadolescent or teenager to say, "You make me so angry" or "I am so angry at you right now I could scream for an hour." Children are creative enough that they might enjoy the challenge of coming up with acceptable alternatives.

Child's Conviction 2: I must learn how to control my tongue so that my words bring life and blessing to others.

What's the nicest thing anyone ever said to you? How did those words make you feel? Mark Twain used to say that he could live for two months off a good compliment. That's the positive power of a Spirit-controlled tongue used to bless others.

For most of us, it takes years of training to shape the tongue into a reliable instrument of blessing. Young children have absolutely no clue as to how to speak appropriately. The young child's tongue is born wild and is prone to saying things in public like "Look, Mommy! That man is so fat!"

Demonstrate how to compliment and encourage others, and then train your child how to do the same. You might, for example, go around the dinner table and have everyone say one or two positive things about each person in your family.

This repetitive training to tame the tongue is exasperating and exhausting. Many parents, often in early adolescence, feel the task is hopeless, and they back off and quit correcting and training.

This starts a trend toward mediocre behavior instead of the pursuit of holiness.

Above all, help your child understand that as destructive as the tongue can be, it also has tremendous power for good. We all need to cultivate the art of encouraging and praising others. What a beautiful gift this will be throughout life.

Dealing with Sibling Rivalry

We are convinced that one reason sibling rivalry exists is so parents will adequately prepare their children for the lifelong relationships they'll forge in a marriage and family. You can use sibling relationships to teach them that they must learn to humble themselves, hear the truth, admit fault, ask for forgiveness, and restore a relationship.

At one point we were in such need of counsel that I spent a couple of hours quizzing some friends, Howard and Jeanne Hendricks, who had already raised and released their children. They understood our situation completely. They had so much sibling rivalry at their house when their children were at home that they wondered if their sons would grow up to hate one another. Yet today those same sons are the best of friends.

Their advice? *"Let them work it out on their own."* Ignore 90 percent of sibling rivalry. Don't always come to the rescue to solve their arguments. Get involved only when necessary for the purpose of training and character development.

This may surprise you—coming from two hands-on parents—but we've taken their advice to heart. We get involved only if one child's worth is under attack, the other child is yelling damaging words at the other, or if physical safety is at stake.

Often your children expect you to solve the problem by ruling in someone's favor, and they will do anything they can to manipulate you to their advantage. But if they are close enough in age that each child can hold his own and no one has an unfair advantage, tell them to work out the problem themselves.

Often we have taken the step of sending our teens to a room or out on a walk by themselves to resolve an issue. They hate that, because this means they have failed to get Mom or Dad emotionally involved or confused. In most of these sibling rivalry tiffs, it's so impossible to assign guilt that even Sherlock Holmes would be stumped.

If their differences are not resolved positively, then discipline both of them. Inflict pain on both warring parties, perhaps with an extra chore, such as washing the same window from opposite sides—this one guarantees to bring a smile and healing.

In one case we tied the legs of our boys together and made them clean the garage together. It's amazing how the common enemy of work can restore the joys of brotherhood!

Here are some other tips on dealing with sibling rivalry:

Clearly spell out the boundaries and limits. No hitting. No saying "I hate you." No bossing each other around. And no cutdowns. Establish and write down nonnegotiable penalties for stepping over the limit.

Have your teens memorize Romans 12:10, 17: "Be devoted to one another in brotherly love; give preference to one another in honor . . . Never pay back evil for evil to anyone. Respect what is right in the sight of all men."

Don't fuel their competitive spirit by comparing them with each other, by playing favorites, or by constantly putting them in situations where they have to compete against each other.

Pray for your children. Ask God to make them best friends. Pray that He will divinely engineer situations where they have to look out for each other; applaud them when they do.

When Benjamin was sixteen, on his own initiative and with our permission, he went at midnight one Friday night to pick up his sister at the pizza parlor where she worked. He wanted to protect her. The next day we praised him at breakfast.

Pray that God will convict them of how they are hurting each other. When Benjamin and Samuel were fourteen and twelve, they were wrestling and battling each other so often that one night they tore a door off its hinges. After we disciplined them and charged

262

them for the damage, we prayed one of those prayers of a helpless parent: "Lord, we feel like we are losing this battle with our boys. Will You do something to knit their hearts together?"

Within several days, Benjamin, the older and bigger of the two, asked to talk with us one morning before school. In the middle of the night, he had dreamed that his brother had been killed in a car wreck. He had awakened crying because he missed Samuel. He felt convicted that he was not really appreciating his brother (an understatement) and wanted to do a better job as a big brother.

Although this experience didn't cure the problem totally, it did temper some of the battling between them. It was another step in the process of our son's growing to maturity, and it was exciting for us parents to see God at work as He divinely orchestrated that circumstance.

It's almost miraculous how the siblings who can't stand each other when they're younger—if their differences are kept under control and if training occurs wisely—will someday, when they are older, become close friends. Don't lose hope. Have faith—it really does happen. If you value relationships, respect, and family members, your training will make a difference. Hang in there.

Child's Conviction 3: My words are a reflection of the condition of my heart.

Do you remember when it was considered impolite to use a curse word in public? Educated, polite people just didn't swear— especially in front of a woman. A couple of generations ago, Rhett Butler's use of a mild-these-days swear word in *Gone with the Wind* caused an uproar. Now four-letter words are commonplace in movies, television, and radio—and in our culture. That makes it even more difficult for your preteen or teen to refrain from such language.

But our youngsters must learn the consequences of filthy or foolish speech. Jesus said, "'For the mouth speaks out of that which fills the heart. The good man out of his good treasure brings forth what is good; and the evil man out of his evil treasure brings

263

forth what is evil. And I say to you, that every careless word that men shall speak, they shall render account for it in the day of judgment. For by your words you shall be justified, and by your words you shall be condemned'" (Matt. 12:34–37).

Dealing with Cursing

Beyond displeasing God, what else makes swearing so disgusting?

One idea you will want to share with your child is that quite a few curse words are related to sex or bodily functions. Take the time to explain this and impress on him that such language demeans the beauty of the sex act as well as the prize of God's creation—the human body.

Don't be shocked if your sons or daughters bring home some words that they've heard from friends. The words used may not be bad per se, but talking about throwing up and other bodily functions in a coarse way is not acceptable for conversation. Our boys have heard more than one version of a mini-sermon entitled "That's not how we talk in this family."

You may need to *help your child find substitute words to use at appropriate times.* The son of one of our staff members at FamilyLife attended a summer basketball camp where the talk was trashy. When he came home he was struggling because those words came to his mind, and it was hard not to say them. So his dad helped him invent some pseudo-expressions. Now when his son dribbles the ball off his foot out of bounds, he'll be heard saying, "Oh, stink!"

After you've drawn the line in the sand about cuss words you need to *have an appropriate penalty ready.*

For a number of years, I've been speaking at our FamilyLife Parenting Conferences and taking an informal poll. When speaking of penalties for cursing, I've asked the adults present what their parents did to tame the tongue. Invariably someone will say, "They washed my mouth out with soap." When I inquire as to the number of adults who were disciplined with Dial or Palmolive, about 30 to 40 percent of the hands go up.

We're not endorsing soap, but occasionally we wonder if parents aren't so afraid of damaging their child's mouth that they've lost sight of the far greater damage to his character and reputation?

Child's Conviction 4: The words I use show respect or disrespect for my parents and others.

I often tried to argue with my mother, and with my forceful personality it was easy for her to feel overwhelmed. On one occasion, I was so angry that I even took a swing at her.

It could have been much worse, however. The one thing I knew I could never get away with was speaking disrespectfully to my mother. I knew my dad would make me pay. Coupled with my love for my mom, that healthy fear was a strong dose of preventative medicine as I related to her.

It's especially important for dads to stand firm against teenage boys who try to use "tough guy talk" to intimidate their mothers. After years of looking up to his mom, a young teenager may suddenly realize he's now taller and heavier, and he may even think he's smarter. A few years ago I needed to step in strongly to admonish one of our sons who was not showing respect to Barbara. "You need to understand," I told him, "that you *will not win.* Because if I let you win in this deal, then you actually lose, because you will not have the character you need when you are an adult."

As important as respect is, *don't jump on every negative comment by your child.* Young people this age, trying out their enlarged ability to voice and hold more sophisticated opinions, will often say things that are foolish. They don't believe it either. You need to smile and let much of it go—as long as no real harm is done to any person.

Watch instead for the particularly acid-toned comments, as well as for a pattern. If your child is talking down to you or using a critical tone consistently, this wild tongue must be "trained."

One Sunday, not long after one of our sons received his driver's license at age sixteen, we were coming home from church and he was at the wheel. I said, "Son, you're driving too fast."

"No, I'm not—I'm driving okay," he answered smugly, in typical teenager fashion.

We rode farther down the road, then Barbara piped up: "You went around that last curve a little fast, didn't you?"

"Mom, I'm within the speed limit."

Technically that was probably true, but he still took a thirty-five-mile-an-hour curve faster than he should have with a car loaded with a large family.

Finally, we commented on his driving a third time. And he said arrogantly and angrily, "I am an experienced driver! Why are you on me like this?"

This little exchange not only bent truth and logic out of shape, but also was disrespectful. Because he had repeatedly shunned our observations about his driving, he was penalized. A two-week grounding from driving realigned his tongue, restored reason, and resulted in a sweeter tongue and more prudent driving approach.

It is good for you to decide in advance how you will deal with situations like this. If you have a plan, you will be better prepared to sidestep your own anger and not end up with a tongue problem of your own by spitting out some words you'll regret.

TESTING YOUR CHILD'S CONVICTIONS

Don't be bashful. I have asked our boys in particular, "How is your language at school? Are you cursing?" I would also ask a brother, "How's your brother's language at school? Is he cursing?" This helps build accountability.

As your teen gets older, sibling rivalry mutates into new forms. Keep stepping into your child's life and shaping his value of people and how his words affect others. You will be like a coach who is training and motivating a player to improve his game just one more notch. Put your arm around him and affirm him for what he is doing right, cheering him on to "love and good deeds" (Heb. 10:24).

Here are some ways to test a young tongue's progress:

Memorize Philippians 2:14–15 and repeat it at least three times a day to help combat grumbling: "Do all things without grumbling or disputing, that you may prove yourselves to be blameless and innocent, children of God above reproach."

We all have bad days, and sometimes as parents we just need to overlook negative comments. But if a grumpy, grumbling spirit persists within a child, it's time to apply the Scripture. We had our entire family memorize this passage one time. Then when any of us would start to moan and groan, someone would pipe up and say "How many things are we to do without grumbling?" *All* things!

Play the Decide in Advance game. Rehearse with your child how he will express himself when he

- Hits his thumb with a hammer.
- Is called a geek at school.
- Is told he is ugly or fat.
- Is told he's a wimp or a sissy.
- Sees his brother or sister do something dumb and is tempted to cut them down.
- A brother or sister cuts him down with "You're such a nerd!"

Reward good behavior / penalize bad behavior with the following exercise. Put a designated number of dollar bills (I usually start with ten) in a jar. Every time your children go to war and can't work it out by themselves, take a dollar out of the jar. Put a dollar into the jar when they go out of their way to be kind to one another or are able to work out a conflict. At the end of a designated time period—we usually go two weeks—the children get to split what is left in the jar. If their behavior is so bad that the money runs out, then dip into both young person's allowances.

Use special occasions to train how to use the tongue positively. Thanksgiving is a great opportunity for this. Ask each family member to write down five things he is thankful for, and encourage him to think about the others as he writes his list. Ask each person to share these aloud, then save the lists in a notebook for review the next Thanksgiving.

Or on a person's birthday, have each of the other family members share five things he appreciates about the person having the birthday. As he practices speaking positively to others, it will no longer feel so awkward to a teen.

CONCLUSION

Sometimes as a parent you will think there is never any light at the end of the tunnel. But our boys are living proof that two totally opposite siblings—who shared a room for eighteen years and fought over everything for well over ten years—can not only tame their tongues but also become the best of friends.

A year ago, Samuel stood up at a campus gathering of three hundred Christian students and began to praise his brother for his courage—Benjamin had decided to take a year out of college and go on a year-long mission trip to share Christ with college students in Estonia. Samuel publicly thanked his brother for his friendship, encouragement, and the life he had modeled. He began to weep as he shared how he loves him and how he was going to miss his brother.

We shook our heads in amazement when we heard that story, realizing our prayers over so many years were being answered.

UNFORGETTABLE LESSON: Encouraging Words

With your child, pick out a relative, neighbor, teacher— someone who you think needs some encouragement and will be appreciative—and work together to write a very nice note to that person. Make sure the note is prepared and signed by your child. Send the note through the mail and wait to see what happens. More than likely a positive response will come back. Use this to show how powerful a "good tongue" is in the life of another person. Point out how good the feelings are when we use our words to encourage and build up rather than to cut down.

And for those who want a special challenge, select a teacher, neighbor, or family member who has been particularly difficult to love. Write that person a sincere note of appreciation and encouragement. You may need to coach the younger teens on this one.

CONVICTION BUILDING PLAN

It won't be easy, but the following questions will shape or solidify your convictions on the words you use and how you use them.

Part One. Answer the following questions individually

1. How was the tongue controlled or not controlled in your home when your were growing up? How was anger expressed? How was your own use of your tongue influenced—even up until now?

2. Review in a detailed way a typical weekend in your home. List any specific moments where you may have habitually sinned with your tongue. Is the tongue more of a problem in your life and home than you may have realized? Discuss your model as a couple and talk about what needs to be a matter of prayer for each of you.

3. Evaluate both yourself and your spouse in the following areas:
    Cursing
    Using trashy words
    Showing disrespect
    Backbiting
    Outbursts of anger
    Criticism

Sarcasm
Pessimism
Gossip

4. Now evaluate your children in each of the same areas:
   Cursing
   Using trashy words
   Showing disrespect
   Backbiting
   Outbursts of anger
   Criticism
   Sarcasm
   Pessimism
   Gossip

5. Now think of what you and your spouse do *well.* What successes have you seen in taming your tongues? What good examples do you set for your children?

Part Two. Conclusions

1. Meet with your mate (or with a friend, if you're single) and discuss your answers to the previous questions.
2. What boundaries do you need to set in your home to tame the tongue?

   (Remember, if you don't draw boundaries around issues related to the tongue, then the ever persistent onslaught of the teenage years will slowly erode whatever standards you do have in place. Go out on a date with your child and begin the process of corralling this little wild beast.)

"And whatever you do in word or deed,
do all in the name of the Lord Jesus,
giving thanks through Him to God the Father."
—Colossians 3:17

17

Trap 12: Mediocrity

If It's Worth Doing, It's Worth Doing Right

If our children are to rise above mediocrity, they need at least one John Mulroy in their lives.

John Flanagan Jr., a retired brigadier general, will tell you that. Flanagan was a teenager when he met a teacher named John Mulroy, but it wasn't until years later in Vietnam that Flanagan fully reaped the fruit of Mulroy's wisdom on the critical importance of extra effort, of going beyond "just getting by."

In 1966 Flanagan flew a mission as a forward air controller for the U.S. Air Force. Alone in a small Cessna, skimming above the treetops, John was trying to confirm a sighting of two hundred to three hundred Vietcong troops. When he arrived at the reported coordinates, John saw no sign of the enemy. After scanning the ground carefully, he was about to end the search. He had done what was expected, an acceptable performance.

Then the memory of John Mulroy's gruff voice halted Flanagan in his tracks, as it had many times before.

While still a teenager attending Archbishop Stepinac High School in White Plains, New York, Flanagan had submitted what he thought was an acceptable class paper to a teacher named

Father John Mulroy. The paper came back with a *C* grade. When John had complained, teacher Mulroy pointed out a long list of deficiencies and said pointedly, "You only did enough to get by. When Christ asks us to go the second mile, he means making that extra effort in *everything.*"

This challenge, and many others from Mulroy, became a turning point for John Flanagan. Over time he became a battler, someone not satisfied with average or getting by. He overcame adversity to graduate from the Air Force Academy and become a pilot in Vietnam.

On this flight mission, once again challenged by the memory of Mulroy's urgings to go beyond mediocrity, Flanagan did not return to base. He used his radio to probe for information and soon discovered a series of mistakes made by another, inexperienced forward air controller.

John located the soldiers on the ground, and he also saw a squad of American gunships zooming in to blow them away. But Flanagan was bothered by what he saw below—something was terribly wrong. Risking gunfire from those beneath him, he dove near the troops on the ground for a closer look. They were not Vietcong, but rather South Vietnamese forces—friendlies!

John intercepted the gunships, blocking them from opening fire. A disaster was avoided, and John won a Distinguished Flying Cross, all because a teacher named John Mulroy long ago had taken a stand against mediocrity.[1]

Is it safe to assume that Father Mulroy was familiar with Colossians 3:17: "And whatever you do in word or deed, do all in the name of the Lord Jesus, giving thanks through Him to God the Father"?

We need to be excellent because we are representing Christ. Our children need to catch a vision for being His ambassador.

The trap of mediocrity snags teenagers today by luring them to become complacent and to settle for being average. The problem is that the average is slipping and spiraling downward—morally, academically, and vocationally.

Teachers could tell you story after story of intelligent teenagers who make little effort to excel in class. Coaches could tell you about athletes who have the potential to be great if only they would work at it.

Your child will find this trap set squarely in his path as he decides whether to study hard enough to make an *A* on the next exam, whether to do an excellent job mowing your lawn, or whether to practice shooting free throws for an extra half hour.

Sometimes our entire culture seems to promote mediocrity. Academically we are readjusting test scores downward to make our students look like they are doing better. They aren't.

Although we have urged each of our children to shoot for the best, all of them have struggled with settling for less. When Ashley was a senior in high school, she said to me (Barbara), "Your senior year is supposed to be fun—kind of a coast. You're not supposed to have to work as hard because you've arrived."

She became mad at me when I said I didn't quite agree with that philosophy. In fact, I made her take advanced classes that she didn't need for graduation, because I knew they would better prepare her for college.

Your child desperately needs someone to step forward and be the John Mulroy who challenges him to rise above mediocrity. Could we propose that you accept the nomination?

DETERMINING YOUR CONVICTIONS

Not long after we began our family we decided we would go away for a weekend and hammer out a statement of values that we wanted to embed in our children. Each of us wrote our top values individually, and then we discussed them as a couple. Although we agreed on the top two or three values, we differed greatly on the other two.

One for Barbara was teaching our children a "strong work ethic," something that didn't even make the radar screen on my list. But after some stimulating discussion around our differences, we embraced this value of a strong work ethic for our children. I'm convinced that our discussion and ultimate agreement has done wonders for training our children to stay out of this trap called mediocrity.

As you consider your own convictions in this area, here are two candidates:

Parents' Conviction 1: We need to model and teach a commitment to excellence.

The stabilizing force in my life was my family. They taught me the standard. Mom always did it right. Dad's character was always rock solid. Both had grown up in families that were rich in relationships and poor by the world's standard. But they both worked hard. At work. At home. And at play. Everything about their lives—from the school board elections and the Little League teams they coached to caring for elderly parents—rejected mediocrity and modeled a comitment to excellence. Barbara's parents modeled the same standard.

So when we began to discuss our standards for our children at home, school, work, and play, we both drew from a deep reservoir called family. Both of us grew up learning what Barbara's dad used to say, "If it's worth doing, it's worth doing right." We hope that our lives reflect that of our parents. We are certainly trying to pass on the challenge to excel to our children.

What are your convictions when it comes to maximizing your potential? Are you easily satisfied with the status quo? Does your child see you as a growing, developing, and hard-working person? Are you challenging him to work to his fullest, God-given potential? Are you being a John Mulroy to your son? Your daughter? Are you calling him or her away from a snare called mediocrity?

When it comes to desiring much more than mediocrity from our children, we need first to examine our own ideas, habits, and performance. Be sure to work through the Conviction Building Plan at the end of this chapter; it contains questions that will help clarify convictions on the trap of mediocrity.

Parents' Conviction 2: We believe God has given us the responsibility of developing children to their fullest potential.

Here's where I'm going to take the opportunity to brag on Barbara.

When our children are a little older they will recognize that she has been the driving force behind much that they accomplished during their time at home. At key points she refused to let them slide into the anonymity of the herd and be average.

She pressed them to be their best. She cheered them on when they struggled. She even home-schooled a preteen and teen to make sure they learned some basics before they had to face junior high. And she was always the one who prodded me to stay up late and help with those science fair projects.

With six children, she sure didn't feel that she was always succeeding. In fact, I can tell you that she continues to struggle with knowing just how much to push and when to back off.

Many times I have watched as she's called a child back to the kitchen to insist a job be redone well when it would have been easier just to finish the job herself. Helping her children reach their potential is a part of her calling as a mom.

Someday they'll rise up and bless her for it.

SHAPING YOUR CHILD'S CONVICTIONS

Before we look at specific convictions, we want to mention what we believe to be four root causes for mediocrity in preteens and adolescents:

1. *Low expectations.* No matter what the task or situation, set goals that stretch (not break) your child and insist on quality effort. Teach and reteach the principle of learning how to be faithful in little things so that he is qualified to be trusted with bigger things. (See Jesus' parable of the talents, Matt. 25:14–30).

Setting higher expectations is often viewed as odd these days.

275

You may have to encourage teachers, for example, to be tougher on deadlines and standards. Don't accept the status quo, which is often average or below average.

2. *Peer pressure.* A study done among 20,000 high school teens concluded that the "kids that kids hang out with have the greatest influence on an adolescent's classroom performance . . . The prevailing attitude among students is that 'getting by' is good enough. 'There is,' the study concludes, 'substantial pressure on students to underachieve.'"[2]

The study further noted, "'At least by high school, the influence of friends on school performance and drug use is more substantial than the influence of parents.' Parents should 'know your child's friends and steer children early in their development toward youngsters who value achievement and school.'"[3]

You will have to determine if your child's friends just want to get by or are more highly motivated. An *A* in math may not be cool with the peer group. If so, you have your work cut out for you.

3. *Ineffective rewards and/or motivation.* Luke 10:7 tells us, "The laborer is worthy of his wages." If your child does a good job, reward it generously. And reward progress away from mediocrity and toward excellence as well. Applaud achievement and quality effort in all areas of life, not just with grades and activities like sports. Life encompasses more than those two.

4. *Inadequate support from key individuals.* Of course you are the key person in making your child want to climb above mediocrity. Be a cheerleader, your child's number-one fan. No one ultimately can love and encourage like Mom and Dad! The world is full of discouraging situations. You need to counteract that.

At the same time, solicit help from others along the way—a teacher, coach, church youth worker. In 1960, when I was a sixth grader, I had a basketball coach who created a rally cry for our motley group of modestly talented players: "State Champs 1966!" No, we didn't ultimately win the championship, but that goal for our senior year spurred me on to do my best. And it contributed to me getting a basketball scholarship to college.

Also, never underestimate the power of an authority figure in your child's life to cause incredible damage. For every good one like John Mulroy, there could be three bad ones. If your child is in a potentially harmful environment, recruit a coach, teacher, or boss at work to help you step in to change the situation.

Following are two important convictions to shape in your child.

Child's Conviction 1: I work for an unseen Boss.

There is much imbalance in the Christian community when it comes to work: We are either driven by it or we suffer from poor work habits that result in mediocre performance. Our children need us to train them with a biblical approach to work.

We are not just working for men but for Jesus Christ. The apostle Paul wrote: "Whatever you do, do your work heartily, as for the Lord rather than for men; knowing that from the Lord you will receive the reward of the inheritance. It is the Lord Christ whom you serve" (Col. 3:23–24).

Our youth need to know that sliding along and getting by with as little as possible will not fool anybody indefinitely. More important, it will not fool God—the One who ultimately is going to determine if a person can be used responsibly for His purposes.

Child's Conviction 2: I need to strive for excellence in everything I do.

Of course when we talk of excellence, we do not mean attaining perfection or applying the same standards to every child. We *are* proposing that, within God-given capabilities, every child be challenged to rise above the crowd, seek higher standards of achievement, and be all that God has gifted him or her to be.

We believe that training a child to step above mediocrity also helps train him not to accept mediocrity in his relationship with God. Luke 16:10 tells us, "He who is faithful in a very little thing is faithful also in much; and he who is unrighteous in a very little thing is unrighteous also in much." A child must be trained to be trustworthy, to fulfill his commitments, to do a good job even when nobody is looking.

Several important topics fall under this conviction—chores, allowances, schoolwork, and jobs.

Chores

Our children have approached their simple household chores with all the enthusiasm normally expressed for a root canal. This is just another training opportunity for a parent, but you need to be consistent and persistent. Following are some guidelines.

Develop a reward/penalty system for chores that are done on time with excellence. A chore that our boys loved to hate when they were still living at home was hauling the trash every Monday to the end of the driveway. This was a significant task; we usually had six to ten cans, and our driveway is pretty long.

Benjamin and Samuel weren't getting the job done consistently, so we decided to make their responsibility a bit more clear. We assigned one boy per month to handle this chore, and if he didn't do it, money was taken from his monthly allowance.

And on top of that, if the cans were not back at the house by sunset on Monday night, a fine of fifty cents per can was assessed. That could involve some serious change—sometimes more than three dollars from an allowance that wasn't very large to begin with.

Once we instituted the fines system, the trash hauling improved rapidly, although we had to keep the penalty policy on the books for years in order to maintain the excellent service.

This penalty reflected our philosophy that a punishment must involve some pain. But prepare yourself for strong reactions. We've heard things from our children like "That's cheap" and "That's unfair." (They will try to make you feel a rung lower than Hitler.) Our response: "You're making the choice. It's your choice whether to comply or not to comply. Now obey."

Another key point to remember is, *Make sure your child knows how to do a job.* You must show him, step-by-step, what to do and what standards he should meet.

278

Inspect what he has done. We have accomplished most of this training in the kitchen.

I have actually made a joke of this when I take the Rainey brood to "Mr. Rogers Neighborhood." I begin speaking softly to them as though I am Mr. Rogers. They hate it.

"Okay now, boys and girls, we're now going to talk about what a clean kitchen looks like," I say. Sometimes, after my inspection, because a pot was not done or plates were lying around, they have to come back three or four times to the neighborhood to finish the task. What torture for any self-respecting teen.

Allowances

We have used allowances over the years to teach our teenagers principles about excellence in money management. When they were about four or five, we gave the children two or three dollars for the entire month, dividing the money and placing it in three envelopes labeled GIVING, SAVING, SPENDING. We gradually increased the amount during grade school until ultimately, by age fifteen or so, they were receiving up to fifty dollars per month for giving, saving, and buying their own clothing, toiletries, and other items.

Along the way they had learned how to do a general budget. It was interesting to watch our teenage boys spend their allowances on things like expensive athletic shoes and then complain that they had no toothpaste.

Some parents make the mistake of giving out such a large allowance that the child doesn't feel the need to work. He has all the money to buy what he needs; there's no incentive to earn extra cash. But this ultimately does not reflect the way the real world works. Each of our children has had to supplement their allowance with outside work.

Some convictions we've sought to teach our children around excellence in money management include:

- God owns it all.
- Giving is an essential part of a Christian's life.

279

- Debt and borrowing are dangerous; avoid them at all cost.
- How you use your money is a statement of your values.

Schoolwork

The issue of grades raises one of the toughest challenges for a parent. How high should you set expectations and how hard should you push without the risk of driving a child off the cliff? We have told all of our children that we anticipated that they would go to college and that getting into college requires good grades and taking tougher classes. At the same time, we have told them that doing an excellent job at school does not mean receiving all *A*'s. It *does* mean maintaining an excellent attitude and making a good effort.

There's no cookie-cutter answer to how hard to press on academic performance since every child is different. But here are some suggestions.

Start with your own heart. Are your motives right or do you want your child to achieve so that you'll win applause from others? Are you pushing so the child will win a scholarship and save you a ton on college expenses?

Academic issues dramatically underscore your need to *really know your child.* What motivates him? Which areas of curriculum are easy for him, and which pose challenges? Also, is he secure in your acceptance, or does he push himself to win your approval? Asking others who know your child—such as teachers, church youth workers, employers, and other parents—will help you determine if your expectations are unreasonable. Above all, pray for God's wisdom.

Consider incentives for grades. Average effort should not be rewarded (unless that's the best the child can do), but above average, superior work should be.

We've learned repeatedly that children are motivated differently. We chose to motivate our son Benjamin aggressively in the area of grades, because we knew he was capable. When he was still in the eighth grade, we challenged him to be the valedictorian of his high school class. And if he did it, we promised him a significant reward. We chose this approach because he was starting to slide on his schoolwork, settling for less. Sometime between eighth and ninth grade he began to take as his own the goal of being valedictorian.

Without this incentive, he probably would have ended up in the top 10 percent of his class; not bad, but beneath his potential. As it was, he ended up number two, salutatorian. He didn't kill himself to achieve this. He just used the talent God had given him and pursued a goal.

Depending on each one's ability, we have motivated our other children with short-term goals and rewards, from a trip, more freedom or money, to an inexpensive CD player. Every child wants something that will motivate him to excel.

Find out how your child learns and studies best. Study habits have been another tension point for us. Fortunately we interviewed Cynthia Tobias, author of *The Way They Learn*, on our daily radio program. She shared how each person has a different "learning style." When we applied these different styles to our children, it helped us understand why one child studies best on the floor with the radio on and why another does best in a quiet room at his desk. This relieved a lot of tension.

Jobs

Life requires work. Work is a lifetime commitment. No loving parent would intentionally deprive a child of the opportunity to learn how to work hard and well, and to understand the rewards that come from work.

Much of the on-the-job training for work needs to take place at home as children participate in simple chores and tasks. Ours started doing small things, like taking the silverware from the dishwasher, when they were just three years old. There comes a time, though, when it's very beneficial for your child to work for someone else. Avoid allowing a child to work too much, with little understanding of what it is doing to his private life and to family.

With appropriate parameters, part-time work can yield solid benefits:

- *A part-time job teaches a child how to work for another person.* As he learns to submit and work under other authority figures, some of them won't be nice, and your child will learn some character issues that God will honor throughout life; for example, how to submit and come under the authority of someone other than parents or teachers.
- *A part-time job teaches responsibility.* This is another character development issue. You really learn at this point how to please your boss and how to follow through on things expected of you.
- *A part-time job can bring exposure to the "real world" while a child is still at home.* As your child goes to work, he is going to bump into issues like possible unethical practices. You will have an opportunity to process issues like this with him.
- *A part-time job can teach your child about fulfilling commitment.* Many young people today have hard lessons ahead of them, because they have not endured some hard situations. I once had a conversation with one of our teenagers who had a job he didn't like. This particular child wanted to get out of his commitment to his employer.

  "Son, I want to encourage you to stick it out and to persevere," I told him. "You can't just quit if it gets a little tough." A stimulating conversation followed. And our son learned an important lesson of fulfilling his commitments even when he didn't feel like it.
- *A part-time job can help a child decide what he likes and doesn't like in work situations.* That really can assist in making college and career choices later.

If your child is about to enter the working world, here are a few suggestions:

Establish guidelines first. Before your child gets a job, establish some boundaries on the number of hours he may work (see our chapter on Busyness) and what he may do with his money.

Children who work and have an infusion of money at an early age when they have no rent to pay or other bills can acquire a warped, materialistic view of reality. Have him plan a budget, with some set aside for savings, giving, and regular needs.

Go with your child to check out the alternatives as he begins to look into part-time employment. Don't assume that a young person understands what to look for.

Some of our most memorable times have come when one of us has accompanied one of our children, usually around his fourteenth birthday, on his first job search. It's a great opportunity for you to give your child some pointers about job interviews and what to look for in a job. You may even get the chance to brag about your child to the employer and increase his chances of getting that best job.

After your child gets the job, talk with him about his first day at work and his first week. Urge him on to excellence by:

- Dressing appropriately for the job.
- Arriving at work ahead of time. (A friend of ours tells his children, "Good things happen to you when you are there ahead of time.")
- Become a student of what your employer expects of you; find out what's important to him and then doing that and more.
- Work hard, regardless of what everyone else does.
- Be honest; don't cheat, lie, or steal. Don't give in to pressure from a coworker or boss to act against your beliefs.

When you take the child to his first day of work, tell him, "You are representing Jesus Christ and our family. You aren't just working for this boss who is selling pizza or tennis shoes or chicken sandwiches. This is how you will combat the power of the flesh, peer pressure, and mediocrity—by being one of the finest workers your boss could possibly have."

Closely monitor the stress that is metered into your child's life because of a job. Make sure your child's employer is not taking advantage of him. Some employers overschedule young people because they earn minimum wage. The employer usually is not concerned with the teenager's grades or other life issues. This has been so important to us that we have driven our children nearly twenty-five minutes one way to a mall where they can work for an employer who cares for them and develops them as people.

Also, some places of employment that typically hire teenagers can become pretty vulgar and trashy. Monitor the moral environment of your child's workplace and use it as an opportunity to instruct him.

TESTING YOUR CHILD'S CONVICTIONS

Here are a few ideas that have worked for us.

Go by your child's place of work when he isn't there and ask his employer how he's doing as an employee. It may give you a chance later to affirm your son or daughter at home.

Use work related situations to teach your child to reject mediocrity and work as unto Jesus Christ. One of our teenagers had a job in sales and was so good at selling that he was earning ten to fifteen dollars an hour, which according to the manager's thinking was too much money. His salary structure was changed twice in a couple of months, and his commission was taken away. We watched as his incentive for selling slid.

We talked about the fairness of what had happened. He didn't quit, but he continued to work hard. This situation gave us an opportunity to teach our son about working as unto Jesus Christ. A hard but important lesson.

FOR THE SINGLE PARENT

Never forget that your model of hard work and commitment to your family will pay big dividends in your child. He will observe your standards and your commitment to excellence, drawing strength like water from a well.

I know of one woman, Marjorie Schulte, who alone raised six children through the turbulent teenage years by taking on a variety of jobs, including a paper route at 4:00 A.M. She was home in time to send her children off to school, and then she took in laundry and did odd jobs for families so that she could be there for her children when they arrived home after school. Today all six of her children are college graduates, including one from Yale. Her fierce commitment to excellence was caught by her children, who today are living lives that honor God.

CONCLUSION

Honestly, the young Raineys historically have not done very well with chores. We've often felt like failures as parents in this area, but they must have learned something along the way.

On the upside of the ledger, however, to a person, our children have been excellent workers outside of the home when they have become babysitters or taken their first jobs. Go figure! All we can conclude is that our perpetual training has somehow worked, even if we don't always see the results in our own home.

CONVICTION BUILDING PLAN

Your entire family will benefit from discussion and action on the topic of mediocrity. Use these questions to prompt your thinking.

Part One. Answer the following questions individually

1. What type of work ethic did your parents model for you? How well did you follow their example as a teenager?
2. How would you describe your work ethic now?
3. In what areas of your own life might you need to apply the

John Mulroy message—"When Christ asks us to go the second mile, he means making that extra effort in everything"?

4. Or are you the other extreme—are you driven to perform? Do you find that your self-worth comes from your achievement? Do you feel that you place too much emphasis on your child's performance?

5. In what areas have you seen your child tempted toward mediocrity?

6. Think through your convictions about some of the following issues:

Work

At what age can your child begin a part-time job?

What is the maximum amount of time you will allow him to work?

Will you allow him to work on Sundays?

Academics

What academic goals can you set for your child?

What will you consider unacceptable on a grade card for each child?

What limits will you set for phone calling or entertainment when there are homework assignments or a test the next day?

Chores

List different chores, set some standards, and think through penalties and rewards for meeting those standards.

Money

How much do you want your child to save and to give?

How much will your child be allowed to use for discretionary spending?

Will you allow your child to borrow from you or other family members to purchase an item?

Part Two. Conclusions

1. Meet with your mate (or a friend if you're single) and share your answers from the first section.
2. What are three to five steps you can take in the next month to begin teaching your child to reject mediocrity?

"Watch over your heart with all diligence,
For from it flow the springs of life."
—Proverbs 4:23

18

Trap 13: Pornography

Stop the Spread of Slime in Your Home

Pornography may be the most alluring trap of all for our teenagers. It certainly can be one of the most destructive.

Children are naturally curious anyway. But when they approach adolescence, and hormones begin streaking through their bodies, curiosity about the opposite sex soars.

Of course, curiosity is a natural, good thing—as are the normal feelings of excitement that accompany sexual awakening. But the trap of pornography can turn innocent inquisitiveness into an obsession with destructive, lifelong consequences.

Whenever programs about pornography are aired on *FamilyLife Today* radio, we receive an outpouring of heartbreaking letters from our listeners. Here's a sampling of the letters we received after our series "An Affair of the Mind," based on Laurie Hall's book of the same name:

I began by having *Playboy* magazines in my early twenties, then I moved on to adult videos, and finally went on-line to adult sites. The last eighteen months have been the worst because of the easy access I had to pornography on the

Internet. I would spend hours at a time to find pictures that would stimulate me. Just as with a drug addict, it took more and more pornography to satisfy my addiction. I began to push my wife away in many direct and indirect ways. I would delay going outside to play with my six-year-old son because I was on the Internet.

My dad had pornographic literature in the house that I found as a young girl. It distorted my view of male-female relationships. I began to see sex as a way to get love. I led an extremely active sexual lifestyle and eventually started working as an exotic dancer. I've been following the Lord for eleven years now, and am married to a wonderful man. But the ghost of pornography still haunts me. Fantasies still plague my mind and interfere with what should be pure love for my husband. I can see the connection now between how I feel and what you said. I am praying for God to cleanse me of the effects of pornography.[1]

This is a major trap for our youth. As parents we must do everything we can to protect our sons and daughters from the jaws of this provocative snare.

The All-American Boy

Pornography can tear apart a home, and it can tear apart a person's soul. And in some cases it leads to even worse consequences.

In the 1950s a boy named Ted grew up in what he described as a normal, loving, Christian home. When he was about twelve, Ted started looking at so-called soft-core pornography found in a local grocery store. And like many boys do, while exploring the alleys and trash piles in his neighborhood, he encountered more explicit pornography, which had been carelessly discarded.

Ted's casual interest in pornography over time turned into a compulsive addiction. And like any type of addict, he needed stronger doses of his drug to provide the same levels of excitement

289

and satisfaction. Ted moved gradually to harder and harder pornography until he was hooked on the worst, the most explicit, printed and film images of raw sexual violence.

To his family and friends Ted was just the all-American boy. He was intelligent, was an *A* student, became an Eagle Scout, went to college, eventually studied law. The desire for pornography was a hidden part of his life. He reached the point where merely seeing violent pornography no longer gave Ted the rush that he craved. For about two years he stood on the edge between fantasy and actually performing the violent scenes flashing through his mind.

One day he snapped—abducting, abusing, and murdering a young woman. Some months later he did it again. Then again . . . and again. By the time he was finally stopped, Ted Bundy admitted having killed more than two dozen women and girls.

Just hours before Ted Bundy was executed at a Florida prison in 1987, in an interview with Dr. James Dobson, Ted explained the role that pornography—and alcohol—had played in fueling and enabling his twisted passions. "Pornography can reach out and snatch a kid out of any house today. It snatched me out of my house twenty to thirty years ago . . . The most damaging kinds of pornography are those that involve violence and sexual violence. The wedding of those two forces brings about behavior too terrible to describe."[2]

Is this just an isolated case? The particularly cataclysmic outcome may be, but police investigators will tell you they are never surprised to find pornography in the home of a sex offender. And who can estimate the number of lives, marriages, and families that are rocked and wrecked each day by this pornographic sewage that seeps throughout our society?

Don't Wait

At what age should you talk to your child about pornography? How should you go about discussing such a disgusting topic, one the child may not have even considered? What should be shared when a child seems so young and innocent?

Like it or not, you must answer these questions and take action when your child is still young. Our children will be exposed to pornography—in a garbage can, on the Internet, from friends, on the newsstand. During elementary school, boys in particular are often first exposed to pornography.

Of particular concern to parents these days is the widespread availability of pornography through the Internet. Just one World Wide Web site that offers pornographic materials reported receiving nearly 1.5 million visits, or hits, a day.[3] By way of comparison, our Web site at FamilyLife considers it a good day when we receive 2,000–3,000 hits.

You need to help your child understand the danger of the pornography trap, but at the same time not do a disservice to God and His truth by making sex seem dirty. This is a challenge.

DETERMINING YOUR CONVICTIONS

Throughout this chapter we will offer many ideas on how to discover and disarm the pornography traps that await your child. But the ultimate and best action we can take against pornography is to keep our own eyes and hearts clean. Ultimately, you are the door of much that comes in your home. Will you be a door that lets in light or darkness?

Parents' Conviction 1: Pornography is a lie. While offering a fulfillment of fantasy, it actually perverts something beautiful created by God.

Imagine being extremely thirsty. You've been lost in the wilderness without water for days. You are wobbly. Your tongue is swollen. You are delirious.

You stumble over the crest of a hill and below you is the sight you have desperately sought. Water!

Drawing on every remaining bit of strength, you hurl yourself down the slope. At the bottom you are surprised to find two small pools. In one the water is green—a thick crust of slime covers the surface. A rotten odor rises to your nostrils.

Not far away is a second pool. The water is clear, and a small, but vigorous stream flows in one end and out the other. No odor there; the pond smells fresh.

Where would you go for a drink?

Sounds simple, right? But when it comes to the topic of sex, our society seems intent on steering us to the polluted pool.

As we described in Chapters 6 and 7, God made sex. It's good. He designed it as the ultimate means of drawing two people together in the marriage relationship. That's the good, pure water.

But nonstop, twenty-four hours a day, every day, every year, through much of what we are served in the media, we are asked to believe that the water in the polluted pond is what's really going to satisfy our thirst.

This is a lie. Pornography twists and perverts the beauty of God's creation. It leads men and women to look at each other as nothing more than sex objects. It causes them to fantasize about sexual relationships with other people. The focus on sensual pleasure becomes a drug that blots out the rest of their lives.

Parents' Conviction 2: We will model integrity before our children by turning away from any form of evil that would pollute our lives and family.

If you want your child to resist the lure of pornography, your first step will be to ponder your own habits. What do you allow to enter through your eyes to find rest in your mind and heart?

Obviously, you need to stay far away from any type of hardcore pornography. But don't stop there. One mistake many parents make is thinking that pornography is just the horrible, crude, sickening material found at the adult bookstore. Increasingly, you will find images in mainstream magazines, television shows, and movies that are not as crude but still sell the same lie that the real water is found in the rancid pond. In fact, our society has become so hardened from the onslaught of sex that we accept as normal what would have been considered pornographic twenty to thirty years ago.

What message is sent to a curious, sexually awakening boy who watches his father leafing through the *Sports Illustrated* annual swimsuit issue? What about the mom who gazes rapturously at the bare-chested movie star hunk appearing on the cover of the latest *People* magazine? These may seem relatively innocent compared to hard-core pornography. But what kind of water is it?

King David, who struggled with controlling his eyes and thought life, offers this insight: "I will walk within my house in the integrity of my heart. / I will set no worthless thing before my eyes; . . . A perverse heart shall depart from me; / I will know no evil" (Ps. 101:2–4).

That verse is printed on a sheet of paper and taped at the top of our television.

Parents' Conviction 3: We will remain prayerfully alert for how this issue may affect our child.

Even though you may do a good job of controlling access of your child to the Internet through your home computer, you must be alert to what other children may be viewing or even through Internet access at school.

Beyond the destructive effects of just looking at pornography on the Internet, lurks the chilling danger of a child being recruited into sexual activity by a pedophile or other sexual deviant. Often these perverse stalkings begin innocently through online chat room discussions. In the Denver area, for example, a sixteen-year-old girl met a man through an Internet bulletin board. Later he persuaded her to pose for a sexually suggestive photo in a park. The man was arrested on suspicion of sexual exploitation of a child.[4]

Our advice: Don't assume that just because your child hasn't had a problem, he doesn't now or won't in the future.

SHAPING YOUR CHILD'S CONVICTIONS

Developing your child's convictions about pornography will take many different forms. We've gone to junior high and high school to talk to teachers who have asked our sons to read what would be rated R in movies. We've sought to expose pornography's lies by talking about its impact on men like Ted Bundy. And we've taken our sons and daughters with us when we've gone to movie theaters to talk to theater managers and protest an NC-17 (formerly X-rated) movie that came to our community.

All of these actions and more can shape your child's convictions and keep him out of the traps.

Child's Conviction 1: I understand that pornography is sin and can destroy my life and my future marriage and family.

You may wonder how much detail to share about pornography with a child without drifting toward prurience.

A great guideline is to look at Scripture and see how the Lord warns us about certain things. He certainly doesn't tell the whole story to provoke our carnality and flesh to sin. For example, in Proverbs we read this description of a woman to avoid: "For the lips of an adulteress drip honey, / And smoother than oil is her speech" (5:3). That is not an explicit description of a prostitute propositioning someone, but it gets the point across.

When talking to a preteen or teen about pornography, you can explain that many people today look at pictures of naked women and men performing sexual activity, but none of this is pleasing to God. Pornography takes something that is beautiful when it occurs between a married man and woman and makes it dirty. At younger ages, say up to about twelve, your child needs only to know that pornography isn't good for him. He certainly doesn't need details that would attract him.

Talk to your child about the importance of keeping his life pure by guarding what enters through the eyes. Jesus said, "The lamp of the body is the eye; if therefore your eye is clear, your whole body will be full of light. But if your eye is bad, your whole body will be full of darkness" (Matt. 6:22–23).

As your child grows older, begin pointing out some of the sexual images you see in the media, in commercials, in magazine advertisements, etc. Here are a few things you could talk about:

- Explain that pornography is any type of media—words, photographs, movies, music—that stimulates sexual excitement. (If you don't care for our definition, create your own; you'll find it challenging to define clearly.) The beauty and the allure of the human body does stimulate such excitement; this excitement is appropriate and good within the marriage relationship, as God intended. Pornography ruins relationships and can lead to destructive compulsions or even addictions. (You might want to share some of the stories at the beginning of this chapter.)
- Without being overly explicit, explain that there are so-called gradations of pornography. Each step is dangerous. What may be harmless looking may be the first step down a slippery slope toward the polluted water. Warn your child of the danger of bringing impure images into his mind and heart. Pornography by its very nature is so addictive, so powerful, that even a casual, innocent encounter can trigger the desire to see more.
- Explain where hard-core pornography is likely to be found—and how to stay away. Explain as well what to do if your child stumbles across a pornographic book, magazine, or Web site.

Is Pornography a Problem for Girls?

Males, who are generally more stimulated by sight than females, will always be the main consumers of pornography. But in our sex-saturated culture, pornography is becoming a problem for females as well.

FamilyLife received a message from a man who had been married for many years before he found out that his wife was addicted to suggestive literature and a harmful, compulsive sexual behavior.

This problem isn't discussed much in the Christian community, because women trapped in pornography see this as such a shameful sin for a woman.

Since girls are sexually influenced more through their emotions than by visual stimuli, a gate opener for a future problem with pornography may be a girl's exposure to romance novels and the fantasy orientation of most TV soap operas and many movies.

When Ashley was in junior high, I (Barbara) bought her some Christian novels because they contained historical information. Ashley became more and more interested in reading these books. Looking through the novels, I discovered that the plot was centered around a romantic relationship.

I finally had to talk to Ashley about reading some of these books. They were making her think too much about "being in love" and having a guy pay her special attention. She was too young to be preoccupied with romance; it just wasn't healthy for her. When you're trying to keep a daughter from early dating and being too focused on guys, there is enough to combat in the culture without dealing with the Christian version of the same thing.

Of course this type of Christian literature would not be considered pornography. But some Christian novels can stir up romantic or even sexual emotions.

A good verse to share with your daughter on this issue is Proverbs 4:23: "Watch over your heart with all diligence, / For from it flow the springs of life." As parents we are commissioned by God to protect these young hearts by helping them develop their own convictions about what they will listen to, read, and watch.

Child's Conviction 2: I will be accountable to my parents for how I entertain myself—what I read, view, and listen to.

Don't assume your sons or daughters are free from the trap of pornography. We know good Christian families who have been blown away by a child's involvement in this snare. Aggressively monitor your child's entertainment habits by asking hard questions:

"Have you been looking at or reading anything at school that you ought not to be looking at?"

"When you're on the computer, are you surfing where you ought not to be surfing?"

"How are you doing in your thought life? Are you steering clear of feeding your sexual thoughts?"

As your child grows up and enters puberty, you will need to discuss this trap on a number of occasions—if for no other reason than accountability. As your child transitions into adulthood, it's healthy for him to know that you are going to ask him these types of questions. The pornography temptation will take on new meaning as the child develops sexually and has the opportunity to be more independent.

If your family computer is linked to the Internet, *make sure the computer is in a high-use room of your home*—perhaps the family room or kitchen. This will allow you to monitor what your child does. Also, *purchase software that screens and blocks pornographic sites.* (See Appendix B for details.)

But continue to be on guard. An article in *U.S. News & World Report* said this about screening software: "Censorship programs won't slow down a precocious teen who has just been handed a smutty new Internet address, nor can they sniff out e-mail with a naughty picture attached."[5] As we were writing this book, an advertisement for a Russian sex Web site mysteriously appeared in our e-mail on our home computer; like junk mail, solicitation by such sites can occur on a random basis.

What If You Find Pornography?

Don't be like one mother who found some pornographic literature when she was cleaning her boy's room and did nothing. She later said with a sigh to a friend, "Boys will be boys."

First, ask God for wisdom in how to handle this volatile subject. Most likely, you will find that your child will react with tremendous shame when confronted with your discovery. Ask God to enable you to express His grace and forgiveness to your child (see Eph. 2:8–9).

If your child is not present when you find the material, show it to your spouse. Talk about who should be the one to talk with the child. Then lay out a game plan that gives your child a chance to tell the truth before you show him what you've found. Pray that God will guide you and grant you the ability to speak heart-to-heart with your teen.

If you find the material when your child is present, then you need to begin dealing with it right on the spot. If your spouse is at home, do this together. Sit down and talk to your child and ask him where he got the pornography and why he is looking at it. Then review with him why this is wrong and inappropriate for him.

Also point out to him the dangers in pornography. Some people are as prone to a compulsive need for pornography as others are to alcohol or drugs.

Tell him you are going to ask him to be more accountable to you than he has been in the past. Continue to ask him hard questions on a regular basis. If your child has a room to himself, consider taking the door off the hinges if needed to eliminate the child's opportunity to shut you out and hide in his room.

TESTING YOUR CHILD'S CONVICTIONS

One night I was in the kitchen making small talk with one of my sons when he was in junior high. For some reason I looked him in the eye and asked, "Have you recently been looking at anything that you should not be looking at—pornography or anything like that at school?"

He looked up at me with a stunned look that said, *How do parents know these things?*

"Well, as a matter of fact," he said, "guess what happened at school today? I got my sandwich and my sack lunch out and was sitting at the back of the room. The rest of the guys were up front by the teacher's desk, and they had a pornographic magazine out and were flipping through it and reading it. One of them yelled at me and said, "'Hey, come on up and look at this.'"

298

At that point I moved closer to my son and said, "Well, what did you do?"

"I put my sandwich in my sack, said no thanks, and walked out the door."

It was time for a pep rally, a standing ovation. "Way to go!" I said. "Do you realize what you did? You were courageous in the midst of peer pressure." I slapped him on the back and gave him a big hug and kiss. It was like he had scored a touchdown at a major championship game.

Questions like the one I asked are a great way to test your child's convictions on pornography. I fear that some parents are afraid to ask because they are afraid of what they will find out. Stay involved by asking.

Following are a few other ways to test convictions.

Play the Decide in Advance game. Create the following role-play situations to teach your child how to respond in the following types of situations:

- Your son finds a pornographic magazine in the trash at a neighbor's house.
- Your daughter's friends are all reading a popular novel that would be rated R if it was a movie. They are all pressuring her to read it.
- A friend of your son takes him to a hideout in the woods (or to his dad's closet when no adults are around) and shows him a stack of porn magazines.
- While using the computer, your child stumbles into a Web site with nude pictures of women and men.
- Your child is communicating with someone in an Internet chat room and someone begins initiating sexually explicit discussions.
- Someone on the Internet asks your child to meet him after school is out.
- At a friend's house your son finds himself in front of a video screen playing a computer game that is sexual in nature. Or

the friend pops an X-rated video in the VCR that came from his father's cache hidden in the closet upstairs.

Keep your eyes open. Discreetly patrol your child's room. If you become suspicious that the child might be hiding pornography, do some serious looking. If you fear that your child has been looking at sexually explicit Web sites, learn how you can search his computer and find out.

Observe how your child looks at the opposite sex. Is the gaze too long and lustful?

Ask him what his convictions are on issues, like R-rated movies, that he'll face as he leaves home. Help him think through what he's going to do when he's on his own and the pressure to conform and go with the flow is powerful.

Discuss the meaning of these verses in Ecclesiastes with your child: "Fear God and keep His commandments, because this applies to every person. For God will bring every act to judgment, everything which is hidden, whether it is good or evil" (12:13–14). Ask, "Is anything we do or think hidden from God?"

Take opportunities on a day-to-day basis to point out how sex is used pornographically in the media to sell products and create inappropriate sexual excitement. Use questions to help your child critique advertisements. Help him to develop his own judgment in seeing what is really being communicated.

If you are concerned that an older child (perhaps thirteen or older) is messing around with pornography, obtain a copy of Dr. James Dobson's videotaped interview with Ted Bundy. As this convicted mass murderer tells of his own slide into an addiction to pornography, the impact is very compelling.

FOR THE SINGLE PARENT

What if you're a single mom with a young son? Should you talk to him about pornography? By all means, yes.

This is another situation where love must take action. Use some good resources; learn as much as you can. Because you love your son, plow ahead and trust that God will assist your efforts.

Ideally, if you and the child's father see eye to eye on this topic, you may be able to present similar content on pornography independently to your son.

If the father does not agree or is uninvolved—or worse, is using pornography himself—what then?

Talk openly to your ex-husband about the dangers and your concern for your son. If he is unresponsive, you can do nothing to change that. But you can impact your son. Share material explaining the effects of pornography with him. Talk about it as long as he will listen, and even sometimes when he won't.

God knows the circumstances and will orchestrate the outcome. You just be faithful in doing your job to warn your son of the dangers of pornography. Lay out the boundaries in your home and encourage your son to resist the temptations, even if his own father presents them.

If your ex-husband is not supportive, consider prayerfully enlisting a male ally, perhaps a man at your church, who could assist in educating and protecting your son.

If you catch your son with pornography, and he's a member of your church's youth group, consider pulling together an intervention group led by your son's youth leader and a couple of other adult men he really respects. As best you can, make sure these men are walking with God and are morally clean themselves. Have them intervene and plead with him, explaining what might happen if he continues to consume this deadly poison.

And of course, never stop praying and asking others to pray too.

CONCLUSION

It was a cool fall morning, but I was getting hotter by the moment. I was reading a newspaper article about *Showgirls*, Hollywood's latest ploy to further lower the standards of decency in our communities. The NC-17 movie was clearly a test by film producers and executives to see what they could get away with.

As I read about the nudity and a brutal rape scene, and then how someone affiliated with the movie was encouraging young teens to obtain fake IDs so they could sneak in, I became further outraged. I had planned on an outing of miniature golf with my three youngest daughters, so we took a minor detour to the local theater where *Showgirls* was playing.

During my ten-minute conversation with the theater manager, I pointed to my daughters and asked, "Would you want your daughters or granddaughters sitting in that theater with a boy and watching that movie?" He had no answer. You could see the shame on his face.

But when he stated that I was the first person in town to protest the movie, I began feeling shame—on behalf of the Christian community I represented. In fact, when I later began calling film and theater executives to protest the film, I learned that during the first week of showings they had received only a handful of protest calls across the nation.

It's easy to feel powerless and to wish someone would protect your community. But there *is* something you can do. When you're confronted with immorality and indecency in your community, don't sit passively and wring your hands about how bad things are.

Stand up. Speak out. Even if the merchants of cultural garbage won't listen, your children will learn from your example. You will help sow the seeds for the family reformation our country so desperately needs.

UNFORGETTABLE LESSON: Tarnished T-Shirt

Take an old T-shirt and cut out a section that is the size of a sheet of paper. Explain to your child that this cloth now represents his conscience. Discuss how white and pure this conscience is and how pure your child wants to keep it.

Now pull out a quart jar that has water that has been colored with food coloring—black (to represent the stain of sin) would be best, but any color will work. Take the corner of the cloth and dip about an inch of the material into the black water, but pull it out quickly. Talk about how that corner is now permanently stained. Discuss how this is what happens when we even take a little bit of sin—in this case, pornography—into our lives. The amount may be small, but the effect is permanent in the mind and heart.

Now take the cloth and dip a couple of inches into the jar, leaving it overnight. The material should soak up the dye and stain even more than just two inches. Talk about the progressive nature of sin and how it permeates our entire lives.

Now dip the entire cloth into the jar. Discuss that this material is now permanently stained.

Conclude by reading Proverbs 4:23 and discuss what it means to guard your heart from pornography.

CONVICTION BUILDING PLAN

Use the following questions to prayerfully hammer out your convictions on pornography and to shape convictions in your child.

Part One. Answer the following questions individually

1. What has been your attitude toward pornography in the past? Did you view much?
2. Are you clean now? Do you have any magazines or videos stashed somewhere that need to be destroyed? Are you visiting Web sites or reading books or magazines that are inappropriate?
3. What is your attitude about messages from advertising and other media that may influence sexual relations with your spouse?

4. What is your response to this idea: "As a parent, I will choose
   not to look at or hear anything that I would not be willing to
   have my twelve-year-old child look at or hear."
5. Study Ecclesiastes 12:13–14 and Psalm 101 to help clarify
   your own standards on what you will choose to look at and
   what you will allow in your home. Where do you draw the
   line in terms of media and literature?

Part Two. Conclusions

1. Meet with your mate (or friend if single) to share your
   answers to the questions you answered individually.
2. Summarize your conclusions on personal standards related
   to pornography.
3. Discuss how you will share your standards with your child
   and how you will make him accountable to you.

19

Trap 14: False Gods

Learning to Cling to the True God

Basketball was like a god to a girl whom we'll call Karen.

Since grade school she had lived only for her sport, and she had been rewarded. In the early 1990s, Karen was rated the top player in her state in her junior and senior years in high school, and she played in two state championship games—one time a winner. Some thought she was the best women's player ever to come from her state.

Then she was off to a major university with a full-ride scholarship. Karen became a four-year starter who helped win conference championships. Karen's last game as a collegian was in the NCAA women's basketball tournament.

A professional team drafted her and offered a superb salary for a rookie. How many young Americans today (and their parents) would give almost anything to live out this dream?

Over the years, basketball had become Karen's god. But after all she sacrificed, with her goals achieved, suddenly she felt empty and purposeless. At a time when she should have felt on top of the world, Karen fell into a deep funk she could not shake.

Months passed without a workout. Karen gorged herself on junk food, and her weight ballooned. The date to report to her pro team passed. After months of lethargy, one afternoon she summoned enough strength to pick up a basketball and take a few shots in the driveway. Only minutes later, discouraged with her performance, she put the ball away for good.[1]

Karen's story illustrates so well the result of focusing your entire life on something which, in the end, does not satisfy. Chasing after any false god never satisfies our soul. On the surface the substitution looks good and offers some of the experiences associated with worship of the true God. But in the end, these frail idols never satisfy us. The truth of God's word cannot be denied: "You shall have no other gods before Me" (Ex. 20:3).

What are some of the false gods our children struggle with? We've identified the top seven. No doubt that list could be much longer.

1. Self. This has to be number one. Everyone struggles with selfishness, but teens often act like the world revolves around them. Our culture feeds the natural urge toward the big ME, and the hybrid youth culture encourages it even more through music, movies, television, magazines, and the Internet.

In fact, this god of selfishness contributes the most to the undesirable behavior we see in teenagers. Don't get us wrong; we love teens, but occasionally their selfish attitudes can irritate even the most patient person. Selfishness had to be at the core of what Mark Twain meant when he quipped about teenagers: "When a child turns thirteen, put him in a barrel and nail the lid on the top. Feed him through the knothole in the barrel. When he turns sixteen, plug up the knothole!"

2. Popularity. Everyone wants to be liked and to be part of a cool group. The desire to belong is what makes peer pressure such a potent force. There is phenomenal pressure to be a people pleaser. Popularity can be a god for our teens if they are troubled or lonely or feeling unloved at home. The emotional deficit can fuel a tremendous drive to seek to be popular at all costs.

3. Success/achievement. In the preadolescent and teen years, success is often measured by achievement in sports or other activities, as well as in grades. Youngsters are looking for approval, acceptance, adoration, and acclaim from their friends and parents, and they can get sucked into making success a god.

4. Approval from the opposite sex. This is a powerful one. During adolescence young men and women long to be affirmed as desirable by the opposite sex. The hunger to be loved can quickly become a false god, especially if they aren't being loved and affirmed at home.

5. Appearance. Young girls, especially, may succumb to this one, although boys certainly want to look good too. Of course this is linked to wanting attention from the opposite sex, and it can be viewed as more important than it is.

6. Entertainment. We live in an entertainment culture that offers us countless ways to stimulate our minds. Our teens are growing up with more options for entertainment than any generation in history, and it's easy for them to be numbed by it.

7. Consumption. Propelled by incessant advertising, our culture worships eagerly at the altar of materialism in great cathedrals we call malls. Whether it is the latest hot CD, Air Jordan shoes, Gap jeans, or eventually a cool car, our children can be snared by their own greed.

We discussed many of these false deities earlier in this book. But with this chapter, we want to conclude the section on traps with the number-one thing you can do to help your child through the teenage years and into adulthood: *Help him establish and develop a relationship with the one true God.*

We've surveyed hundreds of parents at our FamilyLife Marriage Conferences on numerous issues, and the number-one need of parents is learning how to effectively train a child to walk with God. Eventually your child will live on his own, and more than anything he needs a vital relationship with Christ.

In order for your child to embrace his God-given identity, he needs to understand who God is and how God gives us an identity. Here are some key concepts to share:

- God alone is Lord—there is no other.
- God is eternal.
- God is sovereign and has absolute authority.
- God has personality—mind, emotions, and will.
- God is love—He is always relating to man and made man to relate to Him and others.
- God created us in His image—we are made to reflect God's love to others.
- God loves us—each of us is a person of value.

DETERMINING YOUR CONVICTIONS

In too many Christian families, children pick up the wrong message about what's really important in life. By our words and our deeds, are we inadvertently saying that what really counts is a college degree, a good job, a nice family, plentiful things?

Looking back at over a decade of raising six teenagers, we've seen that false gods have proven to be formidable foes, and we're not finished yet. Without a doubt the most important thing we have done is to stay out of the snares ourselves. The battle begins every day when we decide to set Christ apart as Savior and Lord of our lives and to worship the one true living God. Steadily over time as your preadolescent or teenager observes your walk with God and shares this walk with you, he can learn to claim such devotion on his own.

We have assumed as parents that God gave us children so that we could help them grow up. But perhaps He gave us children so that we would finish the process of growing up ourselves? God is shaping you into a model for your children; that's why your convictions are so important.

There are many things we've tried to do in training our children to know, experience, and serve the one true God, but nothing is more important than modeling the following six convictions.

Parents' Conviction 1: Jesus Christ must be our Savior and Lord.

We have chosen to make Christ Lord and Savior of our lives. In our safety-deposit box are the two most important papers we possess. Dated December 17, 1972, both sheets are titled "Contract and Title Deed to My Life."

During our first Christmas together as husband and wife, we wrote that document as a declaration of our desire to give God everything we had and would ever hope to have. Those two sheets of paper serve as a reminder of a solemn covenant to keep as long as we both have breath.

Many are afraid to sign a covenant like that because they think they would have to give up everything. My friend, that is true. Becoming a disciple of Christ means denying your life. But what He gives back—in terms of real life, friendships, peace, and purpose—far outweighs anything you will lose.

Parents' Conviction 2: Regular prayer must be a crucial part of our daily lives.

We pray as a couple every day we are together. Since October 1972 we have ended each day in prayer. That one spiritual discipline has not only kept the walls down between us, but it has built walls of protection around our marriage and our family.

Parents' Conviction 3: We must be the same people in private that we are in public.

We abhor hypocrisy. We aren't perfect, and when we make mistakes and sin, we humble ourselves and ask for forgiveness from our children. Psalm 101:6 says that the one who ministers to another is a person who walks in a blameless way.

Parents' Conviction 4: The Scriptures are God's Word and serve as a daily guide.

We believe the Bible. We read it, make decisions by it, consult it, live by it. And we call our children to it continuously. Again, we don't do it perfectly, but we try to let the Scriptures guide us in our interpersonal relationships, attitude, and perspective of life.

Parents' Conviction 5: Nothing is more thrilling than fulfilling God's mission for your life.

We believe in a divine assignment. Ephesians 2:10 says, "We are His workmanship, created in Christ Jesus for good works, which God prepared beforehand, that we should walk in them." God has a plan for every life, every couple, and every family. We don't believe we are just another family in the six billion human herd, but a family chosen by God and being used by God for a unique purpose and destiny.

We think that one reason our Christian youth today are not making a greater impact is that too many of their parents aren't having an impact for Christ on our world. Again, we are models for our teens. Every Christian needs to possess a spiritual purpose and a mission that transcends and lifts him out of the ruts of life. It's difficult to challenge your teen to be and do something that you aren't courageously pursuing as an adult.

Parents' Conviction 6: We will pass on a godly legacy to the next generation.

We want to pass on to our children not only the knowledge of who God is and the experience of Him in everyday life, but also what it means to trust Him and obey Him (see Ps. 78:5–8). We want each of our children to follow and serve Christ all their lives, so that succeeding generations may know the truth about Him.

SHAPING YOUR CHILD'S CONVICTIONS

In the sixth-grade Sunday school class, we would choose a class verse and asked everyone to memorize it. I would pay one dollar to anyone called on during the class who could recite it perfectly, word for word. This is the best verse we found to drive home to sixth graders the importance of making Jesus supreme in life: "He is also head of the body, the church; and He is the beginning, the first-born from the dead; so that He Himself might come to have first place in everything" (Col. 1:18).

Does your child have a personal relationship with Jesus Christ? If not, pray that God will grant you or others the opportunity to share the gospel. Without Christ and the power of the Holy Spirit in our lives, no one will turn away from worshiping false gods.

But even with Christ in our lives, we all are tempted in the flesh to serve these bogus gods. That's why your child at some point in his teen years needs to develop the same convictions we listed above for you.

Child's Conviction 1: Jesus Christ must be my Savior and Lord.

Child's Conviction 2: Regular prayer must be a crucial part of my daily life.

Child's Conviction 3: I must be the same person in private that I am in public.

Child's Conviction 4: The Scriptures are God's Word and serve as my daily guide.

Child's Conviction 5: Nothing is more thrilling than fulfilling God's mission for my life.

Child's Conviction 6: I will pass on a godly legacy to the next generation.

To build these convictions into the lives of our children, we have emphasized a number of key spiritual disciplines. Here's what we've done with our family.

Prayer

Our approach to prayer at home has been to make it a part

of daily life and events. Of course we've prayed at meals and bedtimes and with individual children when needs arise. We've prayed before tests and tryouts and trips. We pray for overseas missions we've been a part of, for requests that come through our prayer chain, and for everyone in the public schools our children attend. We've prayed as we've driven the children to school, and now that Rebecca is driving to school, we remind her and her sisters every day, "Don't forget to pray." We've also prayed during our family devotions in the morning before school.

Bible Study

Our children grew up hearing Bible stories since the time they were very small. For several years when we still had preschoolers, we helped them learn verses from a Bible memory program. We've done some more formal Bible study with our teens in junior high and early in high school, but it's been sporadic because of schedules.

You might want to try the *Experiencing God* Bible study, youth edition, by Henry Blackaby, or one of the Precept studies for youth published by Kay Arthur.

Young teens often don't feel the need to study the Bible by themselves in their own quiet time. We haven't seen our teens take much initiative until they reach high-school age. The desire for personal Bible study seems to come when they're on their own more, and they see their need to develop their relationship with God, to learn what He's telling them.

We could have imposed more Bible study on our teens, but we really wanted them to see the value of a close relationship with the Lord modeled in our lives.

On a fairly consistent basis I had gone through the book of Proverbs with each child in high school. This book has some of the best wisdom for life issues, such as how to make good decisions concerning the opposite sex, how to make right choices, how to work, and how to be a faithful and responsible steward of what God has given you.

Church

Participation in the life of a church is a must. Your children may not always agree. Our boys went through a time when they didn't want to go. Because they were also involved in other Christian youth activities, we told them they didn't have to participate in our church's youth group but that Sunday worship was not an option.

We also had to set standards for what they would wear to church. For a while the boys wanted to go to church in the sloppiest T-shirts and jeans. The girls have balked as well at dressing nice on Sunday. We've compromised slightly because our church is fairly casual.

Sunday needs to be a special day for many reasons, the most important being the opportunity to participate in a formal time to worship the true God.

Mission

From early on, we let our children know that God has a special mission for their lives. He has gifted them with abilities, personality, and certain qualities that will help accomplish His plan. We want our children to know that it would be better to be a garbage collector in the will of God than to be on the mission field just to please their parents—or for some other reason.

When Jesus gave the disciples the Great Commission, He was in essence giving them a mission. Read His command and words carefully, "Go therefore and make disciples of all the nations, baptizing them in the name of the Father and the Son and the Holy Spirit, teaching them to observe all that I commanded you; and lo, I am with you always, even to the end of the age" (Matt. 28:19–20).

How you send your child to junior high and high school is one of the most important strategic moves you'll ever make. A teenager needs a challenging mission. He needs a purpose that transcends the rush to follow the herd after the lesser gods of popularity, selfishness, etc.

As our children moved into their teenage years, we told them there are two ways to go to school: as a mission field or as a missionary. A mission-field teenager is peer dependent. A missionary teen seeks to reach out to his peers and help them find Christ. Mission-field teens go with the flow of the herd and the youth culture; missionary teens grow in character and conviction, because they are fighting the current.

One way to make Jesus' mandate to go into all the world practical is to become a fellow missionary with your child. Some years ago we began a family project of helping to start a Student Venture ministry on our teenagers' high-school and junior-high campuses. Student Venture is Campus Crusade for Christ's high-school outreach, and we received plenty of help from its staff members as we stepped out in faith. (If you are interested in helping start or support a ministry to students at your child's high school, call Student Venture at 800-678-5462.)

The benefits to our own family have been remarkable. We have found that involvement in a campus group like Student Venture creates a powerful sense of community for a preteen or teenager at school, the very place where negative peer pressure can be overwhelming. Our children have received vital spiritual support through the encouragement and prayer of fellow teenagers, as well as through the adult leaders.

We know that not every parent will start a ministry at their child's school as a way of developing a mission mind-set in their children, but this helped us start our children thinking about those around them who are in need of a relationship with Christ.

Missions Trips

One of the best ways to instill a missions mind-set in your child is to go together on a short-term mission, here in the United States or overseas. In addition to the impact you will have for Christ, you will find that your child will change in significant ways as he moves out of his normal comfort zone and sees the need that others have for Christ.

A year ago I (Barbara) took our three youngest daughters, Rebecca, Deborah, and Laura, on a two-week missions trip to Russia as part of Josh McDowell's Operation Carelift. We were a part of a group of over four hundred men, women, and children who gathered together in Moscow to minister to the spiritual and physical needs of the children of Russia. We went by the busload to schools, orphanages, and family centers to distribute boxes of food, medicine, clothes, and books—and to personally share the good news of Jesus Christ with children.

Our girls had the privilege of handing out good news bracelets and Bibles. Two of them gave the gospel presentation through our interpreter. It was an experience they will not soon forget. We all want to go back, because we fell in love with the Russian people and especially the children.

Our girls now have a far greater appreciation for what we enjoy in this country, and they have seen firsthand what life is like for people in another land. They have tasted both the sacrifice and the joy of being a missionary. For more information, call Operation Carelift at 972-907-1000.

Conferences

One of the most effective tools we have used over the years are youth conferences. These events may only take a few days, but they can grow your child's faith, encourage him to make it his own, and give him a vision for reaching out to students at his school.

In addition to our church's excellent spiritual life conferences for youth, we've sent our children to a couple of highly effective youth conferences.

"Something's Happening USA" is a youth congress organized by Student Venture. Attended by one thousand teens from dozens of states, this prayer conference is held over the Christmas holidays and features some of the most outstanding Christian youth speakers and musicians of our day. Our children say this is by far the most spiritually challenging conference they've ever been to. For more information call Student Venture at 800-678-5462.

"Mind Games" is a workshop organized by Probe Ministries to help teenagers develop a defense for their faith prior to college. Samuel attended this his senior year and wanted to go back the following year. This is a spiritually challenging retreat that gives these teens a head start on developing a God-centered view of life and world issues. For more information write to Probe Ministries, Mind Games Conference, 1900 Firman Drive, Suite 100, Richardson, TX 75081. Phone: 800-899-7762.

TESTING YOUR CHILD'S CONVICTIONS

During our final meeting of the sixth-grade Sunday school class, we would challenge the students to go into junior high as missionaries, to be influencers for good instead of being a mission field. We took each child, one at a time, into a room and had him sit down in a chair facing two doors.

On the floor in front of the chair was a "witness rock." The stone served as a reminder to stay out of the traps and to be obedient to Jesus Christ. It also was to be a witness of a decision that each of these young people was about to make, similar to the rock used by Joshua: "And Joshua said to all the people, 'Behold, this stone shall be for a witness against us, for it has heard all the words of the LORD which He spoke to us; thus it shall be for a witness against you, lest you deny your God'" (Josh. 24:27).

Beyond the stone to the left the child could see an unobstructed view of a door that was cracked slightly open and had a sign reading MISSION FIELD. It was easy to get to and through that door. To the right, the other door could hardly be seen because of chairs, tables, and other debris piled in front of it. The path to that door was hard. Difficult. The sign on this door read MISSIONARY.

All of the young men and young women had a choice. No one was looking on. Each one sat alone in that room by himself, facing those two doors that symbolized how they were going to go to junior high school. Only three would know which door the child selected: The young person. The rock. And God.

These kinds of ceremonies are a part of what is needed for today's youth. They need some drama. Some symbolism. They need to be challenged and called to a truly biblical life.

Did this event ensure that everybody who went through the missionary door cruised with ease through their teenage years? Hardly. But it did give them a sober reference point. A clear fork in the road. An unmistakable choice. You've got to believe that at some point God will use the memory of that ceremony to warn them of the danger of the false gods trap and all the other snares.

You might want to set up a similar ceremony to shape and challenge your son or daughter's convictions.

Following are some other ideas to evaluate how your child is handling the test of false gods.

Monitor your child's schedule. One telltale sign of an attraction to a false god is how a person uses his free time. What really interests him? What does he talk most about? Answers to these questions will fuel your prayers and guide your coaching and correcting.

Keep an eye on where and on what your child spends money. Most children have caught the consumption virus from us adults. Just as a peek at our checkbook and credit card statements will reveal our ultimate loyalties, so watching how a child disperses an allowance and earnings from jobs will tip us off to his. We're not talking about the basic investments in T-shirts and athletic shoes, although those items can get out of hand too. But is there heavy spending on faddish clothing, cosmetics, CDs, concerts, and the like? During the teen years is a great time to begin learning the spiritual principles of stewardship, tithing, and giving to the less fortunate.

Claiming Their Own Faith

How can you tell if spiritual-sounding words coming from the mouth of your child are evidence of a true faith? The truth is, you may not really know until your teen is somewhat older because most children are wise enough to say what they know Mom and Dad want to hear. Testing will determine the veracity of your child's faith, and often that faith isn't severely tested until high school or, for some, even college.

Our children began to experience faith testing in high school. They started coming home with questions like "What does the Bible say about evolution?" or "What does God think about being gay?" We had lively discussions at the dinner table as I played devil's advocate to help them think through their beliefs. We'd direct them to the Bible, and they began to discover truth on their own out of Scripture. That's when faith's roots sink deep.

Always be watching out for a preadolescent or young teen who may be playing church. Our daughter Ashley remembers doing some acting when she was in high school. Here's how she tells it:

> In high school, because of my dad and my family background, I got labeled as someone who had all the right answers. I could go to church and really play the part of the good Christian. I fooled everyone including myself. I wasn't bad at school, but I wasn't living my Christian life either.
>
> I knew I was being kind of a phony, but I didn't know how to get out of it, so I just continued and a lot of my friends did too. There was never a person in my life that was my age who was showing me how to really live it rather than playing church.
>
> In tenth grade I attended a conference and learned from the speaker how to make God number-one in my life. I decided that that was what I needed in my life. I went back and applied it, and it changed my life.

CONCLUSION

A painful experience in the life of our family helped reinforce our need to cling to the true God. Samuel was always the natural athlete in our family. Since I had played junior-college basketball and baseball, I was delighted that our son might follow in my footsteps.

As a child, Samuel played Little League ball for a couple of years with older boys and did well. But when he turned thirteen he really began to excel in tennis. We loved attending his matches and tournaments. We drove hundreds of miles taking him all over the state to play singles and doubles in tournaments. He brought home trophies and ribbons, and he once battled the number-one player in the state in his age group to match point before losing in a tiebreaker.

Samuel was ranked seventh in the state when his game began to slide. His coach didn't understand why he wasn't getting to balls he had earlier reached with ease. Thinking it might be his shoes, we took him to a sports orthopedic doctor for a proper fitting. The problem only got worse.

After Samuel's fourteenth birthday, we took the entire family to the FamilyLife Marriage Conference in Dallas. That weekend we noticed that Samuel wasn't keeping up with the rest of us as we walked to dinner and later when we hurried to catch a plane at the airport.

The following Monday morning we went to a doctor's office with Samuel and were soon numb with disbelief when the neurologist announced, "Your son has a form of muscular dystrophy. He will most likely never be confined to a wheelchair, but he will never run again. His days of tennis and sports are over." Months later, a trip to the Mayo Clinic confirmed the earlier diagnosis.

Although Samuel's disease was not life-threatening, we felt as though there had been a death of a dream for a young man and his parents.

The next four months were tough as Samuel refused to quit tennis. Most matches he tripped and fell face down on the asphalt, losing in straight sets. Many of his opponents, who had no way of knowing what was going on, mocked him and laughed at him. (He and a partner did win a doubles tournament once with a miraculous, come-from-behind victory.)

Finally, Samuel hung up his tennis racket, admitting his playing days were over.

Late one afternoon as I was driving Samuel home from a doctor visit, we were talking about what his disease meant to him as a young man. I was struggling to keep my emotions composed while trying to comfort him. I was battling my own feelings about a fourteen-year-old boy who would never field grounders again. Never play basketball with his brother. Never jog with his dad.

But Samuel ended up comforting me.

In the twilight of late afternoon, he turned to me as we drove home and said with a boyish grin, "Well, Dad, I guess you don't need legs to serve God."

I couldn't talk. As I brushed away a stream of tears, all I could do was reach across the seat and give him a hug.

Samuel is not perfect. He's still spreading his wings and, like all of us, learning constantly what it means to follow Christ.

But riding in the car with me that afternoon, he showed me he was a young man whose identity went far beyond tennis, whose character was weathering a stiff challenge, whose relationship with God and family was sustaining him, and whose mission for God transcended any physical limitations he would face in his lifetime.

UNFORGETTABLE LESSON: Distracting Demo

The goal of this lesson is to show that other things, many of them "good" things, can prevent us from focusing on the one true God.

Set up this demonstration in a room where you have a television set. Bring to the same room a radio and a CD player or tape recorder. You might want to add a buzzing alarm clock too. You can use as many noisemakers as you want. Set the volume on all of the items loud, and then turn them off.

Bring your child into the room and tell him, "We're going to do a fun little exercise to test your attention and hearing. I will stand here by the door and say something; you will stand across the room and try to hear me."

Position your child at the opposite side of the room from where you will stand, and then turn on all the noisemakers.

Go to your spot and *whisper* something like, "I want to take you out for an ice-cream cone."

Your child, of course, will yell, "What? I can't hear you!"

Tell him he can turn off just one item at a time. Each time the two of you should stay in your positions and repeat the experiment: You whisper, and he tries to hear what you're saying.

Finally, when everything is turned off and the room is quiet, your child should be able to hear what you are saying. If not, have him *move closer* until he can.

When you are having that ice-cream cone or other treat, make sure you discuss the following point: God really wants our attention—our worship. He does not want to share us with other gods or things that distract us. Why could you not hear me whispering when the machines were playing? How is this like what happens between us and God? What are some things that can become false gods or idols in our lives?

CONVICTION BUILDING PLAN

Use the following questions to solidify your own convictions about false gods, and to begin developing a plan to shape your child's convictions.

Part One. Answer the following questions individually

1. As you look at your own life, do you see any patterns that suggest you are worshiping any of the following false gods?
   Popularity/approval from others
   Success/achievement
   Approval from the opposite sex

Appearance

Entertainment

Consumption/materialism

2. Now rate your mate in the same areas:

Popularity/approval from others

Success/achievement

Approval from the opposite sex

Appearance

Entertainment

Consumption/materialism

3. Finally, rate your child in those areas:

Popularity/approval from others

Success/achievement

Approval from the opposite sex

Appearance

Entertainment

Consumption/materialism

4. What are some steps you can take to improve your own spiritual life?

5. What are some steps you can take to improve your spiritual life as a couple?

6. Look over the section in this chapter on Shaping Your Child's Convictions. What are some ways you can keep your children attached to God and growing in authentic faith?

Part Two. Conclusions

1. Without condemning one another, share your answers from the questions you completed individually. If you are single, meet with a friend who can offer wisdom and insight.

2. Decide what steps you will take over the next month to improve your spiritual lives and to teach spiritual disciplines to your child.

3. Is it difficult for you to think of starting to improve the spiritual disciplines in your family? Pray that God will give you the strength and the discipline to begin doing it.

Part III

Prayerfully Persevere

20

Will Adolescence Ever End?

Yes! And Life Is Good!

As a parent, there are moments when you wonder if there is any hope. After years of training, shaping, testing, you see a son or daughter wander off track and hear the deadly sound of a trap's jaws snapping shut. It might be a son's nasty outburst of anger, punctuated by a slammed door that shakes the house, or a daughter caught lying about the party she and her boyfriend attended last Saturday night.

You and your spouse, shoulders slumping, may not say the words, but the thought is on your mind. *Are we failures? Are we totally ruining this child? Will he ever grow up?*

We've been there. Done that. Still doing that!

Parenting is not for the faint of heart. The task is long and hard, but there is hope.

Hope is not found in our gold-medal performance as parents. Certainly, we work diligently at being good moms and dads. We pray continually. We stay involved and connected as best we can. We labor to model the standards of truth and integrity that we teach our children. But those good things will never be the source of our hope. Ultimately, our only hope is in God and His faithfulness.

As Psalm 119:89–90 reminds us, "Forever, O LORD, / Thy word

is settled in heaven. / Thy faithfulness continues throughout all generations."

The final teen years, from about age sixteen through high-school graduation, require continued repetition of the basic shaping, testing, and correcting that you have been doing in all the previous years. This is true especially in the sixteenth year. That year, with the arrival of the coveted driver's license, has proved to be a heady experience for each of our four who have passed through it. Each has needed some serious mid-course corrections in that year.

The difference comes in how you do it. You endeavor with perseverance to repeat the instructions that need to be relearned. You can't quit or give up. Meter out the necessary discipline, but be sure to administer these lessons with a healthy dose of compassion for your teen who may be feeling discouraged because of disappointments and failures. Don't become exasperated with your child in front of him. Though you may feel hopeless, he needs you to give him hope that he can make it.

Remember, you may be the only person in his life who really knows his struggles and still believes in him.

Give affirmation for the lessons learned well. And throughout all these later teen years, wisely and prayerfully give your child more and more freedoms, knowing that in a short while he will be on his own.

During the late teens, it's as if you have tied the end of a long, floppy, bungee cord to your child's back. Out the door he goes—in a car, to a job, to new experiences, to relationships with strangers you may not know. Occasionally, you see or hear something and have to jerk the line, maybe even reel a lot of cord back in. But as trust and experience grow, the longer he will stay out at the end of that cord. Finally, you must detach the cord, and the child leaves home for good.

Although the journey through adolescence may seem as long and arduous as the climb up Mount Everest, the trek does end. Just when your aching lungs and wobbling legs seem unable to support one more step, you see the summit. Then the satisfaction is deep, the view spectacular. Adolescence is ending, and your child's maturity begins to break forth on the horizon like the first rays of a crisp morning's sun.

It's a bittersweet irony of parenting that just at the time when the adolescent reaches a new level of maturity and becomes an enjoyable human being that you would love to spend more time with, off he goes.

This happened in a family we know well. This boy, nicknamed B.J., is now a young man in his early twenties. He could have been the poster child for Strong-Willed Boy of the Year. He wasn't a "bad boy"—not even close—but he was intent on marching through life as the one in charge.

In his early elementary years he was frequently the boss. During those years, he began to make war on his siblings, occasionally irritating his older sister but regularly brawling with a younger brother.

Then adolescence hit, and with newly discovered intellectual strengths and a sharp wit, B.J. began enforcing his opinions and will with a new weapon—a biting tongue. Almost daily he clashed and argued with his mother, driving her on many occasions to tears of frustration. His battles with his brother increased in frequency and effectiveness as he became more skilled at intimidation and self-justification. The skirmishes seemed to occur hourly. No end was in sight.

Away from home B.J. was doing great. His grades were excellent, and he was resisting peer pressure. He even took a strong public stand for Christ at school. But he was struggling with his relationships that mattered most.

The border war with his mom became so fierce and potentially damaging to both parties that finally B.J.'s dad intervened. In a pointed confrontation, father went eye to eye, jaw to jaw with his son and demanded more respect for mom or else wrath and consequences would fall like rain. B.J. grudgingly and gradually gave in and relented—a little.

Finally, after years of this demanding relationship, during B.J.'s senior year in high school his mom and dad started to notice some changes in his attitudes and behavior. Now instead of turning discussions into arguments, B.J. began to listen more. A pleasing smile increasingly replaced the self-absorbed scowl. What he'd been taught about faith and life began to become his own convictions and a guide to his actions. Although there were still tensions with siblings, he expressed kindness for his sisters, and B.J.'s brother now seemed more buddy than enemy.

B.J. enrolled at a large state university. He joined a fraternity, and early on he took a personal stand with two others against drinking. He became involved in the Campus Crusade ministry and soon became a leader. Then two years later came his huge decision: B.J. informed his parents that he wanted to stay out of college for a year to participate in a missionary outreach in Estonia. *Where on earth is Estonia?* they wondered.

B.J.'s dad and mom were proud of his decision, but sad too; B.J. would be gone for the entire twelve months. The whole family and many friends gathered at the airport and said goodbye on a hot August afternoon.

The following November, just before Thanksgiving—the first holiday B.J. would be away from his family—he sent greetings by e-mail. Just a few years earlier he had been a headstrong, battling, abrasive, unpleasant teenager. Now this young man, our son, having survived the traps of adolescence, found words like these for his sisters and brother, mom and dad:

> To Ashley: *I can still see your radiant face as you walked down the aisle this summer . . . I count it one of my most blessed opportunities to have been in your wedding . . . Now that you have Michael, my job as protector and big brother is over . . . You are so wonderful, and I want you to know that I love you. Growing up with you is perhaps the most valuable and greatest gift you have ever given me—you have marked me for life. Your love for Jesus. Your desire for others. Your*

devotion for me. All of these things have kept me and encouraged me to pursue our Lord all the more.

To Samuel: *My little brother I used to beat up all the time—and he would go crying to Mom, and then I'd have to re-stripe the parking lot out front or eat dirt and leaves for a month for it—has turned into a mighty man of God . . . You are simply the man, and I truly and honestly look up to you . . . My feeble words fail me trying to let you know how much I love you, so I'll use someone else's: John 15:13 says, "Greater love hath no man than this, that a man lay down his life for his friends." My life is yours. I would do anything for you.*

To Rebecca: *I can't believe that I can hang out with you— my little kid sister—and be able to share anything with you and have you be able to help me and talk with me about it . . . Your desire to serve our Lord is incredible . . . You are a beautiful young woman—both inside and out, and the guy who gets to marry you will be one of the luckiest, most blessed men on earth . . . You are a treasure in my life, and I wouldn't trade it for anything. Wishing I could hug you and see you, and with all the love and affection my heart can muster.*

To Deborah: *Ah yes, my little flower child! You are simply incredible. I can see you right now, your little smile creeping up on the corners of your mouth . . . your face turning red with a little embarrassment . . . You are really growing up into a fine young woman. Your life is reflecting more and more of Jesus' love to everyone . . . I am sure thankful to God for you. You are so awesome and a wonderful sister. Because you are so good about keeping up with me, I don't feel like I am so far away . . . I love you very much.*

To Laura: *I love your laugh and your love for life. Every*

time I come home from school, you are always one of the first to run to me and jump on me and tell me that you missed me and that you love me . . . What other big brother gets such wonderful treatment from his youngest sister? . . . I admit that every time I am around you I always feel better . . . I am convinced that if charging Hell with a water pistol was possible, I think you and I would be the first in line! This Thanksgiving, though I am far away from you . . . I am more and more fond of you and love you more than ever.

To Mom: *I want you to know that if I wrote all day and night for the next hundred years, I could not even begin to say enough thanks and praises to you for all the things you have done for me in my life . . . You deserve much more than I could ever give or say in words, but someday, I shall try . . . I miss you. Your warm hugs . . . your constant smile . . . your words of encouragement. Your wonderful food! Your love for Dad . . . You and Dad have made me who I am today . . . I want you to know that you are the best mom in the whole entire world—and you know what? I know this because I am on the other side of the world, and I know these things now . . . I love you.*

To Dad: *I went for a walk in the woods the other day and thought of you. The numerous times you and I have spent together in the woods. Hunting. Fishing. Cutting down trees—even if some were just a little across the line! Camping. Canoeing. Playing. Man, the memories are intense and wonderful . . . I recalled that many of my lessons I learned growing up were learned with you in the woods . . . Love for Mom. Commitment. A job well done. All of these things I use now as I live in Estonia, and I am grateful for the years of discipline and love and commitment to me. My God has given me the most wonderful blessing when He allowed me to have you as my dad. You are the best . . . You are my dad, and I love you.*

What a blessing B.J.—our oldest son, Benjamin—has become, and how we praise God for His abundant mercy and grace in all of our lives. Only God could have made the changes in Ben's heart and in ours.

We know that Ben is still a young man with many traps still before him. But we've seen enough fruit already to know that *God is faithful.* When the seeds of prayer, involvement, and training are pressed with perseverance into the fresh soil of an adolescent's life, the little plants of faith and good choices watered and pruned with love and encouragement, they will grow to be God's sturdy branches and bear fruit—bushels and bushels of beautiful fruit.

That's our hope, and yours, too, as we parent today's adolescents.

May God's favor be upon you, and may your descendants be mighty!

Appendix A: Understanding Puberty

What's the first word that comes to your mind when you hear someone say *puberty*?

Chaos. Excitement. Panic. Teenager. Moods. Pimples. Pain. Telephones.

Those are a few we might list.

Puberty does involve incredible change and the full spectrum of emotions. But the first signs that our little boy or girl is growing up should not fill us with terror. We need to lighten up and enjoy the marvelous things that God performs in their bodies.

In preparation for this book we consulted a number of sources and collected information from physicians and researchers who have expertise on the physical changes that occur during puberty.[1] The conclusions from these efforts are presented here as a summary of what happens in every child's experience of puberty.

Even the most knowledgeable parent can use a reminder of what's taking place in a child's body at the onset of this time in life, which is unlike any other.

Puberty is essentially the unleashing into the body a tidal wave of hormones that stimulate awesome, irreversible changes.

The biological metamorphoses of puberty have not changed since we all went through it—with one possible exception. Does it seem like puberty starts earlier with many children these days? Virginia Rutter has written, "Since the mid-1800s, puberty . . . has inched back one year for every 25 years elapsed. It now occurs an average six years earlier than it did in 1850."[2] This information only heightens the desirability and urgency of parents to educate their children during the golden years on sexuality and related behavioral issues.

These days puberty begins for girls on average at about age eleven (in some girls as early as *eight* years old) and for boys on average at about age thirteen.

Of course the changes instigated by puberty occur at different speeds with each child—sometimes a girl or boy will mature years ahead of a peer. When puberty begins, girls are usually taller and grow faster than boys the same age. But when male growth accelerates, the boys quickly grow past the girls.

At the onset of puberty, the brain sends appropriate signals to the hypothalamus, which in turn initiates two types of signals: One signal, in the form of a hormone, travels to the pituitary gland to trigger release of other hormones that will result in general growth throughout the body.

A second hormonal signal from the hypothalamus stimulates the pituitary gland to initiate sexual organ development and reproductive capability.[3] The process is complex, and many changes occur simultaneously. It is truly an exciting, confusing, sometimes scary period of adjustment. Most young people have fully completed their sexual maturation by age fourteen or fifteen.[4]

Although psychological development normally does not correlate precisely with the physical changes of adolescence, during these years, young adolescents begin to develop abstract reasoning skills. In other words, they now have the basic tools to reason and make decisions the way we adults do.[5]

In both girls and boys, the development of their sex organs brings on noticeable sexual tensions and feelings. The increase in sexual hormones during early adolescence results in heightened emotional intensity. Girls experience more depression; boys experience more aggression.[6]

Although in a general sense the changes of puberty are the same in both boys and girls, obviously the specific events and their timing are quite different in each sex. So here's a brief overview of what happens in both girls and boys.

Puberty and Girls

The puberty experience we have just described results in a girl growing taller. Her breasts increase in size and round out. Her hips widen, and hair grows under her arms and around her genitals.

At about age twelve, menstruation, the monthly discharge of blood and tissue from her vagina, begins. At the same time, her ovaries, fallopian tubes, and uterus also grow.

When the hormones begin flowing profusely from the girl's pituitary gland, they head for her ovaries. One type of hormone initiates the cycle of one fertile egg being released about once a month until menstruation ceases years later. Another hormone stimulates the development of the entire ovulation system and process that allows the egg to leave one of the ovaries and make its way into a fallopian tube and eventually to the uterus.

Still another hormone is at work in the ovaries to stimulate production of estrogen, which in the female is responsible for bone growth, breast development, increased fat storage, and the development of female genitalia.[7]

After the beginning of puberty, the young female, upon receiving sperm from the male, is able to conceive and bear a child.

Puberty and Boys

In puberty a boy grows taller and heavier. Shoulders broaden, muscles strengthen, and the voice deepens. Hair spouts on his face, under his arms, around the genitals, and elsewhere on the body.

When the hormones begin to flow freely from a boy's pituitary gland, their destination is the testes or testicles. One hormone stimulates the production of sperm. Elsewhere in the testes, another hormone stimulates the production of testosterone, which is responsible for almost all of the outward changes that make a boy start to resemble a young man. These include lengthened bones, increase in muscle mass, growth of genitalia, and development of secondary sexual characteristics, such as pubic, facial, and underarm hair and the deepening of the voice.[8]

The young boy now is capable of ejaculation and more than likely will experience nocturnal emissions—wet dreams. He can perform sexual intercourse and father a child.

FEARFULLY AND WONDERFULLY MADE

Puberty may bring pandemonium, but it also should provoke praise. As David so passionately wrote, "I will give thanks to Thee, for I am fearfully and wonderfully made . . . And my soul knows it very well" (Ps. 139:14). Or as the contemporary translation *The Message* puts it, "I thank you, High God—you're breathtaking! Body and soul, I am marvelously made! I worship in adoration—what a creation!"

As you share the puberty experience with your child, amid the many changes and moods, don't forget to celebrate and praise the *wonder*.

Appendix B:
Recommended Resources

$\mathbf{M}$any of these resources are available through local bookstores or FamilyLife—unless otherwise noted.

To place orders for resources with FamilyLife, see the telephone number and address located at the end of this appendix, page 344.

This resources list for parents and children is organized under the following topic headings:

Anger
Appearance (Eating
  Disorders)
Bible Study
Busyness
Conferences (FamilyLife)
Dating
Media/Internet

Mediocrity (Grades,
  Jobs-Money)
Parenting (General)
Peer Pressure
Pornography
Sex (Sex Abuse)
Spiritual Growth
Substance Abuse

Anger

Lou Priolo, *The Heart of Anger*. Formerly *How to Help Angry Kids* (Amityville, NY: Calvary Press, 1997).

Provides accurate and practical interpretation of Ephesians 6:4:

"Fathers, do not provoke your children to anger; but bring them up in the discipline and instruction of the Lord."

Ross Campbell, M.D., *Kids in Danger/Training Your Child to Tame the Destructive Power of Anger* (Colorado Springs: Victor Books, 1995).
Warmly advises parent on how to help a child manage everyday conflicts and express anger appropriately.

Appearance (Eating Disorders)

Brio Magazine. Each month, *Brio* has articles on modest fashion for girls. Available from Focus on the Family at 800-A-FAMILY.

Remuda Ranch, Center for Anorexia and Bulimia, P.O. Box 2481, Wickenburg, AZ 85358. Telephone: 800-445-1900.
Specializes in treatment for women and adolescent girls suffering from anorexia, bulimia, and related problems. In-patient and out patient programs are operated from Christian perspective.

Bible Study

Cynthia Heald, *Becoming a Woman of Excellence* (Colorado Springs: NavPress, 1986).
Moms and daughters can learn how to pursue excellence in the areas of purity, a gentle and quiet spirit, obedience, and others.

Debby Jones and Jackie Kendall, *Lady in Waiting* Workbook (Shippensburg, PA: Destiny Image, 1997).
This Bible study for high school and college age women examines the book of Ruth and uncovers ten qualities of a godly woman.

Stephen Voorwinde, ed., *Wisdom for Today's Issues*, reformatted (Phillipsburg, NJ: Presbyterian and Reformed, 1996).
Every verse in Proverbs is arranged topically for quick reference. Perfect for those breakfast dates with your teen as you talk about issues he's facing.

Rebecca St. James, *40 Days with God* (Cincinnati, OH: Standard, 1996).
Devotional journal by contemporary Christian music artist Rebecca St. James guides child into insight from God's Word. An enhanced CD (music CD and computer CD-ROM) is included.

Busyness

Charles Hummel, *Tyranny of the Urgent*. Tract, revised edition (Downers Grove, IL: InterVarsity, 1994).

Classic apologetic for saying no to the unimportant and yes to God's priorities.

Conferences, FamilyLife

The FamilyLife Marriage Conference
This weekend conference is more than just a getaway with your spouse. You'll also receive sixteen hours of training in conflict resolution, intimacy, and God's design for marriage.

The FamilyLife Parenting Conference
Get a biblical game plan for raising your children at this practical weekend conference. Also available in an audio series from FamilyLife.

Dating

Elisabeth Elliot, *Passion and Purity* (Grand Rapids, MI: Revell, 1984).

Author tells of her relationship with Jim Elliot and helps young men and women commit daily to Christ in all matters of the heart.

Joshua Harris, *I Kissed Dating Goodbye* (Sisters, OR: Multnomah, 1997).
A handbook for teens and college students struggling with dating issues.

Mike McCoy, "The Interview," audio cassette (Little Rock, AR: FamilyLife, 1997).
Dennis Rainey talks to a dad who interviewed a daughter's date.

Media/Internet

General:

Ted Baehr, *The Media-Wise Family* (Colorado Springs: Chariot Victor, 1998).

Helps you make morally and spiritually responsible decisions about television, movies, and multimedia.

Plugged in. Focus on the Family's magazine for parents trying to sort out the media. Contact Focus on the Family at 800-A-FAMILY.

Internet:

CYBERsitter Blocking software (Santa Barbara, CA: Solid Oak Software, Inc., 1997). The web page address is <http://www.cybersitter.com>.

This Internet filtering software for Windows-based computers will help prevent your children and you from accessing pornographic web sites and downloading other harmful material. Note: If you own a Macintosh, we recommend Surf Watch, available from local computer stores or down-loadable from the Internet.

FlashNet Communications, Inc., 1812 N. Forest Park Blvd., Ft. Worth, TX 76102. For more information call 800-FLASHNET. The web page address is <http://www.flash.net>. FlashNet was the first to introduce the blocking of pornographic sites on the Internet on a company level.

Donna Rice Hughes, *Kids Online* (Grand Rapids, MI: Revell, 1998).

A simple, step-by-step guide to help your child navigate the Internet safely.

"Internet for Christians Newsletter."

Author Quentin Shultze has written hundreds of articles on the media and produces this newsletter available at <http://www.gospelcom.net>.

Magazines:

Focus on the Family Magazines: *Breakaway* (for boys) and *Brio* (for girls) are great alternatives to the teen magazines found on the newsstand. Contact Focus on the Family at 800-A-FAMILY.

Campus Life. This fine magazine deals with the real life issues of high school and college students, including sex, spiritual concerns, friendships, school, and music. Contact 800-678-6083 for information.

Movies:

Movie Guide. This magazine publishes movie reviews each month from a Christ-centered worldview. Contact 800-899-6684 for subscription information.

<http://www.screenit.com>

This timely website tells you everything you want to know about movies, videos, music, and more. Parental Warning: This website describes what is heard and seen and this information, while helpful to you in decision-making, may be inappropriate for your child.

Mediocrity (Grades, Work/Money)

Steve Douglass with Al Janssen, *How to Get Good Grades and Have More Fun!* Revised edition published with Integrated Resources.

In this fictional account, Al and Joanne are mentored by a graduate student who helps them work smarter, not harder.

Cynthia Tobias, *The Way They Learn* (Wheaton, IL: Tyndale House [for Focus on the Family], 1994).

Learn how your child takes in, processes, and communicates information. Audio series also available from FamilyLife.

Doug Sherman and William Hendricks, *Your Work Matters to God* (Colorado Springs, CO: NavPress, 1994).

Discusses theology of work and reveal what Scriptures say about relationships, remuneration, and job fit. Companion workbook perfect for a breakfast parent-child Bible study.

Lauree and L. Allen Burkett, *Money Matters for Teens* (Chicago: Moody Press, 1997).

Book and companion workbook provide tips for learning smart money attitudes.

Parenting (General)

Anne Arkins and Gary Harrell, *Watchmen on the Walls; Praying Character into Your Child* (Sisters, OR: Multnomah, 1998).

Shows how to pray specifically for needs and goals related to your child.

Teresa Langston, *Parenting Without Pressure* (Colorado Springs, CO: NavPress, 1994).

Outlines the importance of written standards in the home. A rebellious daughter in Teresa's family was held to standards of performance and behavior and learned the discipline every child needs.

James Merritt, *Friends, Foes & Fools: Fathers Can Teach Their Kids to Know the Difference* (Nashville, TN: Broadman & Holman, 1996).

A pastor explains how to use the Proverbs as a parenting guide.

June Hines Moore, *You Can Raise a Well-Mannered Child* (Nashville, TN: Broadman & Holman, 1996) and *Etiquette Manager* (Nashville, TN: Broadman & Holman, 1998).

If your child is junior high age, *You Can Raise a Well Mannered Child* will clarify basic manners issues. If you have a senior high student, *Etiquette Manager* is a great training tool to prepare him or her for college or the business world.

Miriam Neff, *Helping Teens in Crisis* (Wheaton, IL: Tyndale House Publishers, 1993).

Author guides parents through the world of teenagers so that they can help their teen make wise decisions. A related questionnaire "How Well Do You Know Your Teenager?" is available from FamiliyLife.

Dennis Rainey, "My Soapbox: Dennis Rainey Speaks to Parents of Teens." Audio Series. (Little Rock, AR: FamilyLife, 1995).

Helps parents tackle topics like profanity, curfews, friends, earrings, movies, and more.

Dennis and Barbara Rainey, "Preparing Your Teen for Life." Audio Series. (Little Rock, AR: FamilyLife, 1996).

Six-cassette discussion on life skills a parent will want a teenager to know before he leaves home for college, work, or service.

Dennis and Barbara Rainey, "Questions and Answers for Parents of Preteens." Audio Series. (Little Rock, AR: FamilyLife, 1994)

Rapid fire answers to real-life questions from correspondence and personal encounters.

Peer Pressure

Greg Johnson, *What Would You Do If?* (Ann Arbor, MI: Servant, 1995).

If you need a jump-start in how to play the "Decide in Advance Game," this book provides 101 scenarios for you and your child to do together. Includes discussion questions and relevant Scriptures.

"'What If . . . ?'/31 Fun Experiences for Families." Audio Cassette. (Little Rock, AR: FamilyLife, 1995).

Thirty-one short audio dramas that introduce real-life experiences to teach values and build character.

Ashley and Dennis Rainey, "Guiding Your Child Through Peer Pressure." Audio Series. (Little Rock, AR: FamilyLife, 1994).

In three-cassette presentation Dennis Rainey and daughter Ashley discuss how parents can help children resist peer pressure.

Pornography

Laurie Hall, *An Affair of the Mind* (Colorado Springs, CO: Focus on the Family, 1996).

Story of a woman's struggle to protect herself and her children from devastating effects of her husband's obsession with pornography. An audio series is also available from FamilyLife.

Jerry Kirk with host Dennis Rainey, "Pornography: The Dangerous Deception." Audio series. (Little Rock, AR: FamilyLife, 1994).

Audio outlines how you can protect your mind, your home, and your community from sexually explicit material.

"Fatal Addiction." Video. (Colorado Springs: Focus on the Family, 1989). Available from Focus on the Family at 800-A-FAMILY.

Video features a riveting, tragic interview with mass-murderer Ted Bundy.

Sex

Stan and Brenna Jones, *How and When to Tell Your Kids About Sex* (Colorado Springs, CO: NavPress, 1994).

Comprehensive book helps parents answer all the tough questions.

Stan and Brenna Jones, *Facing the Facts* (Colorado Springs: NavPress, 1995).

Helps youth understand the physiological changes in their bodies, handle sexual pressure, and gain understanding of God's perfect design.

Josh McDowell, *Why Wait* (Nashville, TN: Thomas Nelson, 1988). The compelling case for abstinence.

Josh McDowell with Bob Hostetler, *The Love Killer* (Dallas: Word Publishing, 1993).

A hideous demon named Ratsbane is out to kill love at Eisenhower High with his weapon called sex. Novel follows three teens battling to stay sexually pure.

Dennis and Barbara Rainey, "Beyond Abstinence: Helping Your Teen Stay Pure." Audio Series. (Little Rock, AR: FamilyLife, 1997).

Audio challenges parents to use sex education to instill values, convictions, and godly character in their children.

Dan Allender, *The Wounded Heart: Hope for Victims of Childhood Sexual Abuse* (Colorado Springs, CO: NavPress, 1992).

Excellent, biblically based insight for victims and those who love them most. There is hope and healing from God. Workbook available.

Spiritual Growth

Jim Elliff, "How Children Come to Faith in Christ," Audio series. (Little Rock, AR: FamilyLife, 1996).

What to teach your child about salvation, judgment, hell, Christ's atonement, and repentance.

Kevin Johnson, *Catch the Wave* (Minneapolis, MN: Bethany House, 1996).

Helps your child understand God's big plans for him. Contains names of reputable organizations doing teen mission trips.

Jerry Solomon, "Sheep Among Wolves: Preparing High School Students to Defend Their Faith in College" (Little Rock, AR: FamilyLife, 1998).

This essay is intended for parents to read as they help their child prepare for anti-Christian worldviews on the college campus.

Substance Abuse

Stephen Arterburn and Jim Burns, *Drug Proof Your Kids*, revised edition (Ventura, CA: Regal, 1995).

This book answers many questions for parents and outlines biblical techniques to help head off problems before they begin. A video presentation is also available.

Milton Creagh, "Masquerade: Unveiling Our Deadly Dance with Drugs and Alcohol." Video and discussion guide. (Colorado Springs, CO: Focus on the Family, 1996). Contact Focus on the Family at 800-A-FAMILY.

In thirty-minute video your child will hear and see the deception of drug use through real life testimony and drama.

Jeff VanVonderen, *Good News for the Chemically Dependent and Those Who Love Them* (Minneapolis, MN: Bethany House, 1991).

Provides an action plan for anyone in your family who has struggled with addictions to alcohol or drugs.

To Obtain Information on Conferences
and
Order Resources from FamilyLife

PHONE: 800-FL-TODAY
WEB SITE: http://www.familylife-ccc.org
ADDRESS: FamilyLife
          P.O. Box 8220
          Little Rock, AR 72221-8220

Notes

Introduction

1. Tom Clagett, "Parenting Survey/Parents of Preadolescents versus Teenagers," FamilyLife Survey, November-December 1997, p. 1.
2. Clagett, "Parenting Survey," p. 2.

Chapter 1

1. This message is a part of an audio series entitled "A Husband of Service, A Father of Sacrifice," Product No.: 766. Contact the FamilyLife Resource Center for more information. Address and telephone number are listed in Appendix B.
2. "Healthy Youth 2000: National health promotion and disease prevention objectives for adolescents," American Medical Association, 1990. Cited in "A Matter of Time: Risk and Opportunity in the NonSchool Hours," An Executive Summary, Carnegie Council on Adolescent Development, 1993, p. 3.
3. J. E. Gans, "America's Adolescents: How Healthy Are They?" Vol. 1, AMA profiles of Adolescent Health Series

(Chicago: American Medical Association, 1990). Cited in "A Matter of Time," p. 3.

4. Kenneth Eskey, "Family is pillar for high schoolers, says study," *Arkansas Democrat Gazette*, June 15, 1995, p. 4A.

5. Eskey, "Family is pillar," p. 4A.

6. Edwin W. Brown, "How one incurable disease affects our youngsters," *Medical Update*, April 1998, electronically retrieved at <http://web2.search-bank.com/infotra>. Article A20497212.

7. Franklin Graham, *Rebel with a Cause* (Nashville: Thomas Nelson, 1995), p. 120.

8. Franklin Graham's story adapted from his autobiography, *Rebel with a Cause*.

Chapter 2

1. Based on the following: Pierre Berton, *Niagara/A History of the Falls* (New York: Kodansha International, 1997), pp. 294-96; T. W. Kriner, *Journeys to the Brink of Doom* (Buffalo, N.Y.: J & J Publishing, 1997), pp. 78-79; and Williah Harris and Judith Levey, eds., *The New Columbia Encyclopedia* (New York: Columbia University Press, 1975), p. 1936.

2. At time of publication of this book, plans were underway to publish the Sixth-Grade Sunday School Class Curriculum. Contact the FamilyLife Resource Center for more information. Phone numbers and address are listed in Appendix B.

3. Berton, *Niagara*, p. 297.

4. Berton, *Niagara*, pp. 297-98.

Chapter 3

1. Jennifer Tanaka, "Drowning in Data," *Newsweek*, April 28, 1997, p.85

2. The book *Watchmen on the Walls* by Anne Arkins and Gary Harrell is a great resource when you don't know what to pray for your child. See Appendix B for information on ordering.

3. Taken from "Men of Action," Spring 92, p. 5. Used by permission.

4. Jeffrey Zaslow, "Straight Talk," *USA Weekend*, Nov. 14-16, 1997, p. 23.

5. Winston Churchill, Address at Harrow School, Oct. 29, 1941. Cited in John Bartlett, *Bartlett's Familiar Quotations*, Sixteenth Edition (Boston: Little, Brown and Company, 1992), p. 621.

Chapter 4

1. Joan Elma Rahn, *Traps & Lures in the Living World* (New York: Atheneum, 1980), pp. 71–73

Chapter 5

1. Dan Korem, *Suburban Gangs, The Affluent Rebels* (Richardson, TX: International Focus Press, 1994), pp. 49-50.

2. Karen Levine, "The age of cliques," *Parents*, December 1995, p. 102.

Chapter 6

1. Victor C. Strasburger, "Tuning in to Teenagers, *Newsweek*, May 19, 1997, p.18.

2. Nancy Gibbs, "How Should We Teach Our Children About Sex?" *Time*, May 24, 1993, p. 61.

Chapter 7

1. Used by permission.

2. Carolyn Smith, "Factors Associated with Early Sexual Activity Among Urban Adolescents," *Social Work*, Vol. 42, No. 4, July 1997, p. 334.

Chapter 8

1. This story originally appeared in Dennis Rainey's book, *One*

Home at a Time (Colorado Springs: Focus on the Family, 1997), p. 121.

2. Joshua Harris, *I Kissed Dating Goodbye* (Sisters, Oregon: Multnomah, Books, 1997), p. 26.

3. Elisabeth Elliott, *Passion and Purity* (Grand Rapids, MI: Fleming H. Revell, 1984), p. 145.

4. The dating contracts were adapted from the original concepts of Jim Cox and are used by permission. Thanks, Jim, for a superb, innovative idea!

Chapter 9

1. Quotation from an audio cassette series on the Book of Jude by Dr. James Merritt, "Keeping Your Guard Up."

Chapter 10

1. "Tidal wave," *World Book Encyclopedia*, Volume 19 (Chicago: World Book, Inc., 1988 edition), p. 280.

2. Marc Peyser, "Time Bind? What Time Bind?" *Newsweek*, May 12, 1997, p. 69.

3. "Charlotte's Web site: Girls, too, need time on computers," *Denver Post*, 3 November 1997, p. 12A.

4. Neil Gross, "Smarts? Why Video Games May Actually Help Your Child Learn," *Business Week*, 23 December 1996, p.68.

Chapter 11

1. Ross Campbell, M.D., *How to Really Love Your Teenager* (Colorado Springs: ChariotVictor, 1993), p. 65.

2. H. Paul Gabriel, M.D., and Robert Wool, *Anticipating Adolescence* (New York: Henry Holt and Company, 1995), p. 24.

3. Campbell, *How to Really Love Your Teenager*, pp. 66-67.

Chapter 12

1. Resources for the section on eating disorders include Gabriel and Wool, *Anticipating Adolescence*, pp. 154-159; Randall

Haddock, "Anorexia & Bulimia—New 'Fads' Plague Youths," electronically retrieved from the Internet on 2/5/98; "Eating Disorders Program," Internet document prepared by The Menninger Clinic, accessed on 2/5/98; and Rachel Kubersky, *Everything You Need to Know About Eating Disorders, Anorexia and Bulimia* (New York: Rosen, 1996).

2. The authors express gratitude to Sheryl and Jerry Wunder for their review of this section.

Chapter 13

1. From *Fatherhood* by Bill Cosby. Copyright © 1986 by William H. Cosby, Jr. Used by permission of Doubleday, a division of Bantam Doubleday Dell Publishing Group, Inc.

Chapter 14

1. "Student Use of Most Drugs Reaches Highest Level in Nine Years—More Report Getting 'Very High, Bombed, or Stoned,'" PRIDE, Inc., Press Release, Sept. 25, 1996. Retrieved electronically from the Internet at <http://www.health.org/pubs/96pride/pr96.htm>, March 13, 1998.

2. PRIDE, Inc., Press Release.

3. PRIDE, Inc., Press Release.

4. David Elkind, *All Grown Up and No Place to Go*, Revised Edition (Reading, MA: Addison-Wesley, 1998), pp. 22, 220.

5. Cited in David Elkind, *Parenting Your Teenager* (New York: Ballantine, 1993), p. 207.

6. John Piper, *Desiring God*, Expanded Edition (Sisters, OR: Multnomah, 1996), p. 19.

7. "Teenagers close to parents not as likely to drink, smoke," Colorado Springs *Gazette Telegraph*, 10 Sept. 1997, p. 1.

8. Ibid.

9. APA Online, "Substance Abuse," p. 2, retrieved electronically at <http://wwwpsych.org/public>.

10. Gabriel and Wool, *Anticipating Adolescence*, p. 62.

Chapter 15

1. Gabriel and Wool, *Anticipating Adolescence*, p. 194.
2. *Current Events*, 31 Oct. 1997.

Chapter 17

1. John F. Flanagan Jr., "The Second Mile," *Readers Digest*, April 1996, pp. 147–48.
2. Connie Leslie, "Will Johnny Get A's?" *Newsweek*, 8 July 1996, p. 72.
3. Ibid.

Chapter 18

1. Excerpts used by permission. Names withheld.
2. Dr. James Dobson, "Fatal Addiction, Ted Bundy's Final Interview," Video, Focus on the Family Films, 1989.
3. John Simons, "The Web's dirty secret," *U.S. News & World Report*, August 19, 1996, p. 51.
4. Carlos Illescas, "Schools fight to restrict access to porn on Internet," *The Denver Post*, October 12, 1997, p. 1A.
5. Robin Bennefield, "When kids prowl the Net, parents need to be on guard," *U.S. News & World Report*, April 29, 1996, p. 75.

Chapter 19

1. Based on a true story. Details withheld.

Appendix A

1. Summary of physiological changes in puberty was derived from Elizabeth R. McAnarney, M.D., Richard E. Kreipe, M.D., Donald P. Orr, M.D., George D. Comerci, M.D., *Textbook of Adolescent Medicine* (Philadelphia: W.B. Sanders Company, 1992). Interviews were conducted by research assistant Michael Escue with J. Kip Parrish, Ph.D.,

and Ed McColgan, Ph.D. The authors want to thank Michael for his assistance in obtaining material for this section on puberty.

2. Virginia Rutter, "The Invention of Adolescence," *Psychology Today*, Jan./Feb. 1995, p. 66.

3. Based on overview compiled by Michael Escue. Primary source: McAnarney, Kreipe, Orr, Comerci, *Textbook of Adolescent Medicine*.

4. "Adolescent" and "Sexuality," *World Book Encyclopedia*, Volumes 1 and 17, (Chicago: World Book Inc., 1988 edition).

5. Joseph Shapiro, "Teenage wasteland?" *U.S. News & World Report*, October 23, 1995, p. 85.

6. "Great Transitions, Preparing Adolescents for a New Century," Concluding Report of the Carnegie Council on Adolescent Development, Carnegie Corporation of New York, October 1995, p. 28.

7. Escue Summary, pp.1–2

8. Escue Summary, p.1.

Index

About the Authors

Dennis and Barbara Rainey are the parents of six children. Dennis helped found FamilyLife Ministries, a division of Campus Crusade for Christ. He is the senior editor of the HomeBuilders Couples Series® and the daily host of the nationally syndicated radio program, *FamilyLife Today*. He also taught a sixth-grade Sunday school class for eleven years where he tested much of this material.

He and Barbara are coauthors of the bestsellers *The New Building Your Mate's Self-Esteem* and *Moments Together for Couples*. They live near Little Rock, Arkansas.

The demands of parenting can put pressure on you—and your marriage. Is your marriage strong or is it as tired as a teenager early on a Saturday morning?

Now's the time to rekindle your love and strengthen your marriage at a FamilyLife Marriage Conference. You will spend an insightful weekend together, doing fun projects and hearing from dynamic speakers about real-life solutions for building and enhancing oneness in your marriage. You'll learn to:

- ◆ Receive your mate as a gift.
- ◆ Clarify your role as a husband or wife.
- ◆ Resolve conflict in your relationship.
- ◆ Maintain a vital sexual relationship.
- ◆ Express forgiveness to one another.

Take time now to plan a weekend at a FamilyLife Marriage Conference. It may be the best thing you can do for your marriage—and your kids!

For more information or to receive a free brochure call 1-800-FL-TODAY or visit our FamilyLife Web site at http://www.familylife-ccc.org

Better Marriages Make Better Parents!

FAMILYLIFE
MARRIAGE CONFERENCE

Get Away for a Weekend to Remember!

FAMILYLIFE
Bringing Timeless Principles Home

Dennis Rainey, Executive Director
A division of Campus Crusade for Christ